"The thing that sets *Moonlighting on the Internet* apart from other books is its authenticity and Shelby's dedication to truly helping people change their personal and financial situations for the better. It's refreshing to read a book of this nature that instead of offering cookie-cutter solutions provides real-world, practical guidance based on what's best for you, the reader, and your personal circumstances."

—Vishen Lakhiani, Founder and CEO of Mindvalley

"*Moonlighting on the Internet* cuts through the usual hype and provides you with a book full of realistic, proven strategies to help you create a second income stream."

—Robert Richman, Culture Strategist and Keynote Speaker, RobertRichman.com

"*Moonlighting on the Internet* lays out the roadmap to begin earning money online and start succeeding. No shiny stuff here, just the facts and blueprints to begin this journey. If you do one thing for yourself this year buy this book. If you can't afford it, steal it. Read it. Follow it. I promise you won't regret it."

—Brent Weaver, CEO and Fo

"*Moonlighting on the Internet* is your g
person can use to instantly increase
of days. If you believe the internet is the new gold rush, you are right. If you think you can't do it yourself, you are dead wrong. Shelby helps you understand the landscape and win. She is not writing about a theory she is giving you her proven secrets to get started today."

—Ronny Lynch, Owner and Founder of Big Baby Agency

"This is the book I wish I'd had when I started my first business almost 20 years ago. Filled with straight talk and proven ideas, *Moonlighting on the Internet* is about far more than making a living online. It is a wise and compassionate guide to creating a business that will feed your soul as well as your family. If you have ever wanted to start a business (online or not), the buy and read Larson's book. It's the startup guide for the rest of us."
—Andy Beedle, Principal of abeedle.com

"*Moonlighting on the Internet* is the perfect starting point for anyone who is in need of adding even just a couple hundred dollars a month working from home. If you or someone you know is stuck on how to get started doing simple tasks that can help bring in extra money every month, I highly recommend this fantastic resource. No theory, proven models that anyone with an internet connection and a few hours a day can get started with."
—Jason Katzenback, Founder of Amazing.com

"Shelby provides real information for real people to get real with *Moonlighting on the Internet*. If you're looking to create consistent income online and practical solutions without all the BS and hype, that's written by someone who sincerely wants you to succeed, then this book is for you."
—Glen Ledwell, CEO of Mind Movies

MOONLIGHTING
ON THE INTERNET

SECOND EDITION

MAKE AN EXTRA $1000
PER MONTH IN JUST
5-10 HOURS PER WEEK

SHELBY LARSON
FOREWORD BY YANIK SILVER

EP
Entrepreneur
PRESS®

Entrepreneur Press, Publisher
Cover Design: Andrew Welyczko
Production and Composition: Eliot House Productions

This publication is designed to provide accurate and authoritative information
in regard to the subject matter covered. It is sold with the understanding that
the publisher is not engaged in rendering legal, accounting or other professional
services. If legal advice or other expert assistance is required, the services of a
competent professional person should be sought.

Library of Congress Cataloging-in-Publication Data
Names: Larson, Shelby, author. | Silver, Yanik. Moonlighting on the Internet.
Title: Moonlighting on the Internet : make an extra $1,000 per month in just 5–10
    hours per week / by Shelby Larson.
Description: 2nd edition. | Irvine, California : Entrepreneur Media, Inc., [2016]
    | Earlier edition published as: Moonlighting on the Internet : 5 world-class
    experts reveal proven ways to make an extra paycheck online each month [by]
    Yanik Silver [and] Robert Olic.
Identifiers: LCCN 2015036271 | ISBN 978-1-59918-576-7 (pbk. : alk. paper) |
    ISBN 1-59918-576-8 (pbk. : alk. paper)
Subjects: LCSH: Electronic commerce.
Classification: LCC HF5548.32 .S554 2016 | DDC 658.8/72—dc23
LC record available at http://lccn.loc.gov/2015036271

Printed in the United States of America

20 19 18 17 16   10 9 8 7 6 5 4 3 2 1

I would like to dedicate this book to my husband and children for being the center of my "Why" and to all of the people working so hard to make our world a better place for ourselves and our families. I hope this book will add wind to your sails. Remember—Possibility has no roof!

CONTENTS

FOREWORD
BY YANIK SILVER

remember waking up at three o'clock in the morning with my first online idea. I nudged my wife, Missy, and said, "Mis, Mis, get up! I've got the idea!" Like any entrepreneur, I always had tons of ideas.

She grumbled, "Just go back to sleep."

I couldn't do it and muttered back something like, "No, no. This is going to be great!"

Instead of rolling over, I actually jumped out of bed, registered the domain InstantSalesLetters.com, and got to work on it. I had no technical skills to put up a site (still don't), but I didn't let that stop me. I simply started working on creating fill-in-the-blank formulas from the best sales letters I'd developed in different industries.

I still remember waking up and seeing $29.95 sitting in my inbox. It was pretty awesome, and the funny thing is, we didn't even have our online merchant account ready, but someone had found our site and ordered.

Within the first month, I made about $1,800. In the third month, it was around $7,800, then $9,400, and on track to do six figures within six months. That's when people started asking me, "How did you do this, and is there any way you can teach me how to do what you've done?"

I didn't expect it, but it turned into my next transition—helping others take their content or expertise or knowledge and sell it on the internet for a profit.

I loved working with so many incredible people and helping them take their passions, knowledge, interests, expertise, and messages out into the world by selling content and information. These students built five-, six-, seven- and even eight-figure-plus businesses in pretty much every conceivable field with my help.

And that diverse background was the catalyst for me to write the first edition of *Moonlighting on the Internet*. I'm proud to say it was a bestseller and helped thousands of people discover real ways they could moonlight and create successful revenue streams for themselves.

To me, life-changing money is usually a couple hundred dollars extra per month. But the problem is you don't know what's legit and what's not. That was just one of the reasons I distanced myself from the online space about eight years ago. I couldn't stand being associated with so many rogues talking a good game but not backing it up with real opportunities for hard-working people.

That's why I'm excited to pass the torch of *Moonlighting* to someone I know and trust, Shelby Larson.

For years, Shelby has been part of a high-level group of entrepreneurs I run called Maverick1000. The idea is to bring together 1,000 game-changing leaders to truly make a difference around the world. And Shelby is a true Maverick with a huge heart. Anytime we talk about business, it's always about the impact. It's about the difference something can make and who will benefit even more than her. In conversations, Shelby tells me repeatedly how proud she is for helping hundreds of stay-at-home moms with her content agency. To me, Shelby is a bit like a super woman, she juggles five kids, a husband, several businesses and a couple pet dragons. But through all of it, she still has time to head up several cause partner initiatives we co-created at Maverick and much, much more.

Not only does she care a lot . . . but she really knows her stuff! At our inaugural Camp Maverick experience this summer, Shelby was one of our "Camp Counselors," delivering a workshop to our attendees. One attendee (camper) literally jumped out of his seat to call his business partners to ask them to change everything they were doing because of what Shelby shared. Now, mind you, this was not a newbie but a seasoned business pro. Shelby has a profound way of being able to contribute to entrepreneurs at any level of their growth.

There's never a perfect time to start. You can always come up with a reason to not do something—but Shelby has now taken away the biggest excuse of not having the right path you need to get going. To me, it's always about the process, not profits, in the beginning. The material in here is not a "get rich quick" method and it's not intended to be—but I know you can begin moonlighting on the internet with Shelby's guidance.

▶ ▶ ▶

Yanik Silver redefines how business is played in the 21st century at the intersection of more profits, more fun, and more impact. Starting with his first million-dollar idea at three o'clock in the morning, he has bootstrapped seven other products and services to the seven-figure mark from scratch without funding, taking on debt, or even having a real business plan.

He is the author of several best-selling marketing books and tools including Instant Sales Letters®, *34 Rules for Maverick Entrepreneurs*, *Maverick Startup,* and his latest, *Evolved Enterprise*. His personal blog is www.YanikSilver.com.

ACKNOWLEDGMENTS

I suppose most authors feel like I do right now—overwhelmed with gratitude for the countless people that served as inspiration or assistance that made this book a reality. It's not even possible to create an appropriate list of people who deserve mention and expressed appreciation, so I will begin by admitting defeat on such a lofty goal.

First words of gratitude go out to my husband, Kerry, and my children, Bean, Carter, Avery, Anna, and Sophia. Thank you for agreeing to go on this crazy journey with me. I look up to each of you every day of my life. Your love, understanding, and support is what fuels everything that I do. I hope some day to be even half as amazing as any one of you.

Heather Sneed—ying to my yang! Having me as a business partner is no walk in the park. We are opposites in nearly every way and you continue to be a blessing in my life. You don't get nearly enough credit for what a true gift you are to my life, our businesses, and our world. Here's to many more years of causing trouble together while making the world a better place.

Yanik Silver—my mentor. My friend. Thank you for passing the torch to me. I'm honored to continue what you started years ago. You, and the Maverick1000 family have changed my life in an irreversible way. You were the one who taught me that possibility has no roof in the first place. Now that theme is the foundation of the legacy I want to leave behind. I am forever changed by taking the green pill.

Howie Schwartz and Dr. Mike Woo-Ming—neither of you probably even know that I'm writing this book, yet I have to publicly state my gratitude to you because you were the ones who picked me up out of obscurity and put me properly on the entrepreneurial path. As I like to say "You created this monster!" I'm so glad you did.

Book contributors—I would not have been able to keep my promise to the readers to never teach on theory alone if you weren't willing to lend your expertise and knowledge to me for this book. This book is great, not because of me, but because of you.

Entrepreneur Press and Promote A Book—I'm so grateful that my publisher was willing to take a chance on me as a first-time author. I'm thankful for your guidance and patience as this book came to life. I'll always treasure my relationship with Michael Drew and Promote A Book who have given me unyielding advice, guidance, and friendship.

World's Best Team! I, truly, have the BEST people who work with and for us. They are top-notch, dedicated, fun people. They helped SO much with this book. Reading chapters, making suggestions, pulling statistics for me—the list is endless. Without you, our businesses are nothing.

Lastly, those who know me well know that nothing is more treasured in my life than "my people." I am so blessed to be surrounded by amazing, inspiring, loving people both personally and professionally. I aspire to be as great an influence in your lives as you are in mine. Those are large, world-changing shoes to fill, but I will continually strive to do my best.

I'm signing this with a heart full of love and gratitude.

—Shelby B. Larson

WHAT THIS BOOK IS NOT

B efore we get into the details about what this book is, I'd first like to cover what this book is NOT. While researching this book, I found myself swimming in a sea of spammy, smarmy, self-indulgent, inauthentic content that has given a lot of training material about making money online a bad name. Content that claimed:

- "Make money from home in your underwear!"
- "Make money while you sleep!"
- "Magic Bullet (insert any number of outlandish claims here)!"
- "But wait, there's MORE!"

Sound familiar? I know it does. We've all read it in books and on the internet. We've seen it on TV and heard it on the radio—those claims about making easy money. That's just not my style. I'm not going to give you a lot of fluff. I'm very real and down-to-earth, and that's exactly what you can expect from this book. These are real strategies, meant for real people like you, who don't have time to waste wading through all the crap out there to figure out what's right for you and how to implement it in your life.

The truth is, I do make money from home, but thankfully for my neighbors and my children, I don't generally do it in my underwear. (Although I have been known to live in yoga pants for way longer than is socially acceptable.) Also, while orders and money do often come in while I'm sleeping, that "magic bullet" solution I found sometimes feels more like being shot with a paintball that doesn't break on impact. (If you've ever been there, you know what I'm talking about. It doesn't kill you, but damn, does it hurt, and it will leave a welt to remind you for a good two weeks.)

I'm not going to lie. When you have a busy life with important people depending on you, it takes some sacrifice to get a plan in motion that will successfully earn income for you. But I can also tell you this: It will be worth it. The beautiful thing is that if you do it right, it's not just going to create an extra paycheck for the short term—it will become an ongoing, continuous revenue stream. Not because it's a "get rich quick" scheme, but because you built something legitimate and sustainable that you can feel good about.

YOU DON'T KNOW WHAT YOU DON'T KNOW

As I write this, I've been moonlighting online for eight years. I have had a lot of wins and a lot of losses in that time. I've created a seven-figure business and multiple six-figure businesses, and I've had a lot of failed businesses in between—or, as I like to call them, "unintentional nonprofits." (I'm actually in the middle of creating my first intentional nonprofit, and I have to tell you, it's a lot more fun doing it on purpose!)

We are going to explore a variety of legitimate business models and strategies for you to make money from home. I refer to these as "Profit Paths." I realize that there are a lot of places that you could turn to learn how to successfully earn money from home. Throughout the book, I have worked to structure the information in a way that takes your lifestyle into account. I realize the knowledge in this book is useless if it's not presented in a way that is applicable for you. For that reason, before we even get into the heart of the various Profit Paths, I will walk you through creating your own Profit Path Profile so that you can evaluate which options are the best match for you.

Well, It Doesn't Look Hard . . .

Do you remember the first time you got behind the wheel of a car? (Or, more terrifyingly, have you had the experience of putting your own kid in the driver's seat for the first time?) It's quite an amusing (if scary) experience. Teenagers are so confident. I love that about them, how fearless they can be. They've seen their parents drive the car a gazillion times, so how hard could it be?

It doesn't seem like it could be all that difficult until you actually get behind the wheel, stick the key in the ignition, and then realize that regardless of the fact that you've seen people drive hundreds, if not thousands, of times, you honestly have no idea what you're doing. You didn't even know what you didn't know until you sat down and decided to give it a whirl.

Even though everything you need is right at your fingertips, you still aren't sure how to put it all together to move forward effectively and safely. This is why the law requires you to go through driver's education. Not just for the know-how, but to gain experience in a safe environment with an experienced educator.

Now, I'd like to add an additional thought to this scenario. How would you feel if the "experienced" educator had never actually driven a car? What if he had spent hundreds of hours watching YouTube videos and talking to experts, but had never actually been behind the wheel? Obviously that would be completely unacceptable.

Driving instructors don't just study other people who were great drivers and then pass along that information to you. They have a history of not only driving successfully, but also teaching other people to do the same. This is an important distinction that you may never have thought of before. While not as life-threatening, why wouldn't you demand similarly high standards of the educators you trust to teach you how to make money online for you and your family?

WHAT DOES THAT HAVE TO DO WITH THIS BOOK?

Because of my passion for providing legitimate work-from-home income to people who can appreciate those opportunities (75 percent of my 200+ staff are still stay-at-home moms), I've found the majority of my success in the service industry. That's covered in Chapter 4: Freelance Writing. While this has been a very fulfilling and lucrative path for me, I recognize that everyone is different. There is not one path that's ideal for everyone.

I have chosen five categories of online Profit Paths that I know are legitimate strategies for successfully creating a second paycheck online. Each chapter breaks down the various Profit Paths, explains the pros and cons of each one, and covers the basics of getting up and running quickly and successfully. However, since I am not personally experienced in making money via all of the paths I've written about in this book and I don't believe in teaching based on theory, I knew I would need a little help.

My solution was to reach out to the people who are the best in the world at the Profit Paths that I have chosen for this book. Some of them have been my mentors, some have been clients, and others I have the great pleasure of calling my friends. They believe in my mission and have generously given me their insights and tips to add to my own. My commitment to you in this book is to only teach based on proven strategies, never on theory.

SUCCESS IS SUBJECTIVE

The beauty of this book is in the variety of people who contributed their knowledge to it. I realize that no two readers of this book are the same, so it made sense to collect stories and strategies from as many different, successful people as possible. I especially wanted contributions from people who define success differently. Success for some of my stay-home mom friends means an extra $500 per month without having to take too much time away from their families, while success to one of my mentors was being able to buy a ticket onto the first Virgin Galactic Flight into space.

WRITTEN FOR YOU BY PEOPLE LIKE YOU

My favorite thing, by far, in writing this book was having the privilege of working with the many successful people who donated their experiential knowledge, some of whom I would call "thought leaders." I love their stories and motivation and the real-world insights they bring to implementing these business models into their full, busy lives.

It's not just the awesome strategies and tactics that I'm going to share with you that really matter, it's also understanding what the trials are and how to avoid common mistakes. Success and failure come in all shapes and sizes. It's important to understand the territory and know how to navigate through it. I know that time, focus, and energy (and often finances) are finite resources and if you're putting those things into one area, then you're taking it away from another. My commitment is to make the shift in focus a smart move for you.

As you read this book and learn more about my story, you will see that from the beginning my personal aspirations were always accompanied by a drive to figure out ways to help others do the same. This is part of my own personal Profit Path, but more importantly, it's keeping me aligned with the vision that I have for myself. I want you to achieve your goals. I want the journey to success to be quicker and easier because you read this book.

Ultimately, I'd like to help you learn how to create extra revenue from home without having to go through all the mistakes that I did and without having to compromise what's most important to you to get there. I never had a book to read or trusted experts to walk me through it in a way that made sense for my life. *My hope is to change that experience for you.*

> *I don't only want to blow the roof off the possibilities you see in your life. I want to prevent you from even thinking possibility has a roof in the first place.*

PART I

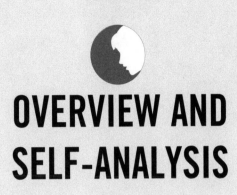

OVERVIEW AND SELF-ANALYSIS

I personally believe that a huge reason that many people fail in successfully making money online is because they spend all their time evaluating the opportunities without knowing how to identify if it's a good match for themselves and their lifestyle. These first three chapters are designed to help you understand how to best use this book and to create a Profit Path Profile. Once you have your Profit Path Profile, instead of just reading about the different opportunities that you'll be exploring in this book, you can actually evaluate which of the paths make the most sense for you and your specific situation.

CHAPTER 1

MY STORY

I actually registered a website just to have a place to send all of my friends and family that constantly ask me, "So . . . what do you do, again?" Even my husband didn't quite know how to answer that question for the first few years that I was making money online. He usually inaccurately responded, "She does network marketing." Which, of course, brought up visions of Amway meetings in some people's minds.

"If I get three friends and then you get three friends . . ." Sound familiar? As you can imagine, that made my friends want to hide the moment I mentioned anything about my work to them. Now, don't get me wrong, while I am poking fun, I don't want to take away from the fact that network marketing companies are legitimate business models. It's just not one of the models that helped me go from a financially strapped and stressed-out mom of five children to the seven-figure business owner mompreneur that I now am.

Wow, don't I look great on paper? You might even think that I'm some super-human Supermom! Of course I sound amazing on paper! I'm not going to put the bad stuff and my collection of failures up there for the world to see. My prospective clients might show up there.

However, I WILL share the bad stuff with you in this book. I will not hold back my collection of failures because I want you to understand and believe that I really will show you legitimate Profit Paths to making money online, but also, I'm not super human. I made a lot of mistakes and suffered a lot of trials. I'm a real person, and the solutions that I'll be highlighting in this book are real, and credible, and work. Even for normal, formerly stressed out, overworked, and tired humans like me.

Here's the five-cent tour. As a busy homeschool mom of five children, I tried a LOT of different models to make money from home. I tried everything from MLM's and other party companies to teaching classes out of my home. I even incorporated my own scrapbook store at one point. I had a little bit of success here and there, but nothing significant and nothing consistent.

At some point, I decided to look into making money online because, like many people, I kept hearing this was a magic bullet solution to our financial woes. The problem was that every time I began researching how to go about it, I was inundated in a sea of hypey claims and I could not figure out how to identify and separate legitimate strategies from scams or systems that would be a waste of my time and money because I just didn't know enough about the online world yet. That being said, I dove in anyway.

HISTORIC FAILURES

Back in 2006, not unlike now, there was no shortage of advertisements claiming to know the best way to make money on the internet. Searching for this topic online brought up a lot of cheesy sales pages of guys in Ferraris in front of McMansions with girls in bikinis. "BUT WAIT! THERE'S MORE!" Those never did resonate with me, but I was determined to figure it out anyway. I made some painful choices:

- I paid money in order to have the opportunity to stuff envelopes from home. /fail
- I paid money to learn how to make money on eBay. /fail
- I paid money to learn how to make money with real estate. /fail
- I paid money to learn the super-secret-magic-bullet-of-making-money-while-in-your-underwear-from-home. /fail
- I paid money to become a mystery shopper. /fail
- I paid money to get access to a vault of PLR (Private Label Rights) information products that I could then resell and make millions!!! /fail

I should probably be embarrassed about this, but I'm not. Because at least I was searching and trying! At the time, I didn't know of any books to help me navigate and weed out the crap from the legitimate opportunities. I had to do my best to figure it all out, and, of course, everything had copywriting designed to make me feel like I had just discovered the thing that was going to CHANGE MY LIFE FOREVER!

I'm pretty sure I spent the equivalent of a small college education by wasting my money online trying to find that magic formula that was going to allow me to generate revenue from home so that I didn't have to sacrifice raising my children in exchange for a little financial relief.

I thought it was this base financial need that drove me into my endless search to find a way to successfully make money from home. While that's partially true, it's definitely not the whole story. The truth is, I had an entrepreneurial fire within me that hungered for success. Not everyone self-identifies as an entrepreneur, and that's okay. You don't have to be an entrepreneur to make money from home. What's important is that you find what drives and motivates you. That fire is important, because to this day it carries me through when things get rough, or worse—boring.

WHEN DID THINGS CHANGE?

While I have no formal training in writing, it's something I've always loved. As an adult, I participated in multiple online writing communities and forums. I mostly wrote fiction and poetry. It was a great creative outlet for me. One of the women who frequented the writing forums informed me that there are people who will pay freelance writers money to write for them online.

The thought had never occurred to me. I think I rambled something eloquent like, "Wait . . . people will pay me money? Like they will give me REAL money if I write for them?" The thought was pretty exciting. Even though I knew nothing about it, I'm always up for a good adventure. This is often how these things start, we stumble into something that we already have some sort of a connection to or affinity for.

This got me researching the eye-opening world of freelance writing online. There was no shortage of information and resources out there, and it wasn't long before I had my first couple of paying clients, because I was a Freelance Writer. (I had a profile online that stated as much, so it must be true, right?)

As it turned out, my friend was right. People would pay me real money to write for them online. I wrote everything from articles about how to walk your dog to blog posts about custom draperies to ebooks on emotional intelligence in children. It was a fun, new world and I was actually working from home and had the paychecks to prove it. Yay me!

I could have stayed with that freelance model. It wasn't long before I had a system and a steady line of clients to help supplement our family's income. But after a while, I started to get curious. Why are people ordering content from me to be published online? What benefits are they getting? That's when things really began to get interesting to me as I started to connect the dots and learn about the vast world of Search Engine Optimization (SEO) and digital marketing.

If you don't already have an understanding about what SEO is, Googling it will give you a lot of information, but you also might find it confusing. The simplest way to think about it is as a commonly used term representing the processes and strategies that you can employ to get your websites and other online properties to rank well in the search engines for the search terms that matter most to you and your business. For instance, if I owned a dental practice in Cleveland, I would likely want my website to show up on the first page of Google when people search for "dentist Cleveland" or "Cleveland dentist" among other terms.

Learning about SEO and digital marketing opened up an entire new sphere of opportunity for me because now, instead of just creating content for my clients, I learned how to also use that content to help market my client's various websites, products, and messages. I was also beginning to realize that no matter what business adventures I might want to start in the future, understanding how to market online would be a critical component of success.

HOW CAN I MAKE MONEY ONLINE TOO?

After a few months of this, people began noticing what I was doing. (I'm not exactly a shy, reserved personality, and earning money from home was the coolest thing that happened to me and my family since I discovered Johnny Depp.) Specifically, other stay-at-home moms were continually asking me what I was doing and could they please do it too.

I tried explaining how I went about freelance writing, but the truth is that they didn't have time, or money (or frankly, motivation) to navigate the barrier of entry the way that I had. So it was as I attended my very first Internet Marketing Conference that I had an idea that changed my life and enhanced the lives of others. I would create a company that outsourced moms as writers.

LAUNCHING MY FIRST BUSINESS

I distinctly remember the day I "launched" my new outsourcing company. I had a website, so it must have been real. I had somehow scraped together enough funds to have someone create a crappy Joomla website for me and I had about a dozen moms who were excited and ready to write. I went out onto the marketing forums that I was now a frequent visitor of and advertised that I was launching a company called Work At Home Mom Outsource and that I was selling the first writing packages barely above cost.

The next morning I woke up and pulled up my PayPal account to see if anyone had bought from me yet, and my previously empty account had $6,000 sitting in it and my email box was flooded with orders. $6,000 was the most money, by a lot, that I had ever seen in any account with my name on it. Now, I think most people would have celebrated, but instead, I nearly had a full-scale panic attack and I started crying.

I called my husband, KJ, freaking out.

"What the heck am I doing? People gave me their money and I've got all of these orders and I've never done this before. Why would they all give me their money? I have all of these moms excited for work but I don't even have a process for managing any of it. I don't know what to do! I have five kids that I am homeschooling and I barely have a successful process that gets everyone out of bed, fed, dressed and educated, let alone figuring out how to manage this make-believe company I have created."

DEEP BREATH

Now, obviously that story had a happy ending. But it wasn't without a LOT of painful mistakes, and a steep learning curve. Truthfully, I got REALLY lucky. Normally, the whole "if you build it they will come" philosophy does NOT work. At the time, I didn't even fully realize the tremendous opportunity that I had stepped into. The online marketing world had drastically changed and people were desperate for native writers who were not tainted by the previous way that marketing content was written.

There are two really great takeaways from this. First, it is NOT typical to have quick success so disproportionate to the amount of effort put in and with such a naive lack of knowledge.

That being said, sometimes those lucky opportunities come around, and if you aren't out there looking for them and taking action, you may never get to experience a success that feels like an unexpected gift that sincerely changes your life forever.

That was something I hadn't heard of many people experiencing before and I've never had such blind success since. It was a blessing and also an intense crash course in Online Business 101. This learning process felt a lot like drinking from a fire hose! While it was not ideal or low stress, it was nonetheless quite effective.

WHY YOUR "WHY" MATTERS

"Gee, Brain, what do you want to do tonight?
The same thing we do every night, Pinky: Try to take over the world!"
—PINKY AND THE BRAIN

Everyone seems to start out thinking that their motivation for making money from home is to do just that—make more money—but that is not usually why you're doing this. You're not doing it to just generically have money in the bank. You're doing it for whatever it is in your mind that you'll be able to do or have or provide if you have more money in your life.

For instance, in 2012, we made a life list goal as a family to live out of the country together one month out of every year. The first year we spent the month of August on Isla Mujeres in Mexico. Some of the highlights for my family were serving in the veterinary clinic, swimming with whale sharks, and releasing baby sea turtles into the ocean.

The second year we spent the month of December in Jamaica. We decided not to give or receive Christmas gifts that year and instead we would give to the people of Jamaica. I'll never forget spending New Year's Eve walking the seven miles of beaches in Negril looking at the thousands of Chinese lanterns float up into the night sky over the ocean carrying people's wishes and hopes for the New Year along with them.

These experiences make it all worth it. This is my big "Why." This is why I work so hard to create my Profit Paths: so that my family can have these life-changing experiences that teach my children to love people and life and dream of ways not only to improve themselves, but also the lives of all those they encounter.

Whatever your "why" is, get in tune with it. I want to show you that when it comes to creating income online, there is no roof on the possibilities. You just need to understand how to navigate through the opportunities successfully.

For me, the benefits of learning how to make money online have grown way beyond that initial motivation. Originally I thought I was just looking for a way to bring in some extra money for the family so things didn't always feel so tight. But in the end, what I got is so much more than that.

I feel a sense of pride in my content marketing company, Content Divas. It provides work-from-home jobs to hundreds of families. That has always been at the heart of why I do what I do. By contrast, Ember Dragon, my digital marketing agency, gives me an avenue to help other people scale their businesses to levels of success they hadn't experienced before. It is a creative outlet that I thrive on. Creating digital marketing campaigns and sales funnels feels like solving big, fun puzzles. I bask in the happiness my clients feel when their businesses grow so well.

Finally, *Moonlighting on the Internet* inspires me. YOU inspire me. There are few things in life that mean more to me than knowing that something I did helped other people create better lives for themselves and their families. This is how I will change the world, one family at a time. My hope is that in learning how to create Profit Paths online, the belief that your potential is unlimited will bleed over into other areas of your life, as it did in mine.

CHAPTER 2

IS THIS BOOK FOR YOU?

Before you read any further, think for a moment about how you wish to use this book. What is your ultimate goal? Do you know what you don't know? In other words, you need to decide whether this book is the right one for you. That's why a huge portion of this chapter is dedicated to defining who I wrote this book for. I really feel like anyone interested in creating their own personal Profit Paths online will benefit from this book, but I took the time to address some specific audiences anyway.

In this chapter, I also encourage you to stop making assumptions that self-disqualify yourself from opportunities and success. You don't think you do this? Of course you do.

I realize that a ton of the information out there telling you how to make money online is spammy and scammy and crappy. My request is that you suspend your skepticism long enough to read this book and believe that the information I'm giving you is legitimate, honest, and completely doable.

FINANCIAL FREEDOM OR BUST

If you're reading this book, then there is some part of you searching, as I was, for something more. You're at least somewhat interested in learning how to create additional streams of revenue online. It may just be a case of mild curiosity and something about this book piqued your interest, or you might be hell-bent on finding a path to financial freedom.

As I wrote that last sentence, an image of you standing on the side of a dusty road holding a sign that says "Financial Freedom or Bust" with an old-fashioned suitcase on the ground next to your boot-clad feet came to mind. Either way, I'm really glad you're reading this book. (I also have no idea why you carry outdated luggage or are specifically wearing boots, but there it is.)

Regardless of where you are in your personal journey or what your motivations are, if you're looking to integrate online revenue into your life, this book truly has some of the best options available for you to explore. The revenue models that you're going to learn about have not only proved successful, but are also designed to realistically fit into your busy, hectic life.

If you read Chapter 1: My Story, then you got a 30,000-foot look at how I got from where I started to where I am today. Almost everyone loves a good rags-to-riches story. Part of why I was chosen to write this book is because so many people can relate to my journey from overwhelmed and indebted homeschool mom of five to successful mompreneur. However, as I was writing my story down, I grew concerned that some of you might assume the book won't be useful for you because your situation is not similar to mine. Rest assured: This book is not just for moms.

IS THIS BOOK FOR YOU?

Stop Self-Disqualification!

It's a typical human behavior to make assumptions that disqualify you from moving forward. There are plenty of reasons we do this, but since I'm not a psychologist, I won't go into them. What I will do, however, is tell you about some of the people I wrote this book for.

All of the people I list below have one thing in common: You have very busy lives with important priorities and people you love depending on you. Like me, you can't sacrifice your current job, school, or family responsibilities to find success online.

The Stay-at-Home Parent

In my opinion, there is no one nobler than a stay-at-home parent. You'll notice I didn't say stay-at-home mom. I know that most stay-at-home parents are moms, but I wouldn't want to leave out the stay-at-home dads. I know a few, and they're amazing. One of the hardships of having a stay-at-home parent in your family is that it cuts your household income potentially in half (or at least drastically reduces your earning potential). Often couples are forced to make the decision between one parent staying home to raise the children or a more comfortable income and, therefore, lifestyle.

Few things make my heart hurt more than families being forced to suffer financially in order to personally raise their children full time. That frustration has been a huge catalyst to my success. I know the world of a stay-at-home parent inside and out. I know how hard you work and how tired you are at the end of the day.

The Hard-Working but Underpaid Employee

This book is perfect for those of you who were like my husband when we started our journey creating Profit Paths online. You work hard at your job, but it never seems as though you have quite enough money to live your life the way you want. Some of you might be stressed out all the time because you never have enough money to simply pay all the bills and make ends meet. (A savings account? HA! What's that?) Others might always get the bills paid, but there's never enough extra for family vacations or cool extracurricular activities for your kids like soccer or dance class or, heaven forbid, DRUMS!

The Unfulfilled Corporate Executive

While most of you reading this book are primarily motivated by financial pressure, this is not the case for everyone. I frequently meet people looking for change who have great careers and plenty of money in the bank. If you're in this situation, the complaints I commonly hear are that you feel bored or unfulfilled. You've achieved "success" as measured by status in a company, title on a plaque, or money in the bank, but you actually hate what you do.

This is an especially tragic story for those of you who have spent a small fortune and years of your life to get the degrees and certifications you needed to achieve what you have. It can be disheartening to wake up one morning and realize that while you've accomplished your goals, you still have aspirations sitting inside you, unmet and unsatisfied. It shouldn't be surprising that the path you chose in your late teens or early twenties is not the path you want now.

The Single Parent

In my mind, few people in existence work harder than single parents. You are probably some combination of all the types of people I have kept in mind while writing this book. You are the main support for your children, the main income provider for your family, and sometimes you're also going to school to provide a better future for you and your family.

In 2012, according to the U.S. Census Bureau, 24 percent of American children lived with only their mom, while another 4 percent lived with only their father. That's more than a quarter of our country's children being raised by single parents. For a good portion of my childhood, I was raised by a single mom. It's an exhausting and often thankless job, and providing resources to help you is a personal motivator and pleasure for me.

The Barely Legal

Despite the controversial title, I'm referring to youth and young adults. Traditional public school and most college tracks are designed to prepare you for jobs and careers working for other people. There are very few resources, especially for youth, to teach you how to become entrepreneurs. In my household, it's actually far more important to me that my children know how to create any amount of income for themselves than it is that they go to college.

How great would it be if by the time your kids get to college, they were already generating even $500 per month online? How much would that alleviate the stress and pressure during this transition into adulthood? Today's youth are more tech-savvy than ever, and it's far more realistic now for kids who haven't even graduated high school yet to learn how to create Profit Paths online. It's also a great way to help put yourself through college or take care of yourself while you're figuring out what you want for your life.

The Unemployable

There are a variety of reasons I might refer to someone as unemployable. At this point in my life I am 100 percent unemployable, and I'm OK with that. I've worked for myself for too long, and now I'm just no good at having a "boss" anymore. I know I'm not the only person like that.

However, there are other reasons you might be unemployable or less employable than others: health reasons, legal issues, disabilities, etc. So many people are in positions where having a way to make money from home would drastically improve their lives. We once had a writer who did freelance writing from home while her husband had cancer so she could still be there to take care of him. That income saved her and her husband from losing their house that year.

The Retired and Bored

I always have a soft spot in my heart for baby boomers and retirees, probably because I have this sense that Social Security will mean nothing by the time I need it. In fact, many people aren't retiring when they are officially able to because they aren't in a place financially to do so.

The real danger for the retired community, besides the growing financial need, is feeling as if you lose your sense of purpose once you retire. I know a ton of you who have looked forward to retiring for years, and then when it actually happened you became so bored you hardly knew what to do with yourself. You've worked hard your entire life, raised your families, and now you don't have to be left on your own to figure out what comes next. This book will show you ways to keep busy and productive by earning money for your household and have fun doing it.

The Shiny Objects Entrepreneurs

"Squirrel!" If you have seen the movie *Up*, that will make complete sense to you. If not, just chalk it up to the author of this book being weird and keep reading.

Because I'm so thoroughly involved in the entrepreneur community, I meet an uncountable number of you who have been trying to create Profit Paths online with varying degrees of success. You know a little bit in a lot of areas, but you just haven't been able to hit your goals yet. You are the people I love because regardless of anything else, I know you have the drive for success. You are out there trying. You recognize the opportunity, but for whatever reasons you haven't been able to channel that drive to your ideal success yet.

When I think of you, I am reminded of professional baseball players. Even the best baseball players, over the course of a year, will still only get a hit on three out of every ten at-bats. Failure is definitely part of the process, but learning how to channel knowledge and energy to create home runs along the way is important, too. This book will help you home in on those missing pieces of your success puzzle.

Successful Entrepreneurs

The thing I love about already successful entrepreneurs is that you are almost always looking for opportunities to create even more success or improve your current portfolio. That is likely one of the reasons so many of you are successful in the first place. You don't balk at opportunities to learn or assume you already know it all just because you've already found some measure of success.

If you already have a great business mind and are a visionary thinker, I am 100 percent positive you can shift that focus to create additional revenue streams or even double or triple your current business by learning new ways to further monetize it. In my opinion, successful entrepreneurs should never want to be the one who knows the most in the room.

Either You're Always Learning, or You're Never Learning

I realize that most people who pick up this book will primarily be motivated by financial need. That's great. It was dire financial need that made me take my business from a hobby business to a serious, long-term sustainable business. (You'll read more about that later.) Need can be a GREAT catalyst. I wrote this first and foremost to help you end that particular pain point in your life. It is a true project of passion for me.

That said, this book is for everyone, regardless of what phase of life you are in or what your motivations are, because I believe that each and every one of you has a well of untapped potential that just needs a little nurturing and guidance. If this book can provide some inspiration or education that helps you make money from home and in turn makes your corner of our world a better place, then it has served its purpose.

YES, BUT . . .

Are you at least one of the types of people I am writing this book for? If so, are you ready to start exploring the possibilities of successfully creating your own Profit Paths? Chances are the real answer inside you is "Yes." I'd love to get excited, knowing this means you're ready to read this book and take action to start making money online, but the truth is I know that many of you are answering my question, "Yes, but . . ."

- "Yes, but I don't know anything about computers."
- "Yes, but I hate computers."
- "Yes, but I don't have any money to get started with."
- "Yes, but I'm totally confused about the internet and don't have time to catch up."
- "Yes, but I'm really busy."
- "Yes, but I only have a couple of hours per week to dedicate to something like this."
- "Yes, but I'm not smart enough, good enough, or talented enough."
- "Yes, but I'm pretty sure everything in this book is a scam."

Whatever it is that follows the words "Yes, but . . ." go ahead and get it out now. Whatever those things are in your mind that are barriers to your success, acknowledge them right now. Heck, you can even write them down if you want. But after you do, crumple them up, tear them up, or burn them. Whatever your excuse is, it's garbage, and you need to throw it away with the rest of the trash. I promise you that you CAN do this. There are paths in this book that are realistic and doable for you and your lifestyle.

That might sound like a bunch of fluffy self-improvement mumbo jumbo, but take a minute to think about it, because it's 100 percent true. You don't have to take my word for it. Throughout this book, I'm going to introduce you to all kinds of people who have had success creating a second paycheck from home in all kinds of circumstances. In fact, some of them have even made the shift to full-time entrepreneur and now all of their income is generated online.

I'd like to start right off the bat trying to counter any objections that might pop up in your mind along the way. The only thing I ask is that you suspend your skepticism and doubts long enough to read this book. Because if you read it with the mindset that it's too good to be true or that it might be possible for some people, but not you, then you will absolutely be right.

Now, I'm not someone who thinks that just because you believe something, it will happen. But belief IS important. When you read about successful people you admire, they have a lot of awesome attributes in common. They're hard workers, they tend to think outside the box, and they all had a vision and believed they could make it happen. Your journey will be so much easier if you believe in yourself and in what you're trying to accomplish—and at the very least believe that what I write about is legitimate and doable. So do yourself a favor, get rid of those "buts," and just answer, "YES."

CHAPTER 3

YOUR PROFIT PATH PROFILE

T he primary objective of this chapter is to walk you through creating your own Profit Path Profile so that as you evaluate the various opportunities you're going to read about, you will be able to consider whether they will be a good fit for you. I encourage you NOT to skip this process, as it will serve you well in choosing Profit Paths for the rest of your life. I also break down how the book is laid out so that you know what to expect and how to get the most out of it. For example, you'll find gems along the way as you read, like this link where you can download forms to go along with this chapter by visiting the resource section of www.MoonlightingontheInternet.com.

PROFIT PATH PROFILE: DON'T SKIP THIS STEP!

How do you know which Profit Path will be right for you? As you are probably aware, many people try to make money online and fail. You've already read about a small portion of the litany of failures in my wake. There are many reasons people don't succeed at making money online, but one of the main reasons is because they don't take the time to really, truly evaluate the different opportunities and consider which is best for them. To be fair, most opportunities out there don't come with a pros and cons checklist telling you which people might be the best match.

If it were only important that you feel properly educated about which opportunities are out there after reading this book, then this would not matter as much to me. However, while education is nice, and one of the goals of this book, the true measure of success for me is if you are able to pick a path and take action with some level of success. For that reason, I'm going to ask you to take a small journey of self-analysis before we move on to the actual Profit Paths that we will focus on for the remainder of this book.

I know it might be tempting to skip this section and forge onward into the meat and potatoes of moonlighting on the internet, but I wholeheartedly encourage you not to do that. This book has so much packed into it that there simply isn't room for fluff. If I emphasize something in here, it means that in my estimation it's very important. I can't stress enough how much more successful you will be if you create a Profit Path Profile through the process I'm outlining in this chapter, so that when you read through the different Profit Paths, you will have a much clearer idea of what you're looking for, what you bring to the table, and what your personal limitations are. If you can trust this process, I promise you will have a more beneficial experience in choosing the right path for you.

Profit Path Profile Form

I have created a printable form that you can fill out while you're reading this chapter so that by the end you will have an initial Profit Path Profile created. You will likely modify this over time, but having it on hand will make reading through the different Profit Paths much more beneficial. Instead of just learning about them, you can more accurately evaluate which ones are best suited to you, your goals, and your lifestyle. For your convenience, I'm also listing the questions here in the book. To download the forms, visit www.MoonlightingontheInternet.com.

BE YOUR OWN BOSS VS. OWNING AN ONLINE BUSINESS

One of the first questions you need to ask yourself is whether you resonate more with the thought of working for yourself or owning an online business. Either way, you're stepping onto an entrepreneurial path. It might seem as though this isn't an important distinction, but it is. Let's explore the differences.

Work for Yourself

While working for yourself does mean having your own business, the distinction is that you are relying on your skills, talents, or resources for your monetization. A great example of this is being a freelance writer. You are writing content for money. You may decide to turn this into a more formal freelance writing business, or you may just freelance casually on the side. Either way, your income is dependent on your ability to write quality content.

Own Your Own Online Business

By contrast, if you were to choose to try your hand at ecommerce, you would be developing channels online to sell products, either digital or physical. So you are definitely still working for yourself, especially in the beginning, but the "thing" you are selling does not rely on your individual work, generally speaking. So while you are still putting time and effort into your company, and therefore working for yourself, your point of monetization is something outside the work you do.

To bring this comparison full circle, there are ways to go from being your own boss to creating an online business. My story is a great example of that. I started out as a freelance writer with no defined company. I just picked up gigs online through freelancing boards and sites. After a while, I created my own business as a freelance writer. At this point, I was still a solopreneur working for myself. The true shift from working for myself to being an online business owner came when I created a content creation company that outsourced other writers to clients. My business was no longer reliant on my personal writing skills to make money. My job at that point primarily became the business owner/CEO.

Honestly Assess Yourself

As you are evaluating this question, try to keep in mind that one answer is not superior to the other. There is a time and a place for both models, and they each have their pros and cons. It's very important that you evaluate this without prejudgment of what you want the answer to be. The true mark of success will lie in your ability to identify which path you'll gain the most from, depending on where you currently are in your life.

And remember, whatever you decide doesn't have to be permanent. I have worn both hats off and on throughout my career, and I believe that will never change. As I write this, I co-own our digital marketing agency, Ember Dragon, with my business partner, Heather Sneed. However, at this time I am the best sales funnel and marketing strategist in the company, so some of our campaigns and contracts depend on my skills as a strategist. I'm actually operating in a dual role at the moment. I was able to identify that this was a smart and enjoyable move for my business partner and myself, my company, and our business plan.

In my opinion, how easy or difficult you find your road to success to be is largely determined by your ability to honestly assess whether any opportunity you see before you is a beneficial match. It's so easy to get caught up in the next big thing, or what I like to call "Shiny Object Syndrome." Really being in tune with your own abilities and limitations, as well as being able to objectively evaluate opportunities without being influenced by emotional excitement or starry-eyed hope, is a skill that will serve you well for life.

PRODUCTS VS. SERVICES

All the Profit Paths we discuss in this book fall into one of two categories, "Products" and "Services." I realize this is a gross generalization, but I feel it's an appropriate way to teach the material, even though there is a lot of room for crossover between the two.

Lowest Barrier to Entry

It is a common and legitimate strategy when you're first getting started to choose the path with the lowest barrier to entry. This is especially true if you have a strong need for a short-term cash infusion. For this reason, most of the time when starting out, the answer to the question about whether you will work for yourself or create an online business will largely go hand in hand with whether you start off selling services or products.

The determining factors are different for everyone. Do you have a skill that you can easily freelance with if you just knew how? Are you connected to a specific market that would jump-start your efforts to sell a product in that industry? Have you already developed a product but have no idea how to market it? Your situation is unique to you, so it makes sense that the smartest path to start on will be unique to you as well.

It might sound silly, but many people don't actually know which Profit Paths naturally have the lowest barrier to entry for them. It's not something that they have had cause to think about before. People tend to put all the focus of their research and analysis on a Profit Path, with little to no assessment of themselves and whether the opportunity they are looking at is an ideal fit for them. Our questions are designed to enable you not only to learn about Profit Paths, but also to evaluate which ones are the best match for you, so you can make the best possible decisions.

Profit Path Profile Questions

As you read through and answer these questions, remember that there are no wrong answers. No one answer is superior to another, and whatever you select right now doesn't need to be permanent or exclusive. You can wear more than one hat! My advice is to answer based on your gut instinct. The important thing is to be honest, so you can select Profit Paths you will have the most success with.

The first two questions are designed to help you identify which type of Profit Paths appeal the most to you:

1. As you read through this section, which of these did you resonate with the most?
   - I like the idea of being my own boss and working for myself by leveraging talents and skills that I already have to make money online.
   - I like the idea of owning my own business by setting up a Profit Path that I will then operate and manage, but that isn't necessarily monetizing my own personal skill set.
2. Is your "gut reaction" answer to #1 in alignment with what is realistic for you in your current life circumstances?
   - Yes
   - No
   - I'm not sure. I need more information to understand and decide.

Before we get into more specific self-analysis, I have to ask: What did you find out? Did your answers surprise you? Is reading this book the first time you have ever thought of "being my own boss" as different from "running my own business"? If so, you're one step ahead of the game because you're able to make the distinction and realize which one is most attractive to you.

PROFIT PATH PROFILE ASSESSMENT: PERSONAL SKILLS, RESOURCES, AND LIFESTYLE

Some people are great at assessing themselves. Some people are great at evaluating opportunities. However, I find most need some guidance to discover which opportunities are the best match for you and your goals. Because this is so critical to your success, I have created three online assessments designed to help you with this process.

One of the first steps to proper self-analysis in preparation for choosing a Profit Path is being crystal clear about what you bring to the table and what your limitations are. If you want to be the best you in this new business adventure and in your home life, you're going to need to be on the level about what your strengths and weaknesses are. As you're reading this book and evaluating your Profit Path options, I want you to go in with your eyes open, knowing what you're good at, where you're lacking, and what your non-negotiables are. Remember, this profile is JUST for you. No one else ever has to see it.

Personal Skills and Talents

This is where you get to take inventory of how awesome you are! Everyone has marketable skills. That doesn't mean your marketable skills will have anything to do with your chosen Profit Path. Hopefully by now you have already acknowledged that you don't know what you don't know. By creating a portfolio, for lack of a better word, of your skills and talents, as you evaluate different opportunities, you'll more quickly be able to assess what things you will need to hire or acquire to be successful, and if that is realistic for you at this time.

Everything should be taken into consideration. This should be a fact-based list without emotion attached to it. Even if you don't at this moment understand how a particular skill or experience could be beneficial, write it down. I'd also like you to write them down without respect to whether you enjoy doing them.

Download a copy of the Personal Skills Assessment from www.MoonlightingontheInternet.com.

Love/Hate Relationship with Your Skills?

Excellent! Now that you have an impartial list of your skills and talents, you get to rate them based on how much you enjoy doing each of them. Next to each talent or skill, rate it on a scale of 1 to 5.

1. I LOVE doing this.
2. It's not my first choice, but I'm good at it, so if it needs to get done, I can do it.
3. I'm neutral. I could take it or leave it.
4. While I'm good at this, I don't want to do it any longer than it takes to replace myself.
5. I'd rather eat dog food than do this skill for any length of time; it's a deal breaker.

One of the reasons this is so important is that being in business for yourself has a lot of unexpected twists and turns. No matter how well you plan, once you put yourself in a role or place a responsibility on your plate, you may get stuck there for much longer than you anticipate. In addition, most entrepreneurial-minded people I know have difficulty, at least in the beginning, of letting go of responsibilities they do well. It's a hindrance to believe that no one will ever do it as well as you, so therefore you will never be able to pass it off. Be realistic about how you feel about your strengths, so that if you end up supplying that skill for longer than you planned, your business or lifestyle doesn't suffer because of it. People who enjoy what they do get things done faster and more efficiently and are happier in general.

Being aware of the skills you bring to the table and how you feel about each of them helps you make long-term and short-term decisions and set goals. It gives you clarity about whom you might need to hire when looking at any specific Profit Path and helps you evaluate what areas you may need to finance vs. sweat equity. It helps you make outsourcing and partnering decisions, and it will greatly impact how you look at your implementation timelines and processes.

Hobbies, Passions, and Experience

One thing that is really exciting about being an entrepreneur is that often the paths with the lowest barriers to entry center on topics you are already familiar with. You may even be a quasi or legitimate expert on the topic. Making money online is exciting. Making money online about a topic you love is even better. That's when your work doesn't feel like work. For this reason, listing your hobbies, interests, and topics you're experienced in is really helpful. When you're evaluating some of these Profit Paths, already being aware of niches and industries that you have some advanced knowledge in will be very helpful to you.

There is no interest that doesn't count. Most (if not all) things have monetizable areas. While you are getting ready to make your own list, here are a few ideas to help you brainstorm.

◀ *Hobbies.* Do you have hobbies about which you are passionate? Perhaps you belly dance or sail or are really into massively multi-player online role-playing games (MMORPG) games like World of Warcraft. Do you show dogs? Do you run a playgroup for moms? Are you an artist? Do you play any sports? Do you love to travel? Are you an avid photographer? Do you sew?

- *Education.* Do you have a degree or certification in anything? Do you have a psychology degree? Are you a certified doula? Did you get a certification or training program in something else?

- *Profession.* Are you or were you at any time a nurse? Have you worked as a dental hygienist? Did you work in a flower shop and can make wicked flower arrangements? Do you have experience in event planning? Have you worked in real estate off and on your whole life?

- *Everyday life.* Are you a fashionista? Do you follow the current music scene? Are you interested in politics? Are you a parent? Are you a corporate executive? Are you an extreme couponer?

These are just a few examples to get your juices flowing. Trust me, if you have something you are passionate about or interested in, there are tons of other people who are, too. There very well may be a Profit Path in that industry meant for you, so be thorough!

Financial Resources

I struggled writing this section because I know a good portion of you will respond to any suggestion to evaluate how much financial resources you have to devote to your new endeavor with a resounding, "If I had extra money lying around, I wouldn't be reading this book in the first place." So before we talk about how much money you do or don't have available, let's make a deal about how we will think about money during this exercise.

Not having as much money as you want is never pleasant. Whether your annual income is $30,000 or $30 million, it's simply distressing. So the invitation I would give to you while doing this exercise is to try to have a positive relationship with money. As long as you or I or anyone is focusing on how much we don't have and how much pressure and stress we feel about that, then we can't be fully present to evaluate how we can improve our situation.

I'm sure you're familiar with the phrase "It takes money to make money." There is definitely truth to that, but that does NOT mean you have to pull money out of your pocket before you make your first dollar. So there is a message of encouragement here. Yes, I definitely believe that in the end it almost always takes money to make money, but there are a lot of ways to start on your path with very little initial investment. That's good news, right?

That said, as you're building your Profit Path Profile, you should take inventory on what capital you could draw from should you need or choose to. Here is the first question I want you to answer with complete honesty: Are you good at managing money? Before you answer, I want to share something with you that may surprise you: In my opinion, whether or not you are naturally gifted at managing money is not as important as knowing whether you are. I'll say it again, a different way. I care FAR less about whether you are "good" or "bad" with finances than whether you have a realistic understanding of your strengths or weaknesses in this area.

I'm not advocating being bad with money. What I'm advocating is getting super real with yourself about it so that if, by chance, you tend to be bad with finances, you can compensate for that weakness. I am one of those people who is not naturally gifted at managing my own finances. I spent years trying to change that, but in the end, the problem was that I'm just not motivated by money. I'm far more motivated by what I can do with money for myself, my family, and the world as a whole.

While I got better through concentrated effort, it's never become a real strength. This doesn't mean I don't understand how to manage money; it's just not a natural gift. The day I got clear on that and stopped feeling bad about it is the day I arranged for other people who are naturally gifted with money to start managing it for me. The truth is that even though I am capable, I'm never going to do it as well as they do because I just don't geek out on it. It's not where my heart is. I really, intensely care that my money is managed properly and I really, intensely care about being part of the process. I just don't have any interest in leading the charge.

So I took it out of my hands and put it into hands more qualified than mine. THAT was a good decision. That is an example of evaluating my situation and deciding there are better fits than myself for that role in my businesses.

So with that in mind, I'm requesting that you take a strong look at yourself and answer the question, "Are you good at managing money?" Release yourself from judgment of whether the answer is favorable or unfavorable and just answer it honestly. If the answer is yes, then great. If the answer is no, then it needs to be on your radar so you can put a plan in place around your finances.

When you're not naturally gifted at money management, you have to be intentional about how you structure the financial management, since you're not well served by leaving it exclusively in your own hands.

Now that that's out of the way, you don't need to feel bad about whether you are personally great at managing money, because either way you're going to make strong, intelligent business decisions so that your finances are in good hands.

90-Day Sacrifice

In the event that you do find a worthy reason to put some capital behind your efforts, my question to you is: How much money could you funnel into your efforts each month if you would potentially not see a return for 90 days?

Remember, I prefaced this with "worthy reason." That means you have identified something that you really do need to be successful that requires money to get. If this is something that gets you to your end goal, how much could you draw from your personal resources to make it happen? Is it $10 per month? $100? $1,000? $10,000?

Whatever number you wrote down, follow that up with where you could get that money. Some people have extra money in the bank to draw from and some people do not. Either way, everyone—I repeat, EVERYONE—spends discretionary money each month whether they have it or not. The point of this exercise is to determine how you could squeeze a little extra money from your budget if you found an opportunity worth investing in. What could you sacrifice to make it happen if you were really serious about it?

Could you cut out fast food? Those $5 daily lattes? Cable TV? What is it? We all have our little luxuries. Again, this profile is just for you. No one else is reviewing it and judging you. But you will want to know ahead of time, if you stumble upon that opportunity of a lifetime, what your plan would be to make it happen. You may never do it, but just knowing what you're capable of gives you the ability to evaluate opportunities in a much more realistic way instead of just dreaming, hoping, and guessing.

Common Financial Starting Points

As mentioned multiple times in this book, we all have unique circumstances, but speaking generally, most people tend to fall in one of three financial categories when they are first getting started.

- *Nest Egg.* You have a little money set aside that you could devote to your project if you felt confident that it was going to be a worthwhile investment. This allows you to worry less about what you can or can't accomplish on your own because you have a little more flexibility to get your Profit Path off the ground.
- *Do-It-Yourselfers.* You will do the majority of the work required through sweat equity, either because you have to or because you (or someone you are closely connected to) have the natural talent and ability to do the work.
- *Hybrid.* Most of you will fall into this category. You'll do some of the work yourself and outsource anything you can't do yourself and can afford to hire someone else to do for you.

Having a clear understanding of what resources you have to draw from enables you to evaluate opportunities properly so you don't get in over your head and end up in a worse situation than you started in. It also gives you the foundation of a plan to create the money you need when a worthy cause presents itself. Finally, when you have limited resources, you want to make sure you are applying them where they will have the greatest impact in getting you toward your goals of sustainable profitability.

Personal Limitations and Lifestyle

When you hear the word "currency," people almost exclusively think about money, for obvious reasons. However, I would like to inject a couple of additional angles on how you view currency.

1. Money is not the only currency required to create a sustainable path of income online.
2. Just like money, these other currencies are not infinite wells.
3. Just like money, you have other priorities in your life that these currencies must be divided across.

Let's look at some of these different types of finite currencies that you should consider.

TIME

Time is by far one of the most precious, sought-after commodities that you possess. It takes time to build a business. It takes time to run a family. It takes time to manage a romantic relationship. The list goes on. You may not think of your time as a currency, but you absolutely must while working to make money online. I would submit that to most people, their time is more valuable than money. It must be treated as the treasure it really is.

How much time do you realistically have to spend each week creating your Profit Path? Can you carve out one hour per week? Two? Five? More?

It's not enough to know how much time you could devote to this; it's equally (if not more) important to have a plan for where you're going to get that time. Just like money, if you don't plan for it, life will suck it away!

My follow-up question is that if the opportunity were good enough, could you temporarily devote more time to creating your Profit Path? Remember, "no" is an acceptable answer. The point of this process is to know what resources you really have available to you and how you would get them if you needed or chose to.

People make the mistake of thinking that money is worth more to them than time when starting a business with few resources. But I actually don't think that's true. I think it's more likely that time is an easier sacrifice to make because you literally don't have access to more cash. It's not that people value their time less; it's that their goal is important enough to sacrifice their precious time for the short term so they have more freedom not to in the long term.

PATIENCE

This is another currency that is not infinite. Busy, driven people get worn down. The more you are balancing on your plate, the more patience will be demanded of you. I can add to this list positivity, coping ability, and energy—these are all critical in all areas of our life. I bring this up because burnout is a very real possibility. Wherever you are spending your various currencies, you are taking away from another area of your life.

For most people, no amount of financial freedom will replace a broken family, a lost love, or poor health. I remember saying to my husband one day, "I think my business has turned into my sixth child, and anyone observing me would assume it's my favorite, because it's getting the most love and attention." Balance is a very real thing, and it's not something that should be sacrificed in the pursuit of financial freedom.

Think carefully about this next set of questions, because most people don't even consider them when creating a Profit Path online.

BALANCE

How will you stay balanced, and how will you know when you're not? I find it very helpful to write down what is important to me when it comes to maintaining balance and what might be red flags that my life has shifted off balance in a way that isn't acceptable. Sometimes you will choose to run with your time and resources unbalanced in the short term to get a dream off the ground. That's OK. The point is that you're doing it deliberately. Trust me when I tell you it is not pleasant to crash because you've been running unbalanced too hard for too long and you have no idea how to course correct.

SUPPORT

Who is your support system? Is it a spouse? A best friend? Does your dog help you stay balanced and happy? Who can you lean on? Who is a resounding voice of reason that can help you evaluate what you're doing and how you're doing it when things get stressful? Everyone needs a support structure, so who is on your "Team Awesome"?

What Are Your Deal Breakers?

The last thing I want you to evaluate in this personal deep dive are your deal breakers and/or limitations. We all have them. A good example is that I have people on my staff who don't work on their Sabbath day for religious reasons. For some of them this is Saturday and for others this is Sunday. This is important enough to them that if building their personal Profit Paths required them to work on the Sabbath, then it wouldn't be worth it. That's a part of their lifestyle that is non-negotiable.

Some of your deal breakers we might have already covered. You may have an allotted amount of time you are willing to devote to your Profit Path, and if it consistently requires more time than that, then it's not a good match for you. Another example is travel. For some people, having to travel frequently would be a deal breaker. For others, the thought of being required to do any public speaking would kill the deal.

So what are your non-negotiable and personal limitations? This is especially important. It's very disheartening to get halfway into a Profit Path and realize it's not going to work for you. Please take some time to compose your own list of deal breakers.

Ultimately, this deep dive into your skills and resources is about really understanding what's important to you and what you bring to the table that you can leverage to make the most intelligent plans for moving forward.

PROFIT PATH PROFILE ASSESSMENT: PREFERRED LEARNING STYLE

You're probably aware that not everyone's preferred learning style is the same. The method for evaluating a person's learning style that I like best is the Myers-Briggs (MB) Assessment. I honestly feel I could write an entire book just on the MB methodology and how beneficial it is. However, there is so much phenomenal information you can research online that I won't take up space diving too heavily into it in this book.

The important thing for you to understand is that Myers-Briggs, ultimately, is a preference test. There are 16 distinct personality types, but all of them fall under one of four personas: Competitive, Humanist, Methodical, and Spontaneous. Each persona has its own preferences, and while the MB methodology teaches us a lot about ourselves, one of those things is our preferred method of learning.

Because your success at creating and implementing a Profit Path is so important to us, we have created multiple versions of our most important material. This way, instead of using the shotgun approach and hoping as many people as possible will be able to use the information, we created four versions, each in the preferred learning style of the four personas. This gives you the advantage of learning in the ideal way for you.

While not a requirement, we highly encourage you to take the Myers-Briggs Assessment because it will enable us to provide you with the highest quality of education, support, and care. You can learn more about the test at www.mbtionline.com.

MOONLIGHTING ON THE INTERNET: PROFIT PATH CALCULATOR

I've put a lot of thought and effort into this book to help you choose a Profit Path that will be a good match for your personal ambitions, lifestyle, and talents. However, as I keep pointing out, you likely don't know what you don't know. As a way to really serve you well, we have also created an additional assessment called Moonlighting on the Internet: Profit Path Calculator.

This is by far the most popular tool we have to help determine which Profit Path makes the most sense for you. It only takes a few minutes to go through and is designed to help you identify, based on your answers, the pros and cons of each opportunity in relation to your specific situation. I think you'll find it useful, even if you think you already know which avenue you would like to pursue first.

You can take this assessment now, before you read through the different Profit Paths, or you can take it after you read the book and see if the suggestions it makes are in line with your own assessment of where you're going to start. You can have confidence knowing that we are committed to providing you with assessments, tips, and guidance designed to help you make the best choice for you, your family, and your future. Visit www.MoonlightingontheInternet.com for more information.

Now, let's get started!

PART II

SERVICE-BASED PROFIT PATHS

The first Profit Paths we are going to explore are service-based. These are paths where you're selling services as opposed to products. Because many of the paths mentioned in this section fall under the freelancing umbrella, I wanted to make sure that you have a good understanding of what freelancing is. So, before we get into the different service paths, let's take a minute to evaluate this topic.

FREELANCING PROFIT PATH PREVIEW

Freelancing is ideal if you resonate with working for yourself and have marketable skills that are frequently in demand. In this section, we explore the following Profit Paths:

- Freelance writer

- Freelance graphic designer

- Freelance tech

- Virtual assistant

Top Level Pros

- Low barrier of entry if you have an in-demand skill

- Low-cost startup

- "Try Before You Buy" without investing too much into it

Top Level Cons

- You are the manual labor

- Fight being a commodity

FREELANCING EXPLAINED

Freelancing is a very common term that you may or may not have heard before. Dictionary.com defines a freelancer this way:

Freelancer: A person who works as a writer, designer, performer, or the like, selling work or services by the hour, day, job, etc., rather than working on a regular salary basis for one employer.

Shelby's Definition: I simply define freelancing as selling your own skills without ties to any one company with full freedom to choose what, who, and how you want to work with your clients. In a nutshell, freelancing is successfully earning income with your own skills. I also almost exclusively consider freelancing a service-based path, and that is how we will address it in this book.

TYPICAL LOW-BARRIER ENTRY POINT

Learning how to successfully freelance online is one of the quickest ways to begin making money online. This is especially true if you have a commonly sought-after skill set like writing, graphic design, or tech-related skills like website development or computer programming. However, if you are reading this and don't think you have a specific in-demand skill set, hang in there and keep reading, because learning how to become a virtual assistant may be a perfect fit for you.

I've chosen to focus on four specific freelance paths in this book, but honestly, there are so many different freelance possibilities that if you have experience in a different arena, you will be able to apply the information we cover here to your own freelance path. Much of the knowledge will be applicable regardless of the type of services you are providing.

PROS AND CONS OF FREELANCING
Pros

- *Low-cost startup.* Freelancing is one of the lowest cost entry points. There are ways to literally get up and running with little to no money out of your pocket upfront.

- *The market is massive and growing.* More than 53 million Americans are doing freelance work, according to a new, landmark survey conducted by the independent research firm Edelman Berland and commissioned by Freelancers Union and Elance-oDesk. That's 34 percent of the entire workforce. (Source: www.freelancersunion.org/blog/dispatches/2014/09/04/53million/)

- *Location independence.* You can literally live pretty much anywhere you want. As long as you can connect to the internet with some sort of reasonable frequency, you are not stuck living in any particular place.

- *Choose when you work.* You get to be in full control of your schedule. Do you only want to work 7 A.M. to 10 A.M. every day? Do you only work on Tuesdays and Thursdays? As a freelancer, you can set the schedule that works for you and honors the commitments you make to your client.

- *Pick your clients.* You get to choose who you want to work with. When you're working for a company, their clients are their clients and you have to work with them. However, when you're freelancing, you get full control over who you work for.

- *Pick your projects.* You get to pick the type of projects that you're going to work on. If you have specific types of projects you like to do or certain niches you prefer to focus on, you have the complete freedom to make that happen.

- *Better income potential.* As you build your reputation and portfolio/ history of successfully completed projects, you have more opportunity to charge more money. Pricing is a delicate thing, and it may take time for you to find the balance of when and how you can charge more, but the silver lining is that it's in your hands. You don't have to wait for an employer to notice, appreciate, and compensate you for your excellent work.

- *Try before you buy in.* One huge benefit of freelancing is that because the barrier of entry is so low, you really can dip your toe in the water and see how you like it before you invest a significant amount of money and time into making it a more serious path for yourself.

Cons

- *Inconsistent income.* Unless you add a recurring model that makes sense into your freelancing business, your income can be very inconsistent—especially when you're first starting out. Sometimes the work is steady, but oftentimes you end up in cycles of what feels like feast or famine.

- *You are the labor.* Your monetization is completely dependent on you doing the work. When you freelance, you are selling your own services. So if you decide to go on vacation, or take time off, your income stops.

- *Lead acquisition is on you.* Until you have a reputation built up that yields repeat business, you have to go out and fish for every client. Part of not working for someone else is that no one else is feeding you prospects.

- *Lower income potential.* What? But you just listed "higher income potential" as a pro! That's right. But this follows the theory of "opposition in all things." Just as there is potential to make more money freelancing, there is also the potential that you will make less money. As mentioned above, incoming work isn't guaranteed. In addition, lead acquisition skills don't come naturally to everyone, and if you're not careful, you could unintentionally pinhole yourself into a lower hourly rate than is desirable.

- *No traditional benefits.* When you freelance it does not come with health insurance, a 401(k), or an HR department to help settle disputes.

- *Commodity complications.* If you are not intentional about preventing your services from being lumped in as a commodity, then you could end up in a situation where you work very hard and get paid too little. (We will talk about ways to avoid this pitfall.)

Conclusion: As a freelancer, you get all the pros and you get all the cons. Regardless if your journey is pleasant or difficult or mixed, you get all the ups and all the downs. You get to live the dream of being your own boss, but the reality is that sometimes your boss is a huge, incompetent jerk.

CHAPTER 4

FREELANCE WRITING PROFIT PATH

already mentioned that approximately 34 percent of the workforce is now freelancing instead of being traditionally employed. Almost 50 percent of those freelancers provide writing as one of their services. Right now there are nearly 4,000 writing-related jobs listed on Elance alone. While there is a lot of competition, there is definitely no lack of demand for quality writers, and frankly, the number of freelance writers who actually do quality work is far smaller than you think. So be encouraged by this statistic, not intimidated by the competition.

SOME QUICK BASICS

In Chapter 15, I'll cover marketing in more depth. However, if you're new to the digital marketing world, having a basic understanding of a few terms and concepts will make reading this section easier.

To be successful as a freelance writer, it's not enough to just understand what the different types of freelance writing are. It's critical to also understand why people are ordering them in the first place. Clients are not paying for content just to have content. They have a purpose and reasons they need that content. Understanding their intentions can determine how happy your clients are with your finished work.

When I give keynote speeches, one of the calling card topics I tend to speak on is the importance of buyer intent. In the digital marketing world, understanding intention is possibly the most important component. You will be hard-pressed to satisfy your clients if you don't understand not just what content they want created, but why. This is very, very important. We'll go into this in more depth in the marketing section of this book, but you'll see me reference it in the specific Profit Paths as well. Understanding intention will give you an advantage over many of your competitors.

Opting In

There are two things that every business cares about online: sales and lead acquisition. One common way that people capture leads on their website is by creating a free offer that is appealing to their target market. Prospects will submit their email addresses to have the offer sent to them. This is called opting in. When someone opts in, they are giving the administrator of the website permission to contact them. Opt-ins are one of the primary metrics that businesses measure to determine the success of their marketing tactics and campaigns.

Copywriting

Copywriting is one of those terms that has different meaning for varied audiences. You could have ten clients ask you if you do copywriting, and each of them would be thinking of something completely different. This causes a lot of confusion in the online writing world. For the purposes of this book, the only type of content that we will refer to as "copywriting" is sales copy. We will use other terms to define any other type of writing.

Call to Action (CTA)

The Call to Action is simply the action any content owner hopes the prospect reading it will take. This could be as simple as "Leave a comment below" on a blog or more direct with "Enter your email to receive . . ." or "Click here to buy."

TYPES OF FREELANCE WRITING

The way that people categorize different types of writing is all over the place. Having started out my career online as a freelance writer, and having owned a content creation company since 2007, it made sense to me to create three overarching writing categories for this book. In my opinion, the most commonly sought-after writing falls into:

1. Product creation
2. Off-site web content
3. On-site web content

To be a successful freelance writer, it is critical to understand the different types of writing that your clients will commonly request. You can find a lot of information online about the different types of popular content creation, but it's equally if not more important to understand why people order the different types and what the end result is that your client is hoping to achieve.

Product Creation

The type of writing that would fall under the Product Creation category is any piece of content your client would sell, give away, or incorporate into one of their offerings. That may not always be true, but all the types of content I'm going to share with you in this section are commonly used as products or parts of products online. This is all part of the massive information marketing sector of the internet.

Some of the more common content pieces requested for product creation are:

- eBooks
- Reports and guides

- White papers
- Newsletters
- Courses
- Supplemental material

This section will explain what these products are, why your clients are ordering them, and what they hope to gain by doing so. Understanding this will help you become a profitable freelance writer.

eBooks

Simply put, ebooks are electronic books. Heck, you may even be reading the ebook form of this book right now! A lot of ebooks are simply electronic versions of books that are in print. However, many people are now writing ebooks that have no print version, and they can be about anything and everything under the sun.

Savvy marketers have been giving away and selling ebooks since before I began working in this space. However, they have become far more mainstream since then. If you go to Amazon and take a look at the many, many books available for the Kindle, you will quickly see that people have grasped the monetization and branding power behind publishing ebooks. (In fact, it's a Profit Path in this book!) With the popularity of devices like the Amazon Kindle, many people actually prefer electronic versions of books.

The quality of ebooks is all over the place. Just like anything that becomes mainstream in the digital marketing space, there are a plethora of low-value ebooks that are basically crap. However, there are also a lot of really great, high-quality ebooks. Assuming you are pricing yourself fairly, high quality is what your client will be expecting you to deliver to them.

Reports

To be honest with you, reports are just miniversions of ebooks. Reports are quick reads, which usually means they cover one topic that the readers are highly interested in. An effective strategy that people commonly use reports for is to offer highly sought-after information in exchange for the prospect opting in to download it. That's definitely not the only reason that people request reports, which takes us back to why it's so important to understand your client's intention, which we will cover in more detail shortly.

GUIDES

I mention this as a separate entity because people will very commonly ask you to create a guide for them. However, unlike the terms "ebook" or "report," there isn't a separate, mostly universal understanding of what they are looking for. When people request a guide, they could be looking for something longer like an ebook or shorter like a report. The only truly differentiating factor is that when something is termed a "guide," it implies to the reader that they will be guided through something.

Here is an example of a report vs. a guide:

Report: *Making Money Online as a Freelance Writer*

Guide: *Freelance Writer's Guide to Making Money Online*

It may not initially look to you as if there is much difference. However, the report version could be a good-to-know informational piece that helps interested prospects begin looking for how to go about becoming a freelance writer. It can give all kinds of information on the "what" without giving any information on the "how" and stay true to the title.

However, if the guide was just an informational piece but gave no instructions on how to successfully make money as a freelance writer online, then it would not provide what the title promises the prospects. This is a subtle difference, but language is very important. Descriptive words make promises in the readers' minds, regardless of the content owner's intentions. Part of being a skilled freelance writer is helping your clients make better products than they are asking for. Often, you will know far more about content marketing and buyers' intentions than your client will.

WHITE PAPERS

Requests for a white paper will require a little clarification. Before ebooks and reports became commonplace in the digital marketing world, white papers had a fairly universal definition. Wikipedia defines a white paper as "an authoritative report or guide informing readers in a concise manner about a complex issue and presenting the issuing body's philosophy on the matter. It is meant to help readers understand an issue, solve a problem, or make a decision."

However, in the marketing world, when many people ask you to write a white paper, they actually want a report. Often they want to call it a white paper because they want the content piece to sound more professional or authoritative. In contrast, you will get people who run in very professional circles who order a more traditional white paper. It is very important for you to get clarity on this before you accept the project.

On-Site and Off-Site Web Content

Content marketing is a huge buzzword right now, not only online among the more guerrilla internet marketers, but also in mainstream corporate America. It should be. With the way online search has been shifting over the past few years, the power of content marketing has grown. This section is devoted to projects that would fall under the content marketing flag.

To understand content marketing, you have to understand why people are doing it in the first place. While there are a plethora of reasons, I have boiled it down to four primary purposes.

1. *Branding.* People use content to help educate their target market about who they are. In the beginning, they may have to teach their target market that they even exist. In the online world, if you want people to know who you are and what you have to offer them, you need pieces of content to populate in front of your target market when they are searching for relevant information.

2. *Provide value.* Once people learn who you are, it's very important that you consistently provide value. The internet is a fast-paced ball of chaos. If your target market is constantly inundated with information and you're not providing value to them, they are not going to continue to give you their time. (Or their money.)

3. *Belief.* If someone is your target market and they can afford you, but they don't opt in or buy from you, then they did not believe you had the solution they were looking for. People have to spend

FISHING AND STRAY CATS

Maybe it's because my dad and brothers are such avid fishermen that the analogy that comes to mind centers on fishing. For this analogy to work, we need to imagine the internet as one amazing lake. In the real world, the type of fish you want to catch will determine where you'll fish. But for our example to work, we need to pretend that every type of fish you could ever want to catch all live together in one lake. In this marvelous internet lake, the website owners are the fishermen, and their potential prospects are the fish.

In order to not walk away from a fishing trip with an empty cooler, you have to make sure you are fishing where the fish you hope to catch hang out and you're using enticing bait. Sometimes you have to rotate through a few different options before you find a bait that really works. For this reason, fishermen tend to have tackle boxes full of different equipment and bait that are all designed to get the job done.

Content marketing is really not too different. The website owners study what is working at enticing their target market to bite and do their best to replicate that. They create different types of content and distribute it intelligently throughout the internet, hoping their prospects will take notice and bite. And just like the real world, they don't tend to randomly toss the content out; they study the most strategic places to "fish" online. It's not too difficult to figure out what type of bait your prospects like. The complication is that unlike reality, where people fish in different bodies of water all over the planet, you're fishing in the exact same lake as every other fisherman in the world.

There are a lot of ways to stand out, but one thing you have to your advantage is that in our example, the fish have much more diverse appetites than real fish do. When you distribute content, you don't only do it about one topic; you put "bait" centered on all the different pain points, solutions, and interests your prospects are searching for. Your tackle box needs to be full of value that meets the various intentions driving the buyers in your market.

At fear of oversimplifying, content marketing is really all about attracting the attention of your prospects, convincing them you're worth looking at over everyone else tossing bait in front of them, and establishing a long-term relationship instead of ending up in the dreaded "catch and release" program. Actually, instead of fishing, what website owners really want is a relationship closer to that of a stray cat that you fed a few times out of kindness, so now it comes back to your house every day looking for more!

time with you before they spend money with you. Strategic content helps move your prospects up the continuum of belief.

4. *Conversions.* Simply put, content is designed to get people to buy whatever you are selling. Opt-ins and sales are the primary ways people measure success, but many people completely miss the mark by only focusing on the numbers. If you understand how to nurture your prospects through content and engagement before the sale, you will make a LOT more money.

In the fast-paced world of the internet, off-site content is primarily used as part of the lead acquisition strategy. It's content that the website owners put out there to get the attention of their target market, provide value, and hopefully lure them to their website, where they can establish a better connection with them. (Fishing and stray cats, remember?) As I write this, content marketing has more power than it ever has before in aiding your lead acquisition efforts.

I could write about the different types of off-site content that may be requested of you, but that list is so huge. On top of that, the types of content frequently requested change and evolve with the whim of the ever-important Search Engine Gods like Google. For that reason, I am choosing not to write on them specifically. Instead, what I want to impress upon you is the importance of learning the purpose and intention behind any piece of content you are hired to write, because that will be the differentiating factor behind whether you do your job merely well, or awesomely.

That said, here are a few types of off-site content that are popular at the time I'm writing this book and are likely to have evergreen uses over time:

- Press releases
- Guest content on popular blogs, websites, and parasites
- Articles
- Authoritative content

I chose these types of off-site content to highlight because I feel they have a good chance of remaining regularly requested by clients. Whether or not they stay evergreen, just knowing what they are and why they are used will help you understand new content ordering trends that may surface in the future.

On-Site Content

The intentions behind on-site content are vast and diverse. Pages on the actual site can be part of the fishing strategies that we discussed in the "Fishing and Stray Cats" sidebar about off-site content. However, the majority of the content on your client's main website will be designed to do three specific things:

1. Provide enough value to keep the prospect on the site and turn them into a repeat visitor with the hope that they will opt in so the website owner can begin marketing directly to them.
2. Turn prospects into buyers.

A WORD ABOUT AUTHORITATIVE CONTENT

There is one thing I would like to address about what I'm calling "authoritative content" before I move on to on-site content. When someone comes to you because they would like to publish an article on a more mainstream, authoritative site like *Entrepreneur* magazine, there are some things you should consider to protect yourself.

First, you should ask if the site has requested the content, or if they are just submitting content and hoping it will be accepted. This matters because those sites can deny content for any reason, including that they already have that topic covered at the time of submission. So it's very important that your success as a freelance writer is not determined by whether or not the piece is accepted, because it's not a factor you can control.

Second, be sure you are educated on the submission requirements of such sites. They often have specific guidelines, and you cannot and should not rely on your client to be aware of those guidelines or be certain they will pass them on to you accurately. If you're going to take on an order like this, you need to brush up on the requirements firsthand.

Finally, make sure your client is educated on both of the above points. Often they have no idea what the odds are of having their content featured on those more mainstream, authoritative sites. You will do yourself, and your client, a huge favor by properly managing their expectations. I advise you to do so in writing so you have a paper trail documenting the decisions made.

3. Achieve organic rankings for search terms that the buyers in their market are typing in so that their successful "fishing budget" can be much lower.

Marketing your website or business is commonly compared to dating, and it really is a great analogy. People need to get an idea of who you are and what you're all about before they're interested in considering any sort of commitment.

Website owners tend to measure conversions in two primary ways:

1. Opt-Ins
2. Sales

I don't disagree with these measuring sticks; however, I submit that the vast majority of people need to spend time with you before they give you permission to contact them directly and especially before they spend their money on you. For this reason, one primary intention behind on-site content is to move prospects up the continuum of belief that the website, product, or business they are looking at has exactly what the prospect is looking for.

You are definitely going to want to read the section in Chapter 15, Business and Marketing 101, about intention(beginning on page 264). I decided to cover it there instead of here because it is important to understand regardless of which Profit Path you choose due to the powerful impact it has on marketing. However, if you plan on trying your hand at being a freelance writer, it is critical for you to understand; knowing how to structure online content around the intention of the buyers in your market can literally save you thousands of dollars in your ongoing marketing budget.

Similarly to off-site marketing, the types of on-site content that may be requested of you are quite diverse, and you will want to do your own research before taking on any writing projects. However, I am going to talk specifically about blogging and copywriting. Both are so popular and so powerful that we offer training on our websites on each as their own Profit Paths. We're not featuring them as Profit Paths in this book, but there are some points worth noting for those of you leaning toward freelance writing.

Blogging

Blogging can be the topic of its own book. In fact, it is the topic of a lot of books! But the thing you need to keep in mind as a freelance writer is that above all else, a blog is a platform. It's a platform that nearly every kind of content you encounter online can live on. Websites need regularly updated content to continue to rank well, and a blog is the easiest way to meet this need. Blog posts are also often the main place on a website where interaction takes place with their prospects. Finally, unless website owners hate money, every blog post should have a CTA on it, even if it's as soft as "What do you think? Leave a comment below and let us know!"

This is where getting in the habit of learning the intention your client has behind the blog posts he is ordering from you is critical. Are they part of a marketing sales funnel? Are they informative, to help move prospects up the continuum of belief? Are they primarily targeting a specific group of keywords to help with website rankings? What is the desired action that your client hopes prospects will take after reading that blog post? If you can get to the root of those questions, your ability to create blog posts for clients can be a source of recurring income, because blogs are not something people tend to have written only once.

Because blog posts have great potential for recurring income for you as a freelance writer, I've created a quick, basic cheat sheet about formatting blog posts starting on page 57 to help give you a leg up for success if you're just starting out and have no experience with optimization.

Copywriting

Copywriting, as I'm defining it in this book, really is its own special beast. Because people use the term in so many different ways, you have to be very clear about what services you do and do not provide. I have found this a frustrating line to walk: You don't want to NOT market yourself as a copywriter, because that would eliminate all the people out there searching for basic website content that they call copywriting. On the other hand, the people who define it the way I do, as sales copy, will have a set of very specialized expectations.

Sales copy is not something that any writer, no matter how skilled, can just roll off the couch and write. I'm a talented writer, and I'm horrible at writing sales copy. (Probably because I hate doing it.) I'm great at outlining it and mapping out the psychology triggers that should be in it, but I'm terrible at actually sitting down and writing it. So if you're interested in providing sales copy services, which are extremely lucrative, you're going to need to do some research, and most of you will need to do a fair amount of training as well. When you are hired to write sales copy, you are responsible for conversions. So if your client is successfully driving their target market to the sales copy but people aren't buying, that's a difficult hurdle to recover from as a copywriter.

The point I really want to drive home regarding copywriting is to be super clear about what copywriting you do and don't do. If you're interested in becoming a sales copywriter, they are very well-paid. You'll just need to get some experience and testimonials under your belt before you can start charging the big bucks.

SEO ON A NEED-TO-KNOW BASIS

I really went back and forth about what to put into this book about Search Engine Optimization (SEO). I am a personal expert on SEO and we will cover some basics in Chapter 15 like on-site optimization and understanding market intent. Truth be told, I could write an entire book devoted to this topic and would need to update it at least annually for it to stay current and relevant. However, while SEO is something I would emphatically recommend when it comes to marketing your own business, it can be considered optional because there are non-SEO-related traffic sources. However, when it comes to successfully writing for clients, there is a certain level of SEO that is not optional. A huge portion of writing projects require you to have a basic understanding of SEO to satisfy your clients' needs.

Because I own and run a digital marketing agency, I've had my head deeply in sync with high-level, advanced SEO, so I will admit I find it a challenge to try to give an explanation here that is basic enough that it will make sense to you if you're new to this online world, but also brief enough to not take up a disproportionate amount of real estate in the book. I'm going to give you some nuts-and-bolts data with no fluff, but only in regard to how it relates to you as a freelance writer. My advice is to read through this section and then go to our website for more resources. This will also give you an appropriate springboard to dive into your own additional research.

The Basics

Search Engine Optimization (SEO) is the art (yes, it is an art) of seamlessly including links and keywords in content so that it rises in the rankings of a search engine. As an example, if a user went to Google and searched "bookstores in New York," you would want your content to include those words so that it will come up on page one of the search engine results. How to make that happen is a bit tricky, and there are a lot of hidden rules and vagueness (Google prefers it that way; they don't want their system gamed). I think it will be easier to start off with what you should avoid, and then we'll move on to what you can do to improve your SEO skills.

In the past several years, search engines have really cracked down on what they deem "low-quality" sites and backlink profiles. I wrote a blog post about the top Google penalties that you will find useful. You can read it here: http://emberdragon.com/understanding-google-algorithms/.

Below is a quick rundown of algorithm changes and how to keep your writing safe (and no, we do not know why Google tends to name their algorithm changes after black-and-white animals!).

PANDA

Purpose: To penalize low-value content sites and reward websites that provide legitimate, high-value content to their readers.

- *Avoid "keyword stuffing" in your content.* In other words, while it is important to make sure your keyword groupings are strategically represented, you do not want to jam them into the content over and over to try to get the rankings you want. Write in a way that people want to read.

- *Don't randomly throw keywords into sentences.* This is a big no-no; your readers should not be able to look at your writing and immediately know what the keywords are. It should be organic and go with the flow.
- *Avoid thin content pages.* It's very important that each page of your website has adequate, relevant content on it.

PENGUIN

Purpose: To penalize websites for over-optimization. This specifically focuses heavily on your backlink profile. This is only going to affect you as a freelance writer if you are creating the anchor text for them as part of your services.

- Keep your "buyer keywords" to no more than 10 percent of the anchor text ratio.
- Run a backlink report on well-ranking competitors to see where they are getting their backlinks from.
- Only create backlinks from sites with good trust flow and that are relevant to the topic the page is about.

HUMMINGBIRD

Contrary to popular belief, Hummingbird is not an algorithm change, it IS Google. I focus heavily on this in Chapter 15, and it is a common topic that I am asked to keynote on at conferences because understanding it, in my opinion, is the difference between success and failure in the digital marketing world. All the ranting I've been doing all through this chapter about intention is not just to create content buyers are looking for—it's also for intelligent optimization purposes.

KEYWORDS FOR CONTENT

Most digital marketing strategies are based on keyword research. Your clients will know (or think they know) the main buying keywords that their market is typing into Google, and they are hot under the collar to get their content in front of those search terms. This is especially prominent with content designed to live somewhere on the web and less vital in products like ebooks that people are buying. Because this is very important to many of the projects your clients will order, you need to have a working knowledge of how to properly use keywords to your client's advantage when you write. While I could write a novel on how to appropriately use keywords, here is a quick and dirty guide that will provide you with the basic idea.

It's important to know what popular long tail keywords the buyers are typing in. The emphasis is on *buyers*. It's great to find a back door to get in front of your target market, but it's low value if it's not getting you in front of buyers. Once you understand the intention behind the buyers in a particular market, this will dictate how you research keywords, long tail variations, and expert verbiage to work into content. Most freelance writers do not include optimization help to their clients. If you learn how to include just a few basic components, it will set you apart from the majority of your competition.

Content Optimization Cheat Sheet

You can download a copy of this cheat sheet in the resource section of www.MoonlightingontheInternet.com. It will help you to properly optimize onsite content pages including blog posts. You can use this as a project form and the information collected will guide you to write an optimized piece of content. It should cover these major points and include the following at the top of every document:

- Requirements
- Meta title
- Meta description
- Meta keywords (5 to 10 keywords)
- Call to action (CTA)

EXPLANATION

- *Requirements.* The top of the project form should have any requirements from the client that are important to that content piece.
- *Meta title.* Each title has to be original for the specific page you're writing content for.

- *Meta description.* This is a super-short snippet about the page/content/topic; keywords are great to include (roughly 155 characters).
- *Meta keywords.* The meta keywords will include keywords from the provided list as well as (and sometimes more importantly) other keywords that relate to the specific page/product/service/topic. You've researched the topic/service/product, so we're looking for phrases you think would be applicable for the page and searcher's intent. (List all of them separated by commas.)
- *Call to action.* Required at the end of each page.

EXAMPLE

Meta Keyword(s): article outsourcing

Meta Description: Improve your rankings and draw in readers with targeted, informative content that is produced by our trained writers and based on well-researched keywords.

Meta Title: The Benefits of Article Outsourcing

Sample Call to Action: To order the highest-converting content offered on the web and for information on our tested and proven organic traffic-generating strategies, visit us at www.contentdivas.com.

TITLES AND SUBHEADS

The keyword MUST be in the title and first few sentences. There should be two to three subheads (depending on the length of your article or blog post) with organic context for the search engines to pick up.

Titles must state exactly what you are writing about. If you say "How to . . .," make sure you give instructions on how, not why, you should do something. Having the title be a mismatch for the body of the content is an optimization no-no.

If you are ever in doubt as to the type of voice the client wants, the default I suggest is a conversational tone. Conversational is not the opposite of professional. You can have a professional conversational tone, but rarely does a client want their prospects to feel as though they are reading from a textbook. If you wouldn't "say it that way," then please don't write it that way.

The first keyword phrase listed must be used three times: Use it in the first sentence, middle paragraph, and last paragraph. The second keyword phrase listed must be used two times throughout the content. All other keyword phrases listed must be used at least once throughout the content.

Important: Do not feel you have to "force" a keyword into your content if that means it will result in an awkward sentence that won't sound natural and will not appeal to readers. It is acceptable to use slight variations on keywords (i.e., filler words such as in, of, at, for, from, and or singular/plural versions) if it allows for more natural conversational writing.

Separate the content with bullet points, indented spacing, and/or lists. This makes for easier reading.

Use the name of the company/person/product/service at least once. Feel free to write from the perspective of the company using "we," "us," "our," etc.

The people reading this content have done an online search for what this company/person offers, and have found what they are looking for. Reading this content should be informative and persuade the potential customer to use this company/person. Do not encourage them to look elsewhere or "visit our website at . . .," because they are already at the website, and should use this company/service!

PRICING: HOW DO I CHARGE FOR MY WORK?

This is one of the biggest questions that people beginning work as a freelance writer have. The truth is that as a freelancer, you can charge whatever you want. The trick is to set a price that makes sense for you and your client and the market. When you do research, you will find the pricing scale all over the place. There are people charging way too much and getting those rates because they've built their business up to do so. An even bigger pain point are the plethora of writers charging far below what they should, which tanks the market value.

Common Pricing Scenarios

There are three main ways that freelance writers charge for their services: per word, per page, and per project. All forms are acceptable.

I'll go through them briefly and give you some points to keep in mind when choosing a pricing method.

1. *Per word.* If you're going to charge per word, it's very important that you set an approximate word-count range with your client and stick to it. For instance, if you're charging 3 cents per word, and your client ordered a short report, you need to have a standard range in mind and clear it with them. I never suggest you set an exact word count in advance because you want the piece to be authentic and write what it takes to make a superior product.

   It's safe to assume (without crazy formatting) that one page of content could be 400 words. So if you're considering a report to be seven to ten pages at 3 cents per word, that would be $84 to $120. It is very, very important to manage your client's expectations upfront and make sure they sign off on the potential costs.

2. *Per page.* Similarly, if you are charging per page, you need to get a page range approved by your client in advance. So, for instance, if you are charging $15 per page, a seven- to ten-page report would cost $105 to $150. The only complication with charging per page is that you run the risk of a client getting frustrated that formatting techniques spread the writing out over way more pages than necessary due to images, spacing, etc.

   For example, if we stick to the assumption that an average word count per page is 400 words, if you charge $15 per page, that's 3.7 cents per word. Let's round that up to 4 cents per word. So if you charge them for 10 pages and they do the math and realize there is an average of 300 words per page, they may find they are being charged 5 cents per word and may feel you intentionally inflated the page count to up your pay.

3. *Per project.* When you charge per project, you figure out a flat fee for a project regardless of length. The advantage is that you can figure out how much you would like to get paid for standard projects and not have to be limited by word count, etc. The danger is that if the project ends up being way more in-depth than

you anticipated, then you won't get compensated for it. You need to accurately figure out how much time and work it will take on your part and price it in a way that makes sense for you and your client.

SHELBY'S RECOMMENDATION

Hybrid. While there is merit in all three methods, I suggest a hybrid approach that combines all three. I pretty much never charge per page. I think it's too much of a variable. Instead, I generally charge one of two different ways. Especially in the beginning, I charged per word and added a per-project flat fee in a way that made sense. So, sticking with the example of the report, let's say it ends up being a 10-page, 4,000-word report. If I want to get paid 5 cents per word, I would handle the situation like this: The difference between 3 cents per word and 5 cents per word is $80. I would charge 3 cents per word, but every report would also have a $100 research and editing fee. I would leverage this in two ways. First, I would let them know that in order to produce the best possible product, you need to be able to research the topic properly. You are able to keep your per-word count lower because you charge this fee to cover your time researching. Also, you are saving them money by not charging your per-hour rate (which is high because your time is your most valuable commodity). Instead, you just charge a flat fee and don't bill any additional fees to the client for research.

Second, let the client know that once they approve the report, it will get edited by a professional editor. So they really are getting a completed document when you're done, and part of that $100 fee is to pay for the editor.

Now that I've been in the writing world for a very long time, I tend to primarily charge per project for anything shorter than an ebook. I do this because at this point, I know how long things take me to write, and I know how much research time is going to be needed. So with the example I just listed above, I would simply charge $200 and list all the benefits they are getting with me. It is very important either way to clearly define what they will be receiving from you.

On my freelancing website, I would list the different types of writing I did with the different price points. In the resources link I gave you for this book, you will find an example of a couple of ways that freelance writers list their pricing on their websites.

ALWAYS display your rates and cost structure clearly on your website. This is very important if you want to be taken seriously as a professional freelance writer. Remember, this is not limited only to how much you charge, but also what your refund policy is and how you handle revision requests, etc. I personally offer a 100 percent money-back guarantee if they are not satisfied with my work. I'll be honest, I have had to make good on this guarantee a few times over the course of my career. The truth is, you will encounter clients that will never be happy no matter what you do or how good you do it. In my opinion, it's better to take the hit and let those clients go. That being said, assuming that you're good at your job and fair in business, just having a guarantee like this will help you close way more clients than you will ever have to refund.

GETTING CLIENTS

Later in this section, we cover some of the larger, mainstream websites that freelancers of all types can frequent to find jobs, but here are a handful of sites that are specific to freelance writing jobs.

Content Divas (http://contentdivas.com)

Pros: You get a wide diversity of projects on this site, so you can build a better resume. Writers also get direct access to editors, the clients, and a very supportive staff. Writers are paid weekly. There are lots of opportunities for other types of work.

Cons: Jobs pay less than you could get freelancing independently, and writers must accept pay via PayPal, although because they use the mass pay option, contractors do not pay fees on their incoming payments. It can sometimes be a slow ramp up to regular work until you have established yourself as a reliable resource.

Write Jobs (www.writejobs.info)

Pros: Almost every second job is for some magazine, newspaper, or publication; there is a minimum pay rate of $10 per 500 words, though average pay is much higher.

Cons: There are many work-from-home jobs, but writers outside the U.S. are disadvantaged by the high number of location-specific gigs.

ProBlogger (www.problogger.net)

Pros: They have a great list of blogging and telecommuting gigs. The rates on offer are usually much higher than what you would find on other freelancing websites. You avoid dealing with the middleman like on Elance or Freelancer, while enjoying high client response rates.

Cons: The search filter isn't that great, so you have to scan every job to find what you're looking for.

FreelanceWriting (www.freelancewriting.com/freelancejobs/online writingjobs.php)

Pros: It has a great search filter and pulls lists from multiple sites and job sources.

Cons: This is a really popular site, so the job quest can be fiercely competitive.

All Indie Writers (http://allindiewriters.com/freelance-writing-jobs)

Pros: The site lists jobs by pay.

Cons: Jobs aren't posted as consistently as on other sites—there are often two- to three-day lapses in postings.

WritersDepartment (http://writersdepartment.com/index.htm)

Pros: This is less of a job board and more of an online hub/community that provides jobs, support, and business resources for freelance writers.

Cons: The site requires an application for access.

Freelance Writing Jobs (www.freelancewritinggigs.com)

Pros: This site saves time by listing high-quality writing jobs from multiple sites and sends you directly to the application phase.

Cons: The response rate is not as high as it is on some other sites (ProBlogger, for instance).

MANAGING CLIENTS AND PROJECTS

While how to get clients is a HUGE question all new freelance writers have, you also need to have a plan for how you're going to manage the client and the project from the point you close the deal through project completion. Every client is potentially a returning client, and you want to make sure they have a fabulous experience.

The Intake Process

Right from the onset of the project, it is critical that you have a realistic understanding of what your client actually wants. You'll get clients with various degrees of specificity on what they are looking for, but they almost always have some idea of what they want, and they are not always great at letting you know what that is. You're getting hired to write for them, but it's a true gift to yourself and your client if you can create an intake process that helps your client paint a picture for you of what they truly want.

Not everyone uses an order form for each project, but I do. I'm a HUGE believer in order forms. There really isn't a wrong way to do an order form. The most important thing is that you design them to get the information that you need. In my company, we have three different ways to handle order forms:

1. *Emailed form*. With some projects, we simply email them a form full of questions and require them to fill it out and email it back to us or upload it to one of our project management platforms. This is especially useful if your client is a little older and less tech-savvy, or if your client wants time to think about it.

2. *Online form.* Google Docs has a free way to create interactive forms. Some of our projects are hosted in this format. We send them a link, they fill it out and hit submit, and the content is compiled and sent to us. This is perfect for clients who are a bit more tech-savvy and for clients who are going to fill out the order form in one sitting.

3. *Phone meeting.* We get some clients onto our recorded phone bridge and talk them through the form. This is ideal if the topic is especially in-depth or the project is very large. It's also a great fit for clients you suspect will be intimidated and not put much information on the form or who will sit on it for long periods of time instead of sitting down and filling it out for you. If the project justifies the budget, we will transcribe this information.

However you decide to do it, getting proper information from the client at the outset will save you the pain of unhappy clients or having to do multiple revisions. Figure 4.1 is an example of our ebook project form.

Basic information: _____

Name: _____

Company: _____

Contact email: _____

Contact phone: _____

Target Audience

1. Tell us about your target audience. Useful information includes whether you have only one target audience or multiple. _____

_____

_____

FIGURE 4.1—**eBook Project Form**

2. Why would they want this ebook? Examples of some possibilities: This ebook solves a specific problem for them. This ebook has information they need in order to accomplish something. This ebook is designed to guide them through a specific process. Tell us as much as you can about the intention behind why your target market would want this ebook. _____

_____

3. What are the objections that your target market may already have regarding this topic? What do the skeptical people in your market think/assume? _____

_____

4. Do you know what questions your target market most commonly ask about this topic? _____

_____

5. What would differentiate someone in this market who IS your ideal target vs. someone who is not? I.e., is there something specific that separates people researching vs. people looking to buy? A good example would be if you sell fine art, art students researching famous artists and paintings would not be your target market, but they may be using the same search terms as people looking to buy fine art.

_____

_____

Nitty-Gritty Details

1. What do you want your ebook to be about? _____

_____

2. Do you have specific keywords within your topic that you want your ebook to center around? _____

_____

FIGURE 4.1—**eBook Project Form**, continued

3. Are you, personally, or a member of your team, a subject matter expert on this topic? _____

_____

4. Do you have links to websites, blogs, or RSS feeds that would be helpful for your writer's research? _____

_____

5. Do you have links to other writing (reports/ebooks/Amazon Kindle Books) that you have found appealing that you might want to highlight as an example of your expectations for your writer?

_____

_____

6. Will you be supplying the writer with research, via written content, video, or audio, or will the writer be pulling the research independently? Please note: If the writer is pulling the research independently, they will need clear directives on information you do and do not consider in line with your philosophy/topic. _____

_____

_____

Formatting Questions

1. Do you already have a table of contents or set topics you want the chapters to center around? _____

_____

2. Is there a Call To Action in this ebook? It will help your writer create an ebook that accomplishes your goals if she understands what the desired end result is that you want your readers to do. _____

_____

_____

FIGURE 4.1—**eBook Project Form**, continued

3. Is this ebook part of a series or a sales funnel? If so, please tell us the other components of the series/funnel. For instance, is there a different product that is designed to nurture prospects into buying/downloading this ebook? Is the main purpose of this ebook to back end your prospects into a mastermind or training course?

_____

_____

4. Are there additional components that you would like this ebook to include besides the standard informational content and images? Examples would be: chapter summaries, action steps for each chapter, cheat sheets, accompanying workbook, etc. _____

_____

_____

5. Is there anything else you would like to tell us about this project and your expectations? Please remember, the more info and details you can give your writer, the better. _____

_____

_____

FIGURE 4.1—**eBook Project Form**, continued

If Your Client Is a Personal Expert

Is your client personally an expert on the topic, or is the content primarily coming from research?

This question is important because if your client is the personal expert, they are going to be way pickier about the voice and sound of the piece and usually hypersensitive to the content because they know the topic inside and out. If my client is a personal expert on the topic, my favorite strategy is to co-create an outline/table of contents with the client and then get them onto a recorded phone bridge to discuss and brain dump on the topics in the order of the outline. Sometimes, if the client has a ton of information in his head but doesn't have it organized, I may do the brain-dump call first to generically talk about the project, form the outline/TOC from that, and then do a second call to talk through the outline in a more detailed fashion.

This strategy has been a huge win for our clients because it guarantees the content will be from their brain and we've had better success in getting it in their voice. When using this technique, you should also ask them for any articles or content they have written, interviews they have given, or videos they have of them speaking on the topic. These can be very useful to you.

Also, you can charge them extra for your time doing these calls; justify this by leveraging the following points:

- It WILL produce a much better product for them.
- You will give them copies of the recording so they can leverage that for other team members or outsourcers, etc.
- Remind them that if they want to come back, you can always produce coordinating blog posts or content to go along with the original product, and you won't have to charge them extra for the basic information.

Now that we've covered some of the types of content that are often requested of freelance writers, let's talk about time-saving research practices. Trust me, if not done correctly, the research phase can take longer than it takes to actually write the project.

HOW TO DO PROPER RESEARCH

Researching is a huge part of any writing project, unless you are extremely familiar with the subject and know everything there is to know already. When doing research, there are a few things it's important to know and avoid.

Avoid Plagiarism

The number-one thing to look out for and be aware of is plagiarism. It is rampant on the internet, so it's important to research your research (using multiple sources) and cite your sources. You also want to be careful when you write that YOU are not plagiarizing someone else's material. It's OK to paraphrase and say something similar, but it is not OK to copy/paste what they wrote and call it your own. Doing so can cost you your job and even lead to a fine or jail time if the victim is serious enough. It's always better to write in your own words with your own flair. That's what you're being paid for—embrace it!

Keywords Matter

Another aspect to remember when researching is to use good keywords. If you're writing about "Diet Coke ingredients," it's not enough just to research "Coke"—be specific and use meaningful sources. Search with intent and a particular area in mind, and you'll find much better sources related to the topic you are writing about.

Not All Sources Are Created Equal

Sources are another hugely important factor when doing research. Keep in mind that not all sources are created equal—if you're trying to gather information on a subject, look for a well-respected site, as opposed to "katiesnottruetheorys.com." You want to make sure you are not writing untrue statements. Remember: Sources matter!

In the end, researching helps you become more of an aficionado on the topic you are writing about. Your ability to do good research could be the difference between what makes and breaks you as a freelancer—take it seriously and always give it the time it deserves. It can be tempting to just write nonsense without doing the work, but when you take that route you risk losing clients and hurting your career. Hard work pays off, and that is certainly true when it comes to freelancing.

Managing Expectations

When it comes to successfully juggling clients and projects, there is nothing that will cause you more pain than not properly managing their expectations. You need to be crystal clear about what they can expect every step of the way. Here are a few of the most important expectations you will want to proactively manage.

First, you should clearly define the timeline for your client's project. While a deadline/project due date is important, a timeline is much more than that. You really should have some sort of intake document that lets them know your process. A good writing project should have regular milestones where you check in with the client so they can approve the direction you are taking with the project. Trust me, if the client doesn't like something you're doing, it's far less painful to learn that partway into the project instead of at the very end, after you have written the whole thing. You should anticipate and appreciate course correction.

Your timeline should clearly identify the different parts of your process along with estimated completion dates. Some of your process may include research, checkpoints, writing, final draft due date, etc. Be sure to pad your timeline. However long you think the project will take you, add on extra time; there is no crime in finishing early, but I guarantee life will get in the way and slow you down.

Next, consider a revision policy. It's important to define what revisions will come out of your pocket and what will cost your client extra money. You can do this however you want, but trust me, this is something you want to have a clear policy on. It is less important what your policy is than it is to make sure you have one and that your client is clear on it.

My personal policy is very clear, but it is dependent on having a thorough intake policy and project form. Depending on the price point, our writing projects may or may not have a revision request included for free. Beyond that, if the client requests a revision because they wanted something they did not make clear or request through the intake process, we charge them for that. However, if we missed the mark on what the client was looking for, that revision comes out of our pocket.

Finally, you will definitely want to request testimonials from your clients. There are few things more powerful than social proof. You should always ask for testimonials, and you shouldn't feel weird about it. They can always say no, and some will even though they love your work. But the more testimonials you can get, the better! Do NOT underestimate the powerful benefit of a testimonial. I think it's also reasonable to offer your client an incentive for testimonials you feel you can use on your website.

CHAPTER 5

FREELANCE GRAPHIC DESIGN PROFIT PATH

To define a graphic designer, first we must define what a graphic designer is not. A graphic designer is not a traditional artist. A traditional artist creates unique images and sounds to evoke an emotional response. The result is then interpreted by the viewer or listener; often, the same piece of work can evoke dramatically different emotions in individuals. This cannot happen with a graphic artist. A graphic designer's job is to communicate effectively through design. The same emotions and message must be communicated to the masses; otherwise, the job was not done effectively.

Google simply defines graphic design as "the art or skill of combining text and pictures in advertisements, magazines, or books." While that's an accurate definition, the type of work you will most commonly be hired for right off the bat will have everything to do with digital products and properties: logos, graphics for website layouts, formatting ebooks, etc.

A graphic designer's job requires specific talents to edit visual concepts and clearly communicate ideas and information to consumers. This is why you can recognize a company just by looking at the colors, logos, and images associated with the corporation's advertising and promotion. It is an art that requires conveying ideas and messages through visual content on websites, posters, book covers, print pages, and more. In any case, a graphic designer's chief responsibility is to use the computer to communicate ideas by using color, images, or logos that represent an idea for advertising or promotions.

TITLES THAT SOUND COOL

In my real life, I'm not very attached to titles. In our company, we make them up. We joke that instead of giving someone a raise or a bonus, they will be getting a cool title. However, when it comes to graphic design, you can actually brand yourself with titles that can help you consistently fetch higher rates. So it's worth exploring. Depending on the industry and the medium, titles vary depending on level of experience. Here are just a few:

- Junior Designer
- Graphic Designer
- UI/UX Designer
- Visual Designer
- Motion Designer
- Digital Designer
- Web Designer
- Animator
- Production Artist
- Graphic Artist
- Mid-Level Designer
- Information Designer
- Interaction Designer
- Product Designer
- Environmental Graphics Designer
- Information Architect
- Package Designer

- Exhibition Designer
- Experience Designer
- Content Strategist
- Executive Level Designer
- Owner/Founder
- Executive Creative Director
- Head of Design
- Chief Creative Officer

Regardless of whether you specialize or what title you decide to give yourself, one thing is certain: You need to understand what graphic designers do and how to find and retain work.

WHAT DO GRAPHIC DESIGNERS DO?

You will find a lot of fancy descriptions for what graphic designers do, but in my mind, graphic designers are visual communicators. They combine art and technology into a seamless field of ideas using images and words and create something that sends a message, represents a brand, or tells a story. That's a very simplified answer. Often they are collaborating with other people like writers, website developers, and creative leads within a company. It really depends on what the specs of the particular job are.

Typically, they do the following:

- Meet with clients and art directors to map out a project
- Give advice on how to reach a targeted audience
- Decide how a message will be portrayed on the screen or in print
- Create images for product identification and message portrayal
- Create graphics (visual and audio) for logos, websites, and product illustrations
- Create designs using a computer or by hand
- Implement/present design ideas to the client and art director
- Decide on colors, text style, layout and images
- Incorporate the client's wishes into the final design
- Review and approve designs before final printing and publishing

The term "graphic designer" obviously covers a broad spectrum. Therefore, most successful designers often choose one area to specialize in. It makes advertising and targeting clients much easier when you have a narrow target audience. Thus, it is important to gravitate to what is most important to you and what holds your interest the most. I don't believe it would be very useful to cover all the different types of art that graphic designers do in this chapter; if you have that particular talent, your questions most likely aren't centered on what you will be asked to do, but more on how you can use your existing talent to create a Profit Path.

SKILLS OUTSIDE GRAPHIC DESIGN THAT MAKE YOUR JOB EASIER

Obviously, to thrive as a graphic designer, you need to have some skills at graphic design. That said, when you're making a Profit Path, you'll need some additional skills to ensure your success. The following are basic skills all graphic designers must develop.

- *Sales and marketing training.* Also referred to as a communication designer, a graphic designer works closely with public relations managers, marketing teams, and advertising and promotions teams. Therefore, many graphic designers will specialize in a particular type of client and industry. For example, some work strictly with entrepreneurs, while others concentrate their efforts in print ads by creating posters. No matter which field a designer chooses, it all falls under the large banner of sales and marketing of products. Therefore, a savvy graphic designer would be wise to read up on basic sales and marketing principles in order to better serve his or her clients.

- *Excellent communication skills.* Graphic designers need to be able to produce rough illustrations, often referred to as "mock-ups," of their designs to their clients using available technology. They must effectively communicate these ideas to clients, customers, and other designers to ensure everything runs smoothly and the final design meets the expectations of everyone involved. Doing so requires thinking outside the box and finding new ways to communicate your ideas to the consumer while still conveying the appropriate message on behalf of the client. This will require you to communicate well, both through writing and speaking. A successful designer can communicate just as effectively in written form as they do verbally or in graphic form.

- *Teamwork.* Since graphic designers work on projects with other designers, marketers, business analysts, programmers, and writers, it is vital to be a good team player. You must learn to collaborate effectively to produce websites, products, and publications.

- *Problem solving.* Graphic design is about more than using the tools of the trade. You will need to know more than Photoshop and Illustrator to succeed. It is not the tools that make you successful; it is your problem-solving abilities that set you apart. To be a successful graphic designer, you must first develop your skills at solving problems in new and creative ways.

GETTING STARTED

When deciding if this field is right for you, it is helpful to consider the qualities and interests many graphic designers share. This may be a bit more difficult considering most high schools do not teach graphic design and most graphic designers do not enter the field until they are in their mid-twenties or early thirties. To make it even more difficult, many potential artists go to design school and find out their education and practice is not what they thought it would be.

So who does become a successful graphic designer? In most cases, designers are excellent observers who find the beauty in everyday objects. They pay close attention as they go about their day with a hyperawareness of the visual and textual clues that surround them. They ask questions, make connections, and observe closely, often wondering how objects and messages combine and what they mean.

But an appreciation of beauty is not enough to become a designer. A true designer wants to take it to the next level: creation. They want to create images they have never seen before. Their observations lead them to wonder how they could incorporate what they see into their work and life. Curiosity is at the core of the designer who can never settle for good enough.

Most important, a graphic designer is both introverted and extroverted. They can work countless hours and days alone, looking at the tiny details of a project without getting bored. But they also can turn this focus outward and relate to people on a personal level to communicate their ideas and shape the world around them.

The good news is that, like many of the Profit Paths in this book, there are many different types of graphic designers. For instance, my 17-year-old daughter is beginning to compete for work on 99designs. com, even though she's had no formal graphic design training. She is a natural artist who is finding work on her own. While this book has information to help you make a long-term Profit Path if you choose, if you have the right skills and drives, you can get off the ground quickly as a freelancer.

Find Your Market

As with some of the other freelancing paths, often you will find it easier to get started if you specialize. Do you have a specific industry that you really enjoy working with? Or do you have a specific type of design that you prefer to do, like logos or ebook covers? This is a great time to look at your Profit Path Profile and identify if you have any connections to a specific industry or group that you might stand out in. For instance, if you worked in real estate offices for five years in the past, you might advertise as a graphic designer who caters to real estate agents and specialize in all their various graphic design needs.

Specialization is a big topic of interest when you research graphic design online. Many successful graphic designers highly encourage it. You may not feel as though you have any specific area that you qualify for or want to specialize in, and that's OK. It's not required, but it's always something to think about while evaluating your options and considering how you want to position yourself in the market.

Find a Work Space

Location, location, location. Ideally, you need a work space that is free from distractions. For the new graphic designer, this often means a separate room in the house. You will need to be able to shut the door to the outside world and let your creative juices flow. Also, you will need this space to protect your projects that are in progress. I realize it goes without saying that anyone working from home needs a dedicated work space, but I've gotten feedback from quite a few artists who say when doing work in the creative field, it is more jarring to have your head pulled in and out of the creative flow.

For example, I can do work for Ember Dragon with regular interruptions from kids, email, etc. But when working on my manuscript for this book, one small interruption can cost me hours of work, possibly even the rest of the day. I find the flow required to do creative work uses a very different part of the brain than I use to do business-type work or strategy. For this reason, I felt it worth mentioning in this Profit Path section. Truly, having a dedicated work space may be critical to your success.

Meeting Clients

You can absolutely create your entire Profit Path online and never meet with a client face to face. However, graphic design is one of those mainstream fields where you could advertise on Craigslist or other local job boards and pick up work with nearby businesses if you want to. In that situation, you will likely need to meet with your client at least once.

When it comes to meeting clients, try to meet at their office if you do not have your own studio. Most likely, they will love you for it. If you're freelancing for a consumer, you could probably get away with telling them you are based out of your home and to expect a family atmosphere when arriving. However, with the easy access to co-work spaces, I would try to avoid bringing clients to your home.

Gather Supplies

First, rest assured you DO NOT need to spend thousands of dollars on technology. The "right" technology will depend greatly on your specialization, but for most designers it begins with the holy trinity of

Adobe's designing software: Photoshop, Illustrator, and InDesign.

In the beginning, you will need a midrange computer with 1 GB of RAM. Unless you are doing high-end animation, 3-D work, and heavy image and video editing, this will work just fine until you can afford the high-end computers designers are "supposed" to have. Don't be put off by the price of a "designing" computer. You won't need one until you can comfortably afford it.

Create a Portfolio Online

This is one of the most important pieces for graphic designers: You have to have an online portfolio. You need a place to send potential clients that will give them background information, examples of past work, client testimonials, prices, etc. If you don't know how to code, there are many platforms such as WordPress or Squarespace on which you can easily set up a website portfolio. However, many freelancers thrive simply by operating from a Facebook page as their main online site.

Powerful Homepage Tips

◀ *Grab their attention.* Visitors will make a split-second decision based on first impression. Your entire website should be about branding you as an individual. Show your voice and personality from the beginning. More than any of the other freelancing Profit Paths in this book, your website MUST have great graphics because they will judge you by how great your site looks.

◀ *Give clients a taste.* Your very best work should be clearly visible and easily found.

◀ *Great headline.* Compelling headlines make search engines extremely happy and get the clickthrough rate you are seeking.

◀ *Introduce yourself.* A little introduction and a short biography go a long way in this business. Showcase yourself as a real person who connects with clients. This is all about building trust. Don't make the mistake of hiding behind your business name. Your About page should be compelling and tell about you (including a photo).

Your bio should not read like a resume. Instead, come across as a person. Consider the client and think about why they are contacting you. What makes you different? What makes you human? Highlight your strengths and downplay (or leave out) your weaknesses.

- *Create a welcome video.* When the client sees you on video, it creates an instant relationship. They feel they have met you, and the beginning of a bond is formed. Many designers love this option.

Success Stories

Success stories can give your prospects a peek at what you do for your clients. Because graphic design is so visual, before-and-after images speak volumes. You really can't underestimate the power of really fabulous before-and-after images. However, you could also take a couple of your favorite projects and give a little more detail that will highlight how you work with your clients, not just the great work you do.

Here are some tips to create success stories that make you more than just a commodity graphic designer:

- *Show the beginning product.* This is what most people refer to as the "before" image. Identify the client's problem. Instead of just showing the picture, you can add content emphasizing what the client was looking for. What problem were they looking to solve? What was their desired end result?
- *Showcase the "After."* In addition to displaying your design, emphasize how the image you created does indeed solve the problem the client came to you with. Show how your design helped them meet their goals.
- *Show your thought process.* Include sketches of your design in progress. This gives your prospects an idea of how your thought process works and how you think through what they are requesting to meet their needs.

This is a great place to add the client's testimonial as well.

Client Testimonials

Client testimonials are your references. Without them, a new client may feel concerned about your ability to do the job. No one wants to feel as though they are your first customer. Solid testimonials provide an unbiased third-party opinion on your work. It tells the prospective client that your former clients were pleased with your work and that the claims you are making are valid. Very rarely, if ever, will a freelance client actually check references on a graphic designer. They will see your portfolio and read your testimonials, and the rest relies on their direct interaction with you.

FINDING CLIENTS

In the beginning, you will not have the valuable resource of referrals. So we are going to talk about how to get your foot in the door and start building a client base who can refer you to others. Steady work will come, but it is important to know that it is uncommon to have full-time income right out of the gate when you're in the startup phase.

There are many ways to drum up business online, but here are some that have been proven effective over time. In Chapter 8, there is an extensive section on different freelancing job sites with tips on finding clients through them. However, there are a couple of sites that specialize in connecting clients with freelance graphic designers.

Compete for Work Sites

One of my favorites is 99designs (http://99designs.com/). We had our logos for both Moonlighting on the Internet and Ember Dragon done on that website. Here is a great article 99designs wrote about how to find the right projects for you using their site, build client relationships, and have fun (https://99designs.com/designer-blog/2010/11/12/finding-design-projects-opportunities/).

Other sites I haven't used but that have good reviews are:

- *crowdSPRING* (www.crowdspring.com). crowdSPRING is a traditional crowdsource site for graphic design. It's similar to 99designs with a slightly different model.
- *LogoGarden* (www.logogarden.com). LogoGarden's unique spin is that they cater exclusively to entrepreneurs. They provide standard graphic designs that the budding entrepreneur will

need like logos and business cards.

- *Design Observer* (www.designobserver.com/jobs). This website is primarily graphic design, but there are other jobs requested as well. One major benefit of this platform is that the job postings are instantly listed across other popular graphic design job websites.

- *Coroflot* (www.coroflot.com/jobs). This one also heavily caters to people looking for more traditional employment, as opposed to freelancers. You can view and search more than 2,000 creative company profiles and job listings.

- *Behance* (www.behance.net/joblist). This isn't exclusively graphic design jobs, but I put it in this section because that appears to be the primary focus.

While compete-for-work sites are great resources for finding jobs, especially when you're first starting out, don't underestimate your ability to put yourself out there and get work through networking with other professionals.

Conventions/Mixers

While this may be out of your comfort zone, there is no better way to make connections and gain leads than attending functions. People like knowing who they are working with and like being able to put a face to the name. Going to these places alone will ensure you talk to others and meet new people. The next day, send a quick follow-up email saying it was nice meeting them, but don't solicit any business. Do be sure to add them to your LinkedIn profile! I built my entire business up to this point primarily through word-of-mouth. Graphic designers have an edge in networking situations because most people understand what a graphic designer is. You don't have to spend a lot of time explaining what you do the way that, say, virtual assistants do.

Sell Your Art Online

Etsy, Squarespace, and Pinterest are perfect for artists selling their work. Create several pieces for sale to stretch your abilities and promote your services.

A QUICK NOTE ABOUT SPEC WORK

According to the Graphic Artists Guild, spec work is an unethical practice for designers. Essentially, it is a client asking you to do work for free in hopes of them liking your idea and awarding you the job. Since ideas are the heart of your business, this means you will be giving away your work for free hoping they will like it. If asked for a spec layout, you should politely refuse. Most savvy clients will not even ask, but some more uninitiated prospects might need a polite education on why submitting sketches is unacceptable. If, for some reason, you do decide to do spec work, then place a copyright notice on all sketches (no full illustrations) and date and photocopy everything. These are your ideas and should not be taken lightly. (Note: This is different on sites where you are competing for work, like 99designs.)

PRICING A JOB

Determining how to create your pricing structure can be complicated and scary when you first start out. You want to keep yourself priced competitively and still make a profit. As a freelancer, the sky is the limit as to how you structure your business, but in general there are two different ways to structure your fees: hourly billing or flat rates.

Hourly Rate

Charging hourly has the benefit of getting paid for the time you actually work. This works great for those who are not good at estimating how long it will take to finish a project and for when unexpected problems come up. When you charge hourly, you get paid for the exact time you work and will need some sort of tracking system to determine billable hours.

When you're billing by the hour, you still have to calculate the hours the project will take in advance and succinctly present them in a way that makes sense to the client. If you run into problems and it takes longer, you'll need to be able to talk your client through that or eat the extra hours. On the flip side, when you get the job done under the estimate, that's always a nice horn to toot for your clients. Many designers don't like to have to deal with the micro-management feel of that. It can feel a bit like letting the client take a peek behind the curtain where all the magic is happening.

Fixed Rate

When you're working on a fixed rate, you're still ultimately basing the project fee on the hourly rate. Ultimately, you're figuring out how much work the project is going to be and how much you want to get paid for it. Even when you're charging a flat fee, clients want to know how you're calculating the fees anyway. Instead of giving specific line-by-line details, here are a couple of things to help justify your fixed pricing:

Approximate hour window of time (example: six to eight hours labor).

How many rounds of feedback and revisions will be included?

The danger of fixed rates is that if you run into a snag and the project goes way over what you expected, you could eat a lot of expenses on a project. However, you will get much better at estimating as you go. Obviously, when the job takes way less time, you get to pocket the difference. So this method has pros and cons.

Hybrid

Many designers will use a hybrid pricing metric where they charge a flat fee for the initial part of the project, which could include a consultation, research, pre-approvals, etc. Then they charge an hourly rate for the project from that point on. You also have the freedom to ebb and flow between the different pricing options depending on the project and the client. It's common to charge a "high maintenance tax" for clients who you know are frankly going to be a pain in the neck.

Establishing Your Rates

It is not uncommon for designers to charge different rates for different types of work. For instance, consulting may bill out at $50 per hour while your design rate may be $100 per hour; more sophisticated types of design like animation may bill out even higher than that. At the time I am writing this book, the prices are all across the board. So you are definitely going to want to do your own research and find out what the competitive rates are for the type of work you want to do in the area you want to do it.

That said, I think a safe average from what I'm seeing is anywhere from $75 to $150 per hour. That probably means there are a lot of jobs in the $25-to-$50-per-hour range and then a few designers who charge $300-plus per hour. What's important is that you figure out what's competitive for you and make sure your policy is very clear from the outset. Finally, ALWAYS take a deposit upfront; a 50 percent deposit is very common.

DESIGN PROCESS: MANAGING CLIENTS

When you begin the design process, you don't have to provide a consultation. However, many freelancers like doing this, and it does help the clients feel they are getting more of a white-glove experience. The initial consultation is extremely important and, in most cases, will be your first contact with the client. The consultation allows you to hear directly from the client about their needs. This will not only help ensure your final product is in line with what they are looking for, but will also help you determine how much work the project will involve.

I highly recommend offering a free 30-minute consultation upfront via phone or Skype. The Skype call gives you the face-to-face interaction if you want it, and since it is free, you can easily set up a Skype account for consultations with potential and current clients. The 30-minute time limit is also important, as you do not want prospects eating up valuable time asking questions with no intention of actually hiring you. It's a good idea to set up a communication structure designed to weed out potential prospects who aren't very serious, so you only get on calls with likely buyers of your services.

Once they have hired you, you can set up a Pinterest board just for them. This allows them to pin logos, images, and designs they like. While you should never copy these images, you can use them as a starting point to get an idea of what graphics they like. This is the perfect way to get into your client's head and learn their taste.

CREATING THE PROPOSAL

Your project proposal is essentially your sales pitch. It should clearly convey three important items:

First, your proposal needs to convince your prospect that you thoroughly understand what they are looking for. This is very important. Many times clients know what they want but have a hard time conveying it to you. Reiterating it in your proposal gives them the confidence that you are on the right track—or gives them the opportunity to correct your vision so it's in line with theirs BEFORE you establish the final price with them.

You need to confirm that you are the best person for the job. You want to highlight what they are hiring you to do, and follow that up with the information that shows them you will be providing them with quality work to meet their needs and desires.

You also want to clearly define your pricing, processes, timeline, etc. It is very important to be completely clear from the beginning so you can accurately manage their expectations from start to finish.

Remember, this is not a contract, so you don't need to include any legal jargon or terms and conditions. When done right, your proposal will look nice, add to your sense of professionalism, and inform the client of everything they need to know to get started. As a designer, it always helps to also make it branded and looking nice.

So what goes in a proposal?

- *Cover page.* This includes the title, client's company name, date, point of contact whom the proposal is being prepared for as well as your logo.
- *Body.* Begin with a friendly and upbeat introduction to the project thanking the client for his or her time. Add specific details relevant to the client and the project. As you get deeper into the proposal, you will want to include the project scope.
- *Project scope.* This is where you get detailed about the prob-

lem and the solution for the company. You will want to do a point-by-point presentation of everything required for the project and how you plan to handle it. This will show you pay attention to detail and thoroughly understand the client's needs.

◀ *Fee summary*. This is the breakdown of all the services you will provide the client. The summary will include itemized prices along with a project total. This section will also give an expiration date. This is important because you do not want to hand a proposal to a client and then have him or her come to you several years later wanting the project completed at those prices. Generally, a 30-day time limit is sufficient.

◀ *Fee schedule*. This section is where you define how you will be paid. Detail at what point in the project you will expect deposits, triggers for payment, how you expect to be paid, and overall milestones of the project. This is also a good place to include estimated completion dates.

◀ *Background*. The background section is optional but highly recommended as a final way to sell yourself as the best candidate for the job. Finish up with your experience, specialties, and a general background summary.

◀ *Next step*. The final section is your call to action, with the next steps laid out plainly for the client. This lets them know how to start the project.

This should go without saying, but your proposal must be 100 percent error-free and professionally branded. This can easily be done in Microsoft Word or Adobe InDesign, but it is much easier to use software like Bidsketch (www.bidsketch.com). Bidsketch allows you to fully customize the proposal and save it as a template for future use. Once set up, all you need to do is change the client details, saving you valuable time and money. Additionally, Bidsketch has the bonus feature of allowing you to digitally send your proposal to the client to click and approve for you to start!

CLIENT AGREEMENTS

A client agreement or contract is an essential part of design work. It protects both you and the client from stress that neither of you needs. It sets up a clear black-and-white statement of what you will provide, what the client will provide, and how you will get paid. Starting a project with that kind of assurance should make both you and the client feel better about it.

A client agreement is different from a proposal. Remember, a proposal contains no legal jargon and is not binding. The client agreement is a binding document, which both you and the client sign. Unlike the proposal, this is not a sales tool and should contain very specific language. I recommend you hire an attorney or, at the very least, have one read over the contract and conditions before sending it out.

You can use pre-fab terms and conditions, which can be found on the website for AIGA (www.aiga.org/standard-agreement), an association for professional designers. Unfortunately, the pre-fab documents can be overkill and may scare off smaller clients. However, places like RightSignature (https://rightsignature.com) work much the same way as Bidsketch, and you can send the documents to the client via email for a digital signature. You can then download the signed PDF and have a legally binding document at the ready. Honestly, if you do a search for sample contracts, you will find PLENTY to review that will help you create your own.

GETTING THE JOB DONE

Presenting your work is the final step in selling. Your job is not done once you have "finished" the project. Now you need to present the final product in a manner that sells the project. You don't just want to send images with no explanation at all. Explain why you chose these images and those colors, because the client will be showing them to everyone and their brother for opinions. Without a solid explanation of why you did things a certain way, you are opening yourself up to criticism. You have some options when it comes to presenting your work:

◀ *Presenting in person.* This will give you a chance to sell the product and explain your decisions. Go in confidently with the product in the final form. If it is digital, present on a laptop. If it is print, bring in a printed copy. Most important, don't make the newbie mistake of giving a "tour" of the design, showing *what* you have done. Instead, explain *why* this object is here and *why* it is that color. Explaining your decisions disarms the objections before they occur!

◀ *Presenting remotely.* Many graphic designers never meet their clients face to face, so all communication is done via the internet. Here are some tools that make this easy:

  - *Annotated PDF.* This is perfect for explaining the why behind a project. Start with a cover level and an introduction to the project with the stated goals. Then insert the designs. You can use Adobe Acrobat's "sticky notes" to mark right on the design why you chose what you did. This way the client gets the benefit of your presentation while looking at the design. Even better, when the client shows it around, everyone else will see your presentation and understand why things are the way they are.

  - *Screen-casting.* Screen-casting is almost like being in the same room. You can get software that will record your screen and your voice. This way you can show the sample designs and explain your thought process as you record the video. Then when you email it to the client, it is like they are in the same room with you hearing the presentation. My favorite free option is Jing (www.techsmith.com/jing.html), but I absolutely love Snagit (www.techsmith.com/snagit.html), which you can try for free for 30 days with a one-time fee of $49.95 after that.

No matter which way you decide to go, don't present unfinished work. Clients are not always the creative type, and they may not see the same potential in the design that you do. No matter how excited you get, keep a lid on the process until it is finished.

Revise

Revisions are part of the Graphic Design Profit Path. There are some things you can do to streamline the revision process, allowing you to finish the project in two or three rounds.

First, ask questions. Try to fully understand exactly what the client wants. It's good to have a preset list of questions that you think will help you understand their expectations. It's never a bad idea to have them show you more examples of what they're looking for. Be sure to ask about color preferences, font styles, and target demographics.

Next, write down your goals for each revision and have it in writing how many revisions are acceptable before an additional fee will be charged. I have found three revisions is the magic number; everything should be squared away by the third time.

Start with the black-and-white concept. Present two or three options, and have the client pick one they like. This will be set up for color options and revisions to come.

Then move on to revision. The first two rounds of revisions involve fine-tuning the concept incorporating the client's feedback. On the third revision, everything should be approved and set and you can move on to finalizing color. On the final revision, you can present three to five color schemes for the client to choose from.

Finally, know when to give in. At some point, there may be a disagreement in the creative flow. All you can do is give your opinion as the expert and try to make them understand your choice. But when a client digs in, all you can do is back down and let them have the final say. After all, they pay the bills and it is ultimately their decision.

Finish Up

Once your design is finished and you're ready to send it over, you'll want to know how to give it to the client properly. If the files will be printed, they need to be sent in CMYK mode with a minimum of 300 dpi resolution. If the images will be on the web, send them in RGB mode with 72 or 96 dpi. If you're sending a CMYK for print purposes, it never hurts to also include an RGB version in case they want to put it online at a later date.

There are seven file types you will want to send to your client after finishing the job, depending on what they purchased. Remember, purchasing a design from you can be lower-cost, meaning they only bought the right to use that image, or they could buy the entire image from you, which means they now fully own it and you can never use the image again. Depending on what they purchased from you, the following file types are commonly requested and sent:

- AI (Adobe Illustrator)
- EPS (Adobe Illustrator)
- PSD
- TIFF
- PDF
- JPG
- PNG

Sending files like AI, EPS, or PSD lets the client edit simple parts of the design like colors or shapes if they ever need to.

SUMMARY TIPS

Here are a few quick tips to help you map out the best way to work with clients on this particular Profit Path.

1. *Manage expectations.* Make sure to get clear information at the beginning consultation—design styles, colors, examples of things they like that others are doing.
2. *Set clear deadlines.* Make sure to ask the client for specific dates and times they would like to see drafts and the final product. Many do not understand the time required for even the simplest of graphic tasks, so establishing clear deadlines helps to manage the client's expectations, along with allowing you time to plan your schedule for this and any other jobs going on.
3. *Underpromise, overdeliver.* Unexpected things ARE going to happen. Always add some time into client quotes and your own schedule for things that don't go the way you think they should.

4. *Multiple drafts are inevitable.* You are almost guaranteed to make at least one change before the final product. Be open to the alterations they are requesting. If you don't agree with a change request, always approach it as a suggestion: give a valid reason why the design element may not work, and be sure to provide some possible alternatives.

5. *Provide variations.* Provide a couple of options for the client upfront. Maybe offer a safe version you know meets the client's expectations and then maybe give them a riskier version you can envision based on their needs. Sometimes clients don't know that they don't know what to ask for.

6. *Don't take critiques personally.* Graphic design is very subjective—as an artist, you tend to protect the work you have done. You have to remember that this is all about the client being happy with the end result, so if they don't love your first draft, collaborate with the client to make sure the end result is something you are both proud of.

7. *Be well-rounded.* Clients love having someone who has some knowledge outside just graphic design. They can use you as a resource, and this will help improve your long-term relationship with them (and potentially referrals).

8. *Stay current.* Media/graphics are always changing and new things are always coming out—make sure to stay up-to-date and always be willing to learn.

9. *Set boundaries.* You know your limitations, so make sure you're not taking on too much work. Though it may seem right at the time, because it means more exposure (and more money), make sure to keep everything in balance. Taking on too much will add unneeded stress that will just end up hurting your creativity.

CHAPTER 6

FREELANCING FOR THE TECHNICALLY TRAINED

If you are technically skilled, there is a world of Freelance Profit Paths that may be open to you. Trained technicians command high dollar figures, and hanging out your shingle as a freelance tech expert can be an attractive option. In this section, we're going to look at how someone who either is already technically skilled, or who has some skills but wants to know what's possible as a freelancer in this field, can find work and prosper. This section will be a little different because the types of work under the flag of "technically trained" are quite diverse. There isn't a universal "how to."

I'm defining the technically trained as those of you who are skilled and knowledgeable about the technical side of the digital world. This will range from "Hey, I know how to install WordPress sites" to "Hey, I can fix the computer or networking issues in your company" to those of you who are offended by the idea that installing a WordPress site is tech because

MEET THE EXPERT
MIKE CLINE

Mike Cline is the CEO and founder of Tech Guys Who Get Marketing (www.techguys whogetmarketing.com). Mike is a dear friend of mine and has a fascinating tech company with a really fabulous internal culture. He has scaled his company up to the place that many of you starting down this Profit Path dream of. He's my favorite "go-to techie."

you could personally design and build your own SAS. This section is for those of you who know that "java" is not just a cute word for coffee and "rails" aren't just tracks that trains drive on.

For the most part, I'm not even qualified to give you suggestions outside the basics because the knowledge I would need to have is far above where I'm at. So if you're heading down one of these Tech Profit Paths, I'm going to assume you are solid in the "how-tos" of your skills, and what you need from me are the "how-tos" of making money with your skills online.

WHAT FREELANCE TECH JOBS ARE AVAILABLE?

OK, assuming you are passionate about computers, possess a background in information technology, are naturally analytical, good at problem solving, or have a gift for attention to detail, there are a few freelancing paths in the tech arena that may be just right for you. Let's start with a quick list of 15 well-paying Profit Paths to investigate further.

1. *Web Developer.* Designs, builds, and maintains websites and is responsible for the way websites function.
2. *Software Developer.* Participates in every aspect of software development, from wireframes to programming to QA and testing.
3. *Mobile Developer.* Participates in all aspects of mobile device-specific software development. These can be games, apps, and mobile versions of existing websites.
4. *Programmer/Coder.* Specifically focused on writing code to support functions of a computer or mobile software program. The word programmer is a professional term, whereas coder has more of a shoot-from-the-hip connotation.
5. *Information Systems Manager.* Oversees the computer activities of companies and implements technology that can help these entities meet their goals. This is similar to the role of a CTO in a large organization.
6. *Systems Analyst.* Assists with the efficient and effective use of computer technology specific to the company's function and goals.
7. *Computer Hardware Engineer.* Researches, designs, develops, tests, and oversees the manufacture and installation of computer chips, circuit boards, and computer systems. A computer hardware engineer also works with computer peripherals. To work directly with the public, one must have a license.

8. *Support Specialist.* Helps companies' customers or staff solve computer-related problems. May help with difficulties computer users are having with software programs, operating systems, computers, or peripherals.

9. *Webmaster.* Maintains websites and supports ongoing design, analysis of user data, implementation of new content, and responding to user feedback.

10. *Computer Technician.* Installs hardware and software, performs preventative maintenance, and solves problems people have with their computers.

11. *Systems Administrator.* Has responsibility for the upkeep, configuration, and operation of computer systems and servers. A systems administrator is also responsible for the uptime, performance, and security of client systems.

12. *Software Architect.* Makes high-level design choices and dictates technical standards, including software coding standards, tools, and platforms.

13. *Database Administrator.* Administers the installation, configuration, upgrading, monitoring, maintenance, and security of databases for a company. A database administrator must also oversee the development and design of database strategies, system monitoring, and database performance and capacity.

14. *Network Administrator.* Prevents unauthorized access, misuse, modification, or denial of a computer network. Network security oversees the authorization of access to data in a network.

15. *Data Science.* Oversees advanced analytics, data mining, customer segmentation, predictive modeling, reporting methods, and data quality.

It is important to understand that having a technical skill to market and knowing where to look for your first freelancing jobs is just the start. Employers that are looking to hire freelancers on job sites generally want skilled workers that are experienced or have a positive feedback rating on the site in question.

A good strategy to build a portfolio and client base is to accept jobs paying less than you are really worth at first in order to get your foot in the door, do good work, and receive positive reviews. Build a reputation this way and then start going after better-paying jobs charging what you are really worth. Freelance tech people are often scrutinized a little more thoroughly than other types of freelancers. Getting those first few jobs under your belt with positive feedback will make your journey a lot easier.

Another virtual guarantee with tech freelancing is that you will likely be interviewed before prospects make the decision to hire you. For that reason, it is important to develop quality interviewing skills and keep an updated resume. This becomes more true as the type of technology services you are providing become more advanced. Coding a piece of software for someone is a whole different arena from writing a report for them to give away.

The last thing I will say before we get into the specifics of this Profit Path is that of all the freelancers people hire online, they find it most difficult to find great tech workers. There are a ton of talented people for hire, but finding the right person in the right location and within your budget can prove tricky. It's a common pain point. So you really do have a great chance to carve out a name for yourself in the digital freelancing world.

A DEEPER DIVE INTO TWO SPECIFIC PATHS FOR THOSE WITH A DESIRE TO LEARN

As I was preparing for this book, it became clear there are a lot of talented individuals who don't have training, but have a strong leaning toward digital technology. So I wanted to explore two common paths in more detail so those of you reading this who have interest but no formal skill in web development or programming can get an idea of what it will take to become a freelancer in these areas.

Web Developer

If you have a strong interest in website development, the good news is that you're choosing a Profit Path with a LOT of paying clients looking for quality freelancers to hire. The first thing you should know is that a huge portion of websites these days are built on WordPress. So the barrier to entry is much lower than it was five or so years ago.

There are many different ways to learn the skills you need, from formal classes to books to websites. However, if you're looking to become a more legitimate website developer, you'll want to master a few more things than just how to navigate WordPress development. There are three skill sets you can consider the building blocks for modern websites and their front-end functionality. You should learn them in this order of priority:

1. HTML
2. CSS
3. JavaScript (it is important to know JavaScript itself and not just jQuery)

As I write this, there is a new language becoming so popular that some people feel it will replace Java. Understanding the different types of languages and projects will help you recognize which tech skills and knowledge will help you the most.

Web development jobs are generally divided into front-end tasks and back-end tasks. The front end is made up primarily of HTML, CSS, and JavaScript components. These components build the pieces of the website the user sees and interacts with. The front-end tasks may also require photo manipulation in Photoshop or some other photo editor. Understanding how the site will function between the different web browsers (Firefox, Internet Explorer, Chrome, and Safari) is an essential skill.

Back-end tasks will require additional skills in at least one server-side programming language such as PHP, Python, Ruby, C#, JavaScript (yes, this can be a server-side language as well), etc. Skills that allow you to interface with databases to organize, store, call, and manipulate data will increase your value to your customers. Some examples of databases are MySQL, Ingres, MongoDB, Oracle, and PostgreSQL, among others. These components are used to build the behind-the-scenes parts that provide the functionality of the website.

Also, there are online tools that can assist you with choosing a programming language and a database flavor. There is a lot of information online about different languages. As often as new technology changes, it is important to stay abreast of trends in programming languages and strategies.

Here is a quick list of the most commonly used programming languages:

- HTML5
- CSS
- PHP
- Ruby
- Ruby on Rails
- Python
- Java
- C
- Objective-C
- Swift
- C++
- C#
- JavaScript

Programmer

Although we just discussed programming languages that are useful to know if you want to become a freelance web developer, programming goes far beyond the basic mechanics of a website. There is such a huge market for talented programmers. People are looking to hire them all the time. So where do you start if you're completely green?

The rest of this book is primarily focused on how to freelance skills you already have, but I want to make sure you know how to get started if you're walking into this industry from the ground up. You could actually get educated with the intention of freelancing as opposed to getting a traditional job with a company. Learning a programming language combined with good habits can be a lengthy process. Do not let that stop you if this is truly where your passion lies, but understand that the time needed to invest in this Profit Path is longer than other Paths. The first thing you need to do is familiarize yourself with the industry by dispelling a couple of myths.

Myth 1: There Is a "Best" Programming Language to Learn

There really is no "one best language" to start with. The first language you learn will often have no long-lasting effect on your programming path down the road. What matters most are the core programming concepts you learn, which can be applied across any future languages. Regardless of which language you choose, you will find someone online saying their language is the best one to learn first. This is the nature of the world we live in. Just roll with it.

Myth 2: The First Language You Learn Will Decide How the Rest of Your Programming Career Will Go

Regardless of which programming language you begin with, understand that they will vary in style and syntax, but the concepts you learn in your first language will translate to other languages down the road.

Let the Path Determine the Language

The first step in becoming a programmer is to select a programming language to learn first. (Remember I said there is no one best language to start with. The following is just a suggestion to help guide you in your decision.) You should first think about the type of projects you would like to work on. That will provide you with a list of languages that will help you toward your goal of making a Profit Path out of these skills.

Many programmers I know suggest a good language to start with is Python. Python is a great first experience: It is a very well-rounded language with applications on the web as well as on local machines. It integrates well with lower-level languages such as C and offers a smooth transition into higher-level languages such as Ruby. Most important, it has a very supportive online community. This will prove essential when questions arise during the learning process.

There are many paths to becoming a programmer, and it is important to pick the path that best fits your learning style and your chosen platform. You can learn programming the traditional way, through college courses, online courses, books, YouTube videos, etc. People new to programming should start with a single language and go through the path that best fits their learning style, but be sure to begin at the beginning and follow through right to the end of that path. Do not skip ahead or try to take shortcuts.

There are many online lists of practice exercises and project challenges to tackle while you are learning. You can challenge yourself with more complex programming projects from competitions held for programmers. Gamification is a fun and effective way to learn new skills.

Maybe you want to focus on programming games, or mobile apps, or maybe complex websites. There are programming languages specific to mobile development, such as Objective-C or Swift for iOS, Java for Android, and C# or JavaScript for Windows Mobile devices. The C++ language is widely used in video game development. And as described in the Web Developer section above, websites are commonly built with HTML5, CSS, and JavaScript.

All programmers should eventually gain experience in multiple programming languages. Once you are comfortable with your first language, move on to another that differs in some fundamental way, offering a new functionality. The more languages you learn, the better equipped you will be to choose the right tool for any given task. This is the hallmark of a good programmer. Often the jobs you get exposed to along the way will dictate the order in which you learn new skills and languages.

As with a foreign language, just because you can read a programming language does not necessarily mean you can program in it. To really know it takes much practice and repetition. You must be able to use the language effectively for it to become a marketable skill.

The fastest return on investment in the Technical Freelancing Path is determined simply by being able to truthfully say, "I already know a programming language."

Where to Learn

If you want to learn to program in your spare time, check out one of the websites below, where you can find free lessons ranging from basic math to advanced programming. My 17-year-old daughter taught herself basic HTML from free online courses, so it definitely is possible.

Some of these courses include:

- Khan Academy (www.khanacademy.org)
- Tuts+ (http://tutsplus.com)
- Codecademy (www.codecademy.com)
- Treehouse (https://teamtreehouse.com)
- Lynda.com (www.lynda.com)

Remember that the web is full of resources to learn any given technology. And the best tip I can share with you when attempting to learn anything new is: Be patient, be persistent, and know how to Google!

TIPS FOR SUCCEEDING IN THE FREELANCE TECH PROFIT PATH

As a freelancer, you'll be competing with many other people for jobs, so it's incumbent upon you to not only present yourself well, but also make it clear that it would be a mistake NOT to hire you! Here are several tips to help make that a reality.

Assemble a Killer Personal Portfolio

This one can be a bit tricky at the outset, as you need to make sure you have permission to show work you've done previously for an employer as a sample of your work. Going forward, make sure anything you do as a freelancer you have the right to show. Be careful about signing NDAs (nondisclosure agreements), as they can sometimes bite you in the you-know-where.

Put your best, most recent work in your portfolio, and make both a print and online version of it for best results.

Get Glowing Recommendations

Ask clients to give you written or video testimonials, as these can very often make the difference in whether you're considered for a job. If you've done quality work for them, this should be no problem. Moreover, they'll be likely to use you again and again, as well as refer you to others.

Be Sure to Charge What You're Worth!

The temptation for those starting out freelancing is always to undercut the market with their rates. While this might work initially, you'll find yourself stuck at that discounted rate and hard-pressed to justify charging more when they come back to you. Decide on your base rate and stick to it. You understand what the work entails, and they don't. Explain what they're getting for their money, and demonstrate why you're worth it.

You will always get clients who will lowball you, and who will expect you to do a job on the cheap with the promise of more and better-paying work in the future. This almost never works out, so be willing to decline jobs. On the other hand, make sure what you're charging is within the normal parameters of what is currently being paid to freelancers. There are quite a few freelance rate calculators available online, so be sure you are not shooting for the moon. Your rate should be more than you would earn at a regular job, as you have overhead now, too.

Also, of all the different Freelance Profit Paths, Tech has the largest complications due to low-priced overseas workers. People assume that coding is "safe" to outsource overseas because the written English language is not a significant part of the job. The truth is that most people in the United States would rather hire a U.S.-based freelancer but believe they can't afford them. Part of your job is to show them why you actually are a better fit all around. Even if overseas workers are cheaper, they commonly require a lot more revisions and therefore end up costing more—and the clients don't have a positive experience.

Diversify Your Client Base

Revisiting the "NEVER have a single point of failure in your business" rule, it's essential that you diversify your client base as much as you can. It's great to have clients who have projects so large that they eat up most or all of your time, but there will come a day when either you're done, or they head in another direction.

What do you do then? If you plan to remain a freelancer long term, then make it your business to always have a steady stream of leads coming into your business. If your work is in high demand, you can take only the highest-paying jobs or perhaps hire a subcontractor or two and realize a little passive income. Wouldn't that be a nice problem to have!

GETTING WORK

There are numerous freelancing opportunities for all the above roles—and far more that I haven't even mentioned. How can you find these opportunities? You will find many people looking for these skill sets at online marketplace sites, which we cover in Chapter 8; these are some of the sites I have personal experience with. These are great places for people new to the freelancing field to start taking jobs and gaining experience. The wonderful thing about these opportunities is that they can be started while you're still working your full-time job. This will allow you to get a feel for the amount of time you'll need, build your portfolio, and find out what sort of income you can realistically expect. These experiences will help you narrow down the type of projects you are passionate about.

It is important to understand that having a technical skill and knowing where to look for your first freelancing jobs is just the start. Employers who are looking to hire freelancers on these sites generally want skilled, experienced workers who have a positive feedback rating on the site in question. In order to build a portfolio and a client base, a good strategy is to accept jobs paying less than you are really worth at first to get your foot in the door, do good work, and receive positive reviews. Keep in mind that "accepting less than you're worth" doesn't mean working for dirt cheap. Doing so brings down the standard pay rate for your entire industry. However, it is quite common in the beginning for people to have skills worth an exceptional premium, yet lack freelance work history and testimonials to consistently justify higher-end rates.

Build a reputation this way and then start going after better-paying jobs charging what you are really worth. It is important to develop quality interviewing skills since most if not all of these Paths will involve at least one interview with prospective employers evaluating your skills.

Approach these interviews as the opportunity to show off your work and how right you are for the job in question.

Learn New Skills and Stay Up-to-Date

While it's tempting to simply concentrate on the work at hand, if you're going to build a viable freelancing career, you'll need to keep up-to-date on what's going on in the tech world. As you know, this field changes so fast it can be very hard to keep up with, but you must, as clients will be asking you about it, and you need to look well-informed. Consider it a business expense (timewise) you're putting into your future earnings. Learning new skills can also help make you even more marketable. If you find a certain professional certification will help you get some jobs you might be missing, consider investing in it.

Professional Networking

For a freelancer, this is one of the biggest areas of opportunity. Almost everyone you run into these days either needs a freelancer or knows someone who does. If you're not out there talking to people, they will not know how you can help them and will likely find someone else.

While it can be hard for some tech types to venture out into that land beyond the computer screen and actually connect with people, if you want to make the big bucks, this is where the action starts. Start by attending local business gatherings and chamber of commerce mixers. It might be a big stretch for you at first, but when the referrals start flowing in, you may feel differently!

You should also consider attending highly ranked internet marketing conferences. Online, you are just one in a sea of people advertising their skills. But at a conference, you can talk to people, hear exactly the type of work they are looking for, and get a good feel for their experience working with freelance tech up to that point. It is invaluable to be able to listen to people in your target market talk about what they are looking for and what their pain points are. This will enable you to structure yourself as a better solution for them. Plus, you get the opportunity of making yourself and your skills known to them personally.

Create an Air of Legitimacy

People need to believe that you aren't going to take their check and never talk to them again. Create a real business presence; this includes at the very least business cards, a business checking account, a website, a dedicated business email, and a phone or Skype line. All the paths in this book are legitimate Profit Paths, but the Tech Paths veer closer to the more traditional side of business. When you meet with a prospective client, make sure to present in a professional manner. Most businesspeople you will come in contact with and try to solicit work from won't appreciate or hire someone they feel is not a pro.

IS TECH FREELANCING IN YOUR FUTURE?

Unlike freelance writing or virtual assistant work, tech-related jobs are highly specialized and not easily spoken of in general terms. If you find that even your spare time is spent poring over technical things, you may be a good candidate for this Profit Path. It pays well, and since you already have most of the skills needed to do the work, you can be in business very quickly. A lot of the information covered in the other Freelance Profit Paths will cross over to this section as well. The Quick Action Steps are:

1. Do some research to see what types of projects are a match for the skills you wrote in your Profit Path Profile.
2. Get an idea for the competitive rates for those projects.
3. Set up your online presence.
4. Go get your first client!

CHAPTER 7

VIRTUAL ASSISTANT PROFIT PATH

"A virtual assistant (typically abbreviated to VA, also called a virtual office assistant) is generally self-employed and provides professional administrative, technical, or creative (social) assistance to clients remotely from a home office." —Wikipedia.com

In my opinion, a virtual assistant (VA) is anyone who can help a business in a virtual manner (i.e., at a separate location). Despite the title "assistant," a VA can do much more than a regular assistant, like a receptionist or secretary. In fact, a VA can do any type of work needed to support a business virtually.

Like all freelancers, a VA is a self-employed independent contractor who is willing and ready to help professionals in a variety of tasks to run a business. These tasks can include anything from administrative work and bookkeeping to social media and project management. The only difference between a VA and a traditional office assistant is that the VA will never set foot in the client's office and does all the work from a remote location, generally their home.

Some Clarification

There is some crossover into specific freelancing paths when we start getting into the topic of the Virtual Assistant Profit Path. If you read any books about becoming a virtual assistant, you will find a lot of information about specializing. The common school of thought is that specialization is almost always more profitable than generalization. However, when we get deep into the topic of specializing, in my opinion that often takes you into more specific freelance paths. For instance, if you have website development skills, you would likely never title yourself as a virtual assistant because your services will carry a much higher price tag if you title yourself a website developer.

Ultimately I included the virtual assistant section because it is such a realistic path for people who might not have strengths in one specific, high-demand skill like freelance writing or graphic design. Being a virtual assistant is a catchall for pretty much any skill a business might hire you for, and that fact alone makes this a profitable path for a wide variety of people.

The great thing about the Virtual Assistant Profit Path is the limitless possibilities. This extends to the types of services you can offer, the markets you choose to serve, and whether you work solely for yourself or whether you contract with VA companies and let them funnel clients to you. This is one of the most customizable Profit Paths I know of.

GETTING SET UP AS A SOLOPRENEUR VA

As mentioned, anything that needs to be done in a business can be outsourced to a VA. However, some of the more common skills needed to be an effective VA include basic office and administration skills, writing skills, and knowledge of social media management, as these are always in high demand. Still other "must haves" include being a self-starter, excellent organization, effective communication skills, attention to detail, and an ability to follow directions carefully.

Here are a few of the more specialized skill sets many clients are seeking. These are just examples, but if you have strengths in these areas, you may want to consider marketing them on a more specific freelancing path as opposed to running under the virtual assistant flag:

- Content writing
- Web design
- Email marketing
- Social media management
- Blog and website management
- Multimedia production (podcast, YouTube Videos, etc.)
- Ghostwriting
- Graphic design
- Research
- Editing
- Tutoring
- Desktop publishing
- Counseling
- Audio/video editing
- Copywriting
- Bookkeeping
- Project management
- Transcription
- Programming
- Data Entry
- Sending out correspondence
- Appointment setting
- Online filing
- Making phone calls
- Website maintenance

Top Skills for VA Employment

The following is a more complete breakdown of VA work and the categories they fall into.

- Email management (reminders, autoresponders [AWeber, Mail Chimp])

- Correspondence (business letters, thank-you notes)
- Database building
- Receptionist
- Calendar management
- File management
- Dropbox
- Research
- Coordinating travel (creating itineraries, hotel and flight booking, car rentals, restaurant reservations, travel visa requirements)
- Transcription (including voice mail)
- Taking down minutes of meetings
- Creating basic reports
- Preparing slideshows (PowerPoint presentations)
- Liaison between team members
- Set up, manage, and update social media accounts (Facebook, Twitter, LinkedIn, YouTube)
- Blogging (create, manage, and publish blog posts; guest blogging/ghost blogging; filter and reply to comments on blog)
- Answer support tickets
- Audio/video editing (removing background noise, adding intros and outros to videos)
- Basic photoshop/image editing (not graphic design)
- PowerPress (podcasting WP plugin) installation
- Podcasts (creation, set up on iTunes, insertion on blog post)
- Content writing
- SEO writing
- Press release writing
- Newsletter writing
- Copywriting
- Article marketing
- SEO/web marketing (directory submission, article spinning, site analysis, keyword research for blog content, competitor analysis, landing page setup/creation, webmaster submission, sitemap submissions, on-page and off-page optimization for a post/page, off-page optimization for blog commenting, creating backlinks/

link building, weekly/monthly Google Analytics and traffic reports, monthly keyword ranking reports)

- Social bookmarking (Digg, StumbleUpon, Reddit, Delicious, creating a social bookmarking tracking sheet)
- Forum participation/moderation
- Graphic/web design (designing logos, banners, icons, ebook covers and headers; designing infographics from provided content; designing websites and creating mockups; designing landing/sales/opt-in pages)
- Web development (site maintenance/security and troubleshooting, CRM integration and social media integration, payment gateway integration, install and support an email ticketing system)
- Support and develop WordPress (PHP) websites (install WordPress plugins and themes, WordPress theme customization, WordPress functionality and plugin enhancement)
- Bookkeeping, accounting, and other financial support (file taxes, handle expense reports, set up online bill payment service with payment authorization, manage accounts receivable, update accounting software as bills are paid, audit bills to prevent overpaying, reconcile bank statements, enter credit card transactions, prepare invoices, track past-due payment notices and follow up to collect, make and/or enter deposits, prepare end-of-month reports)
- Teleseminar planning (set up teleseminars, coordinate the speakers, make sure everything runs smoothly, record the event, arrange to sell or share the presentation as necessary)
- Event planning and coordination (get details on venues, coordinate speakers, send out announcements, track attendees, send out reminders, coordinate registration, ensure availability of equipment at event)
- Human resources support (place ads, sort through resumes, conduct phone interviews, narrow down the field of applicants)
- Personnel (verify past employment, call references, prepare and send welcome package to new employees, track dates for employee performance reviews)

- Payroll support (verify payroll requirements, check taxes, check tax and payroll forms)
- Project management (keep all subcontractors, employees, and team members on track; use calendars, scheduling tools, emails, and phone calls to make sure deadlines are met)
- Database management and data processing
- Writing, editing, and proofreading
- Expert industry insight (keep an eye on the competition, provide updates on industry, perform product research)
- Customer service (set client appointments, act as a customer support representative, email clients, maintain contact with clients as a go-to person)

Other task categories come into play when a VA specializes in an industry:

- Medical VA
- Legal VA
- Real estate VA
- Nonprofit VA

Know Your Strengths

If you completed the Profit Path Profile I walked you through in Chapter 3, you have already compiled a comprehensive list of your strengths, interests, and weaknesses. This will help you get very specific about the type of VA work you would like to get involved with and become known for. Take a good look at what areas you are lacking in and decide if you need to find a strategic partner to help in those areas or if you need to educate yourself to be better prepared to serve your market. That said, it is fully acceptable to only offer the services you are great at and not worry about the rest.

Service Specialization

I know I said I'm not going to focus on specialization in specific services because by doing so you really should move into more of a freelance model to fetch a higher price tag. However, there are different levels of specialization. For instance, if you are a talented web developer, then yes, I would advise you advertise yourself that way. That said, you could lump certain skill sets that you have or that you acquire to then advertise yourself as a specialized virtual assistant.

One example would be that you don't have enough skills to advertise yourself as a full social media expert who can create and implement successful social media campaigns, but you know how to create sophisticated pages on popular social media platforms like Facebook, Twitter, Pinterest, etc. You're also great at tracking social media posts on the various platforms and making sure comments are responded to, etc. You may even know a specific industry well enough that you can do some regular posting for clients. So you may advertise as a social media VA. There are so many companies that have zero social media presence, and to have someone doing even the bare-bone basics in this arena would be better than the nothing they have going on right now.

Likewise, if you really enjoy working with people and you are articulate in writing and understand the basic mechanics of email and help desks, you could advertise that you are a customer service VA. This is a great help to any company, since I believe that a company truly is only as good as its customer service.

I frequently hire marketing virtual assistants. They don't know enough to be in charge of marketing campaigns, but they can help manage my clients' work. My marketing VAs are invaluable to me. My point is that there is a level of specialization you can do as a virtual assistant that will allow you to charge a higher fee and make your marketing message more specific.

Market Specialization

Market specialization is different from specialization of skill sets. This is where you choose specific industries to focus on. Again, this can make you more valuable to your market. The idea here is that an accountant will be far more likely to hire a virtual assistant who specializes in helping successful accountants than a VA who is just a really great VA. Take that one step further: What if you were an accountant or worked for an accountant for many years, but now you're working as a VA who

REAL-WORLD EXAMPLE FROM BRANDING EXPERT MICHELLE VILLALOBOS

If you ever talk to a really great branding expert, they will tell you that specializing is always more powerful than generalizing. My friend Michelle Villalobos is one such amazing expert. We both gave keynotes at ONTRApalooza 2014. When I was listening to her presentation, she was using life coaches as her example. She asked how many of us knew a life coach. Everyone in the audience raised their hands. Then she asked how many of us knew multiple life coaches; the majority of the room raised their hands again. Her point was this: If someone knows you are a life coach, you become a dime a dozen in their mind.

She then told the story of one of her branding clients who came to her as a general life coach wanting to create a better brand. She started talking to this woman, Suzanne Yvette, and her story was very intriguing. She is both a breast cancer survivor and a former military servicewoman. So instead of being a generic life coach, she specifically became a coach who specializes in coaching women through the three phases of breast cancer. You can see part of her branding here in this screenshot from her website (www.suzanneyvette.com):

Her brand is brilliant and her business exploded because now when encountering women with breast cancer, her name pops into people's heads, so it became very easy to refer people to her. Michelle had case study after case study just like this, across multiple markets.

It is natural for you to feel like saying, "I can help anyone! I don't want to limit myself!" I understand the feeling. But as a marketing expert, you'll need to trust me on this one. Specializing almost always leads to more business because you stand out and people know who to refer to you. You won't just blend into the background of the millions of virtual assistants in the world. As branding expert and author Sally Hogshead likes to put it, "Different is better than better."

To get more awesome branding guidance, you can visit Michelle's site at www. michellevillalobos.com.

specializes in assisting accountants because you've decided to work from home so you can raise your children?

Businesses like the thought of hiring people who really understand their specific market. It makes them feel they are getting higher-quality assistants, and they are likely right. They are willing to pay more than they would for a generic assistant, because a specialized assistant is bringing something more to the table that is of value to the business. It sends the message that you can fill your clients' needs in a way that a generic VA cannot. You will know what the client needs, how to help the client, and can even recommend other VAs for other aspects of the job when necessary.

Profit Path Questions

Do you have a specific market you would really like to serve? This may be a market you understand because you've been involved with it in the past, or it might just be one you're interested in, or one you have a connection to that gives you an easier "in." If you're considering this Profit Path, take some time to look over your Profit Path Profile and identify if specializing in a specific market, at least in the beginning, might make sense for you. In my opinion, your freelancing career will be far more lucrative if you specialize than if you don't. I also believe that everyone can ethically "fake it until you make it." Everyone has life experiences that can be drawn on and used to help position yourself in the marketplace.

SETTING YOUR RATES

Virtual assistants have no standard rate of pay. Some virtual assistants, even in the U.S., make less than minimum wage, while some, especially those who specialize, can average $25 per hour or more. It is not unheard of to make $100 per hour if you position yourself properly. You need to be smart about it. You do NOT need to make less than minimum wage just because you choose to go down an unspecialized path. But you do need to be intelligent about how you position yourself in the marketplace.

While places like Fiverr have VAs for as low as $5 per hour, they also have virtual assistants listed for $25 per hour. What's the difference? Positioning. I can't emphasize enough how much positioning matters. To successfully position yourself in any marketplace, you need to first understand the aspects of the market that matter.

Worldwide Competition

First, it is important to understand that virtual assistant work is worldwide. Therefore, you will be competing against people who can and will SERIOUSLY underbid you. In Third World countries, $3 an hour is a fair price, and many people are willing to work for that. Unless you come across a company wanting a native English speaker, this will be one of the biggest obstacles. If you are offering a skill sets commonly found in low-paid, overseas workers, you need to position what you bring to the table as a U.S.-based virtual assistant. You don't want to be paid at the same rate they are, so you can't allow yourself to be lumped into the same category. Even if you're offering the same service, it's up to you to position yourself in a way that offers much more value.

To successfully increase your wage and maintain clients, follow these tips:

◀ *Keep an eye on the competition.* This will let you know what others are charging and what type of service is expected. You don't have to charge the same as your competitors, but understanding the market averages will help you set your rates.

◖ *Keep your prices competitive.* I cannot emphasize this enough. Do not severely undercut your competition to get work. I know this sounds like a great plan, but by doing this, you lower the overall average rates in your industry.

◖ *Set your rates based on tasks given.* A flat rate may seem like a good idea, but some tasks are more complex and take a greater skill level to complete. While hourly rates are fine, set the rate based on the tasks given and the level of specialization for those tasks. Bigger clients requiring more skill will be more than happy to pay the higher price for excellent service.

◖ *Don't always charge by the hour.* Some jobs like writing should be paid by the assignment and not the time given. The key is to provide value for your service. Charging a set amount per 400-word blog post is much more acceptable than charging by the hour for the same task. The key is to think about the task and create a pricing system that makes sense for both you and your client. Usually VA work does not fall under a one-size-fits-all pricing structure. A VA is all about the win-win.

FREELANCING AGENCIES AND CERTIFICATION PROGRAMS

While membership in an organization is not absolutely necessary, it can be very helpful in the beginning. Associating yourself with a professional society can gain you the credibility and clientele you are seeking at the beginning of your VA career.

Two organizations worth noting are:

1. The International Virtual Assistants Association (http://ivaa.org)
2. The Administrative Consultants Association (http://administra-tiveconsultantsassoc.com)

Certification Programs

There are a few places that offer training on becoming a successful virtual assistant. Here are some you can look into:

◖ *Moonlighting on the Internet* (www.MoonlightingontheInternet.com)

◀ *Assist U* (http://www.assistu.com)

◀ *International Virtual Assistants Association* (www.IVAA.org)

◀ *Virtual Assistant Training* (www.virtualassistanttrainingacademy.com)

Virtual Assistant Companies

Virtual assistant companies do exist, and they work one of two ways. The vast majority of them work by finding clients for you, and then taking a cut of what you're paid. However, some companies hire virtual assistants more on par with a contractor relationship. They consider their clients to be theirs and hire VAs to work with their clients. So you'll work as a VA servicing their clients. Both types of companies charge the client and pay you an hourly wage/salary based on the tasks performed. You can expect anywhere from $7 to $15 an hour working through a VA company.

I own companies that use both methods. Content Divas and Ember Dragon hire virtual assistants to serve our clients. However, Moonlighting Moms specifically connects clients with high-quality virtual assistants we train and outsource. The virtual assistants and clients choose each other, and the VA sets her own rates. We ensure the pool of virtual assistants is well-trained and high-quality, and the VAs get a plethora of clients that are attracted to our brand and reputation. Both methods have merit.

The biggest pro of working for a VA company is that you do not have to put time, energy, or money into lead acquisition. The biggest con, by contrast, is that you'll often make more money being a solopreneur if you are good at lead acquisition. My advice is to not put yourself in a box. Work for an agency *and* do solopreneur VA work. You really can have the best of both worlds.

I must remind you that at this stage in the game, we hire all our virtual assistants in-house, so while I haven't personally tried the other companies listed below, these are some of the more popular VA companies:

◀ *Moonlighting Moms.* We specialize in business-related virtual assistants with an emphasis on services in the digital marketing world. You are required to get certified to our standards before we will outsource you to our clients. No, we don't only accept moms as our virtual staff.

- *Zirtual* (www.zirtual.com). These VAs perform a variety of administrative assistant tasks: responding to emails, paying bills, ordering gifts, dealing with customer service, and so forth. Most are college-educated and based in the United States. All applicants must pass an extensive vetting process that tests their communication skills, tech savvy, and resourcefulness.

- *Red Butler* (https://redbutler.com). A concierge service with VIP perks. Red Butler assistants do regular business and personal assistant services along with special perks. Through their connections, clients can request anything from "Oil of Olay baths" to Lil Wayne singing "Happy Birthday" to their kid. The Red Butler Card also activates special VIP privileges at hotels, restaurants, clubs, bars, and other entertainment venues.

- *Fancy Hands* (www.fancyhands.com). This service allows team members to coordinate meetings, make purchases, and do research along with managing their personal lives. Fancy Hands specializes in helping you take control of your business and life and allows multiple users to take advantage through a single user access.

- *eaHELP* (http://eahelp.com). Based in Atlanta, eaHELP specializes in executive assistants and the administrative tasks that a traditional EA would do: everything from simple calls and emails to calendar management and travel planning. Clients rest assured knowing the VAs have a minimum of five years' experience and went through a rigorous screening.

- *Virtual Assist USA* (http://virtualassistusa.com). Based in Pittsburgh, Virtual Assist USA has a 35-person VA team working to make your life easier. The VAs have hundreds of skill sets, and no matter how many VAs a client deals with, it will only receive a single invoice from them. They strive to provide long-term administrative assistance through remote support.

- *Time etc.* (http://web.timeetc.com/powerful). Applicants are required to go through an intensive vetting process and take key skills and an IQ test before clients hire them out by the hour. Unlike most VA businesses, a client can pay by the hour instead of by the task and is not subject to a monthly plan.

◄ *TaskRabbit* (www.taskrabbit.com). TaskRabbit differs in that it allows users to outsource their tasks and to-do lists to persons in the neighborhood. If you do not live in a TaskRabbit neighborhood, the company also offers VA services to plan vacations, do research, proofread, and more standard remotely accessible tasks.

FINDING CLIENTS

The biggest obstacle to becoming a VA is finding jobs and clients. There is no proverbial "job board" waiting for you to go click on leads and start working. It is much more complicated than that. Being a VA means building relationships and getting a reputation as a good worker. Then the jobs will start to come.

Unfortunately, many people are stuck in the "employee" mindset. They want to clock in, do a job, get paid, and go home. This is why they ask, "Where do I find a job?" Even with the freelance sites, you have to track down clients, bid for jobs you want, and sell yourself as the best possible choice. As a business owner (which you now are), work does not usually fall in your lap. You must either be willing to put the time into hunting down leads and find work to keep a steady pay stream flowing, or start out working with a virtual assistant company.

Because being a virtual assistant can encompass so many different services and lends itself well to charging by the hour, there is a unique opportunity to sell your services in time blocks. Time blocks are an excellent way to get a commitment out of a client. You can offer blocks ranging from 5 to 40 hours per month and let your clients choose when to use the hours.

Additionally, allow for a recurring program to make the transition from month to month easier.

You can offer a discount for upfront payment. Clients are more likely to buy more services if there is a discount involved, and it's often easier to get them to pay upfront if you incentivize doing so.

CHARACTERISTICS AND TRAITS YOU NEED TO KEEP YOUR CLIENTS

Keeping clients requires loyalty, and that means you will need to demonstrate other skills besides expertise and knowledge. Here we talk about the traits outside your specific marketable skills that will inspire loyalty in your clients and keep them coming back again and again.

Reliability

Reliability is a must in a virtual assistant. No matter how qualified you are or how cheaply you work, you *will* lose clients if they can't rely on you. This means they need to set it and forget it. When they give you a task, you must work on your own to get it done without reminders and without any hand-holding. You are supposed to make their life easier, and if they have to constantly stop what they are doing to check on you, you will lose a client.

Accuracy

Accuracy is very important. Mistakes are human and will happen. But you must avoid unnecessary mistakes like typos and subpar work. If your client has to go back and check your work, you are not saving them much time.

Integrity

Integrity is everything when it comes to intellectual properties. Plagiarizing is unacceptable and will cost you clients (if not more). Additionally, be true to your time frame. If you promise work by Thursday, then it must be done by Thursday; if a delay is absolutely unavoidable, you need to pre-emptively communicate that. I try to get things done a day early just in case something comes up at the last minute so I have a little extra wiggle room.

Kind and Friendly Personality

Rapport with your clients will take you farther than you could imagine. Always stay positive, no matter how the client acts. When you are positive and uplifting, you show confidence in the midst of their crisis, which will gain you respect.

Resourcefulness

A valuable virtual assistant is the go-to person for information. You don't have to know everything about the business, but you need to have a system in place that allows you to find out. This can be as simple as having a specific point of contact at the company that you can go to when you need information. However, once you ask a question once, be sure to document it so that you don't have to ask for the same information repeatedly. Being able to answer the majority, if not all of a client's basic questions helps make you an irreplaceable part of their team.

An "Ideas" Person

This goes along with resourcefulness. You want to have ideas that make the company better. When you think about the client's business, you show you are more than a typical assistant. Plus, when you come up with a strategy to make the business better, many times the client will put you in charge of it, keeping you working and making you even more valuable.

Help Grow the Client's Business

Along the same lines as the last two points, if you can make a client's business grow and they increase their income, you will have a job forever. The extra income you provide the client will make you a priceless member of their business.

Follow Through and Follow Up

Stay on top of every task, even when your client does not. Small tasks can often fall through the cracks, but it is your job not to let that happen. For example, I had a client who needed to approve all bookmarks before I posted them. If I did not get approval after two or three days, I would send her another email with the bookmarks attached saying, "In case you missed these, these bookmarks are awaiting approval." I did this on more than one occasion, and she even thanked me for keeping her on task.

Work Well Under Pressure

Never let a client see you sweat. This is a joke, but it is true in more ways than you think. You want each client to think they are your only client, no matter your workload. This means not taking on too much because a stressed-out VA passes the stress on to the client, which is exactly what you are trying to relieve.

Ability to Multitask

Probably one of the top five things a virtual assistant must do is take on multiple tasks for multiple clients and keep them all moving forward. It takes organization, efficiency, and good scheduling, but it is critical for virtual assistant success.

A FINAL WORD OF CAUTION

A virtual assistant is not meant to be a personal assistant at the beck and call of the client. Many times, businesses struggle with the difference between a traditional employee and a VA. A virtual assistant has other clients and cannot drop everything for one client like a traditional business assistant. This is where setting boundaries is vitally important. VAs are especially easy to unintentionally abuse because they are often the "catchall" for tasks that a company doesn't employ a dedicated team member to do.

The client needs to respect your time as much as you need to respect their time. This is the only situation in which you might have to tell a client no or that this is not a good time. Small businesses and new virtual assistants alike struggle with this. You physically cannot be at the beck and call of your clients. Therefore, you must set clear boundaries.

You will need to set hours for when a client can call; off hours they can email you information. Personally, when a client wants to call during off hours, I set a higher rate. This allows me to have my personal time and it allows them to get hold of me in an emergency at the higher price.

CHAPTER 8

FREELANCING WRAP-UP

When pursuing a Freelance Profit Path, it is of the utmost importance to brand yourself, particularly in the online market. Think of it as your online persona. This persona needs to be professional, attract employers, find work, and be exceptional at what it does. You are in the business of selling yourself and must be remembered to build clients and gain a favorable reputation. It is most difficult in the beginning because you have no feedback. One place you can start is on freelance job sites.

POPULAR FREELANCE JOB SITES

Freelance job sites offer the newcomer the fastest and easiest way to find work. These sites require you to set up a profile with as much information as you can provide. Prospective clients come to browse and choose freelancers based on the profile, services needed, and feedback left. Competition can be fierce. However, they do allow you to connect to clients and build up a portfolio when finding work elsewhere.

There are a TON of freelance websites where freelancers can find work. Here are some of the more popular ones:

- *Upwork.* Formerly Odesk (www.upwork.com). This site offers a little something for everyone—writers, virtual assistants, accountants, consultants, designers, developers, customer service specialists, and more! Their focus is more on mass amounts of low-paying jobs, as opposed to their sister freelance site, Elance. Upwork recently announced that they intend to phase out Elance and run all of their crowdsourcing exclusively from Upwork.

- *Elance* (www.elance.com). Elance and Upwork are owned by the same people and are two of the top freelance sites in the world. Elance has the potential to offer very high-revenue projects if you stick with it and produce good work.

- *Fiverr* (www.fiverr.com). This site offers a plethora of one-of-a-kind opportunities, as well as the usual writing and virtual assistant jobs. They also specialize in music, graphic design, and computer programming.

- *Guru* (www.guru.com). This site lets you categorize yourself by skills so prospective clients can find you, instead of the other way around. If you have a week to work on a website design layout, you can post your profile saying just that and a client looking for the same thing can hire you to help them. Very simple!

- *Workaholics4Hire* (http://workaholics4hire.com). The name may seem a little unsophisticated, but since 1999 this site has provided freelancers with quality work and quality pay in the areas of specialized skills, project management, and support services for web-based business owners.

- *Ziptask* (www.ziptask.com/home). Ziptask differs slightly from the other freelance job sites listed here, as it acts as a middleman between the client and the freelancer. The client tells Ziptask what they are looking for, and Ziptask finds the perfect freelancer. Once completed, the work goes to the client without the freelancer ever interacting directly with them. This process has its pros and cons, but a lot of freelancers are very happy with the opportunities they receive through this site.

◀ *Freelancer* (www.freelancer.com). Great for project-based work, as opposed to one-off assignments. If you like to take on big tasks that take time to complete, this is a great place to start.

◀ *Toptal* (www.toptal.com). This place boasts it hires the best of the best—the top 3 percent of software developers. Once you've been in the game for a while and honed your skills, this would be a great place to graduate to.

◀ *Staff.com* (www.staff.com). This site is more focused on full-time hiring. If you're looking to make freelancing your main career, this might be a great place for you. But if it's a side project to make a little extra cash, stick to the other freelance sites.

OPTIMIZING YOUR FREELANCE PROFILE FOR SUCCESS

It's not enough just to sign up for a bunch of freelance sites and let the chips fall where they may; you've got to stand out and make a name for yourself. There are thousands upon thousands of competitors out there, and though you may think your work speaks for itself, that's hard to do if no one ever sees it. Here are a few tips to get you noticed in the crowded freelance world:

◀ *Have a catchy title.* Just saying your name or job title isn't enough. Grab their attention in some way—be funny, be creative, be you! I've seen multiple people list out their titles and one of them is "part-time Super Hero," "part-time Rock Star," etc. You can do a search on LinkedIn and you'll see some creative titles.

◀ *Talk about what you can do as opposed to who you are.* Don't waste all the allotted space on explaining where you're from, how old you are, etc. Tell the client what you can do for them—they are the ones scanning your profile and selecting you, so make it count!

◀ *Treat every client and project like they're important.* Most sites allow for feedback from clients, and if you don't work hard on little projects and get bad reviews, bigger project clients are going to see that and hire someone else. Every client is important.

◖ *Sell yourself.* If you went to school or earned certificates or accreditation in some area, make sure your profile reflects it! Even though it may seem irrelevant, it shows the client that you can accomplish your goals.

Now, I can't promise you'll immediately get a ton of work on any of these sites, even with the optimization tips, but if you work hard and keep at it, good things will come your way! The number-one quality of a successful freelancer is persistence. In addition to establishing an online profile via freelance sites, you should also beef up your social media presence. Below are a few ideas.

Twitter and Facebook

Use hashtags to track tweets and Facebook posts about freelance writing gigs that fit your niche. For example, if you want to write in the blogosphere, use #FreelanceBloggingJobs to see what people are tweeting/posting about.

Pros: This demonstrates resourcefulness to employers and is an excellent social networking opportunity (and job searching really is all about networking!). It also gives you a chance to get in touch with people who regularly tweet about freelance writing jobs.

Cons: It's not the most efficient job search method, it has a variable response rate, and the listings will offer no information about pay or location.

Guest Post on Blogs

As a guest blogger, you establish yourself as an expert in the field and potentially drive traffic to your site. (By the way, this is great for search engine optimization.) It also allows you to get your name or company name in front of potential clients. To find guest blogs:

1. Do a Google search on blogs related to your specific niche.
2. Contact the person in charge of the blog and present a topic idea.
3. Use the person's name when contacting them. A generic "Dear Sir" or "To Whom It May Concern" shows a lack of research and comes across as a form letter.

4. If you want to gain clients and not SEO rankings, stick to blogs your potential clients will read. This means targeting business blogs.

5. Make your blog stand out by setting up Google authorship. It is super easy to do and increases your chance of your article actually getting read.

LinkedIn

LinkedIn allows you to find groups with prospective clients and answer questions, which puts your name out there. Here are some tips to help you get maximum benefits from LinkedIn:

- *Fill out the profile completely.* You need to have as much information as possible on this form.
- *Get recommendations from everyone you have worked with.* Recommendations are gold for the LinkedIn community.
- *Follow groups and answer questions.* You need to be an active part of the community to get your name out there and make those all-important connections.

Online Networking

This is often the trickiest step; getting that first client. Networking with your target audience both online and off is a good way to reach them. Additionally, content marketing and presenting yourself as an expert will help you convert your audience to clients. You can also join freelance organizations that have busy job boards to find new clients.

Maintaining your freelance street cred, especially online, means you must provide value. Content in the form of reports, audio or video programs, webinars, and online courses are all great ways to provide value to potential prospects. It's also a great way to build a lead list. Provide the content for free and then market your business consulting services to your subscribers in subsequent messages. The content helps position you as an expert and gives you access to qualified prospects.

Then focus on your word-of-mouth marketing. Once you've gotten the ball rolling with your first few clients, embrace a referral or affiliate business model to drive more business in your direction: provide some sort of credit or incentive if clients refer new clients to you.

Finally, continue to provide value. There may come a time when the client will no longer need your services. However, that doesn't mean you cannot continue to provide value to them. Content, like a monthly newsletter, will continue to provide information to your past clients, and they'll be more likely to refer you to a friend or associate because you're in continuous contact with them.

TIPS FOR SUCCESSFUL CLIENT MANAGEMENT

Not every freelance model includes consultations with clients, but many do. What works for me may not necessarily work for you. However, over the course of the years, I have discovered some things work better than others when doing a consult. For example, when I take control of the conversation and tell them what I do, it tends to go poorly. Clients are looking for solutions in one form or another. I have found it is much more effective to take a passive role and ask the client what they are looking for before I do much talking. This allows the client to feel listened to and understood from the very beginning.

My biggest piece of advice is to listen carefully. You will want to understand what the client's needs are and honestly evaluate whether you can meet them right from the beginning of the conversation. Keep accurate notes and refer to them whenever speaking to a client.

Consistent Client Communication Is Key

Selling services is a very different beast from selling products. Your job starts the moment you accept the assignment. Therefore, I cannot stress enough how important great communication is. Everything you do is being judged, and if you want the client to come back, you need to be professional from the moment you accept the assignment until you deliver the finished project. You can do this in five easy steps:

1. Confirm the job and tell the client you will have it finished by the due date. This lets them know you have received the job and are starting.

2. At the halfway point, confirm with the client the date of completion and assure them everything is going as planned. At this point, get answers to any concerns you may have.

3. On the delivery day, let the client know you will be completing the project on schedule.

4. Deliver the job on time.

5. Follow up with the client to make sure everything was received and completed as expected.

These steps hold even on rush jobs. Especially on rush jobs. You will want the client to know you have taken the job and it is going as expected.

Three Fail-Safe Objectives

1. *Give solutions.* Ideally, everything will go as planned, but that is not always the case. When something does go wrong, bring it to the client along with a solution to the problem. If you're designing a website and the WordPress theme does not allow you to do what the client wants, then you will need to present ideas to fix the issue.

2. *Learn from projects.* Once a project is over, take time to reflect on what went well and what could have gone smoother. This time will help you better organize your company and give you valuable feedback for the future.

3. *Get feedback.* Ask for feedback from the people you worked with. The project manager may have ideas to make things go more smoothly, while others may feel they did not have enough information. Whatever the feedback, it is always a positive experience. If things went well, great! If things went askew, then it is a prime opportunity to learn.

Handling Objections and Rejection

Rejection will happen no matter how good you are. The key is to diagnose the rejection and try to turn it into a positive. For example, a client may say the ideas are fine but the price is too high. You could simply ask what their budget for the project is and then offer them solutions based on the budget they gave you. This could very well turn a no into a yes.

Another good approach to rejection is selling yourself as more than a task completer. You want to sell yourself as an invaluable idea person as well. Let them know you are committed to making them more successful and will continue to come up with ideas to make their business grow. Demonstrating this during the consult and showing testimonials and references can go a long way toward getting hired.

Whatever the outcome is after the consultation, email them thanking them for their time and for considering you. A no on one project doesn't mean they won't hire you in the future. Keeping a variety of thank-you email templates on hand will make the task much easier, as most scenarios repeat themselves frequently, and your level of professionalism will go a long way toward forming a bond with the client later on.

Stay Organized

We freelancers wear a number of hats, and in order to succeed, you'll need to get very good at organizing your business activities and finances. Fortunately, there are many great tools to help with these tasks. Here are a few of my favorites for freelancers:

- *FreshBooks* (www.freshbooks.com): A financial tools suite
- *Google My Business* (www.google.com/business): An entire suite of useful web and mobile tools
- *Quote Roller* (www.quoteroller.com): Terrific tools for creating and managing quotes, proposals, and contracts
- *Dropbox* (www.dropbox.com): A wonderful file storage and sharing service
- *Snagit* (www.techsmith.com/snagit.html): The best screen capture utility for images and simple videos
- *Mozy* (mozy.com/#slide-8): A terrific online backup solution

Consider Buying Business Insurance

Didn't think about this one, did you? Most freelancers don't, and when something goes horribly wrong, as it sometimes does, you are up the creek without a paddle. Good insurance can be had for $200 to $500 a year. Consider it; it could save your business.

SUMMARY: BASIC STEPS TO GETTING STARTED

1. Identify ideal clients and target markets.
2. Get specific about the type of business you'd like to work with. For example, you might choose to work for prestigious corporate clients who have an increasing need for virtual assistants because of downsizing and outsourcing of jobs that were previously done by employees. Or you might choose to take interesting and creative jobs providing virtual office assistant or virtual personal assistant services for busy professionals such as authors, entrepreneurs, real estate agents, doctors, or lawyers. You might even become a virtual assistant for professional associations or nonprofit organizations.
3. Define your service offerings and rates.
4. Decide whether to offer your services as a freelancer or through a virtual assistant company.
5. Pull together references and testimonials from former employers and clients.
6. Set up work procedures.
7. Determine how you will work with your clients. Do you require a consultation with the client first to get on the same page and avoid miscommunication? Do you want a signed contract between you? Do you want to provide several options for payment or stick to one that is best for you? Do you want full payment upfront, half upfront, or at the end of the project, task, or service?
8. If freelancing, set up your web presence (website and social media profiles). The website should include:
   - A homepage
   - An introduction to who you are (video is best, so the client can immediately feel connected)
   - An ethical bribe with high-value content speaking directly to your customer

- A blog
- A menu of services
- A client needs assessment form
- A calendar link to schedule consultation: When a prospect clicks to submit their completed needs assessment form, they are instantly redirected to my calendar link, TimeTrade (www.timetrade.com), to schedule their complimentary consultation, while simultaneously my email inbox shows me I have a prospect, and an immediate follow-up email tells me the day and time of the scheduled consult—all in one fell swoop.

9. Set up a system for customer relationship management (CRM). There is CRM software designed specifically for VAs called DigitalSorbet (http://digitalsorbet.com). It allows you to track your work, keep clients informed, and create and manage invoices. It also allows for feedback on completed work, getting paid online, storing files, and capturing leads directly from your website.

10. Set up time tracking and invoicing software. If you set up this type of system from the get-go, your business will run much smoother and easier (trust me!). I recommend using Toggl (www.toggl.com), Harvest (www.getharvest.com), FreshBooks (www.freshbooks.com), Zoho Books (www.zoho.com/books), or Wave (www.waveapps.com), as they all allow you to track time and invoice clients seamlessly (with the exception of Wave, which doesn't have an area for you to track time, so you'll need to use another online timer if you go with them).

11. Set up project management software. Whether you need a way to organize your own business information or projects for clients, project management software is invaluable in keeping you focused and organized. Check out Insightly (www.insightly.com), Podio (https://podio.com), Trello (https://trello.com), Asana (https://asana.com), DigitalSorbet (http://digitalsorbet.com), Teamwork Projects (www.teamwork.com/projects), Slack (https://slack.com/), Producteev (www.producteev.com), and

Redbooth (https://redbooth.com). You can also go the simple route and use Google Drive (www.google.com/drive), Evernote (https://evernote.com/), Remember The Milk (www.remember themilk.com), Wunderlist recently acquired by Microsoft (www.wunderlist.com), or a combination of those.

12. Set up a payment processor. If you're making money online, you need a way to collect money online. PayPal (www.paypal.com/home) is typically the best (and expected) way to go. There are several PayPal alternatives out there, though, such as Square (https://squareup.com), Stripe (https://stripe.com), and Dwolla (www.dwolla.com).

CHAPTER 9

CONSULTING/RESELLING PROFIT PATHS

The Consulting and Reselling Profit Paths are ideal for you if you like the idea of selling services to businesses but don't necessarily want to fulfill those services yourself. These paths are also ideal for those of you who are strong at selling and who thrive working one-on-one with clients.

On the plus side, these Profit Paths do not require you to be a personal expert on the services you are selling, fulfillment of services is not your responsibility, and the setup is a low-cost model.

On the downside, though, outsourcers sometimes fail you, you must be comfortable selling services you may not fully understand, and it can be harder to control the outcome of a project.

CONSULTING AND RESELLING EXPLAINED

Consulting is a broad term because it can apply to just about anything. People get hired as consultants for a large range of topics. Because the

MEET THE EXPERTS
MIKE COOCH AND JOSH CLIFFORD

Mike Cooch and Josh Clifford are two of my favorite people. But I didn't just fill this book with pictures of my favorite people. I put them here because they own an excellent company called Local Income Lab (www.localincomelab.com), which teaches people how to successfully become local marketing consultants.

focus of this book is to cover legitimate Profit Paths that a wide variety of people could quickly get up and running with, I am going to talk about consulting and reselling services in relation to digital/online marketing. However, much of this information will cross over into other specializations. If you have a specific skill set or experience in a different industry where there is a market for consulting, this section will be valuable to you as well. Some examples are financial consultants, sales consultants, and tech-related consultants.

Dictionary.com defines consultant as a person who gives professional advice or services to companies for a fee. I actually wouldn't change this definition, but I would clarify that in my opinion, selling advice can be different from selling services. They often go hand in hand and are sold as a package deal, which is why I'm grouping consulting and reselling into the same section. That said, you do not have to be qualified to supply both guidance and services. You have the freedom to decide which type of business you would like to provide. Since this section is primarily going to lump the two together, let's take a moment to explore them separately.

Consulting

I consider consulting to be the business of selling advice, guidance, and knowledge that you have acquired through experience and/or education. One thing I really like about consulting is that it's a very well-known practice in the corporate world. People automatically understand what consultants are and why people hire them. You do not have the added complication of needing to educate your target market on what a consultant is. You may have to convince prospects that you are worth hiring for their specific situation, but you probably won't have to explain what it is you do.

Business-savvy people understand the painful costs of making mistakes. They also tend to know their own personal limitations. So it is not a foreign concept to hire a consultant when expanding their business into a new arena. I chose to focus on marketing consultants because businesses that realize they need to monetize their online presence commonly have no idea how to do that. They realize it will take an investment, sometimes a significant one, so it is very common for them to hire a digital marketing consultant rather than just blindly ordering services or hiring an ad agency.

While I do feel reselling services in conjunction with your consulting is a smart tactic, it is not required to be successful. Many businesses are happy to pay for someone to give them a road map of sorts so that when they start investing money into their digital marketing, they feel they are doing it in an intelligent way. It's very intimidating to oversee something you have no frame of reference for. Hiring a consultant to help them determine what they do and don't need and what they can expect to pay for the results they want removes a level of mystery and worry that is commonly associated with buying digital marketing services.

Reselling

Being a reseller of services is almost always paired with some level of consulting, because your prospects will have some questions about what you're selling and why they should buy those services from you. But since that's just a typical part of any business I'm not going to label it consulting, because you're not really making money off your advice. Also, I feel the need to make a distinction between reselling services and becoming an agency, which I cover extensively in Chapter 9.

In this chapter, being a reseller means the following things:

- You have identified at least one service that you can confidently resell to your target market.
- You are not doing the legwork of the service yourself, but have instead found a reliable source to outsource the work through. (Otherwise you're freelancing, which as we covered at length in the previous chapter, is a viable option.)
- You do not have the outsourcers in-house. You are reselling someone else's work, and most likely you are white labeling those services. In other words, your prospects probably have no idea who you outsource through.

While I wanted you to understand the difference between the two and your options to combine or separate the guidance from the services, to keep things simple we will use the term "consultant" to encompass both consulting and reselling services for the remainder of this book.

PROS AND CONS OF CONSULTING

Like freelancers, consultants are masters of their own economic fate with all the same pros and cons when it comes to being your own boss and having the freedom to choose the clients and projects you want to work with. So I won't be covering those basic pros and cons again, as that would be redundant. But there are some additional pros and cons specific to consulting.

Consulting Pros

- *You don't have to be the personal expert.* One of the great things about being a consultant is that you don't actually need to be a personal expert at what you're selling—but you do need to be able to represent yourself as though you are. I know that sounds shady, but stick with me through this chapter and understand that I would never encourage unethical practices or strategies. We will explore how you can provide stellar consulting and services without being a personal expert yourself.

- *You are NOT the worker bee.* You are getting paid for your brain, not your hands. This is my way of saying that you are getting paid for what you know instead of what you do. From your prospect's perspective, they may be paying you for your knowledge and for the services you are providing, but in reality, you know you are not actually the one doing the work. You have a trusted outsource solution.

- *You can leverage other people's success.* You don't have to have a history of success to get started because you can leverage the case studies and success stories of the outsourcers whose services you are reselling. Some people refer to this as "Social Proof Jacking."

- *You enjoy a low-cost setup.* The costs to get up and running are relatively minimal. You'll need an online presence and a way to get in front of your target audience, but that's about all.

Consulting Cons

- *You may not be the personal expert.* While this is definitely a huge pro, it can also be a huge con because you have to know enough about the industry to evaluate your prospect's situation and make accurate recommendations of what services they need to accomplish their goals. It also can be challenging to provide quality control for a service you are not an expert at.

- *Outsourcers sometimes fail.* It is inevitable that at some point one of your outsourcers will fail and you will be left holding the bag. You get all the accolades and benefits of the great work your outsourcers do on your behalf, but the flip side is that if one of them fails you, that's also on you as far as your client is concerned. You can be left scrambling to figure out a quick replacement solution.

❮ *High competition and skepticism.* Over the years, marketing consulting has become a huge target in the biz op space. The result is that you will have a lot of competition. Depending on the type of consulting you are doing, you may not have a lot of competition that is an actual threat to you, but it exists nonetheless. In addition, businesses have been approached by a lot of marketers who don't know what they are doing, so a level of skepticism has crept into the marketplace. You will have to fight being lumped in with these incompetents. We will talk about how to avoid this pitfall.

❮ *Less control over the outcome.* Because you're not doing the actual work, you have less control over the outcome. We will talk about strategies to keep your finger on the pulse of what is happening with your client's work.

The Bottom Line

Ultimately, being a successful consultant requires the following strengths:

❮ *Working knowledge.* While you may not be the personal expert doing the actual work, you need to acquire and maintain enough knowledge to evaluate your client's situation and make recommendations that accomplish their goals.

❮ *Great sales ability.* You need to be very good at selling yourself, your business, and your services.

❮ *Great people skills.* Being a consultant requires regular contact with your clients.

❮ *Project management.* You need to be able to manage the work you are running through outsourcers for your client. This requires the ability to manage multiple moving parts and a high level of organization skills.

Consulting is part of my personal path. I started out as a freelance writer and moved into consulting, which led to the creation of my digital marketing agency. Now it's come full circle, because I'm frequently hired JUST for my consulting on top of everything else I do, and my track record allows me to charge a high-end fee for my brain.

LOCAL VS. GLOBAL MARKETING CONSULTANTS

Instead of separating these out into two distinct sections, I'm going to talk about both together. They are very similar, except that with one you are solely focusing on local, brick-and-mortar businesses in your area, and in the other you are primarily working with online businesses whose target market is nationwide or web-wide.

Helping Local Businesses Get Started Online

Did you know there's an entire cottage industry built around helping local business owners create and maintain an online marketing presence? Some people call this "local consulting" or "local offline consulting." For most local businesses, their primary prospects all live within a specific geographical location. Dentists are a great example. It would be highly unusual for them to get patients who live more than 20 miles away from them. Most will live within 10 miles.

I usually encourage people who want to go down this path to start with their favorite businesses in their area. Local business owners are far more likely to trust patrons they already know. This can also be a very gratifying experience for the consultant because they are helping a business they care about. Many businesses know they need help monetizing their online presence, but they don't know how and don't trust the barrage of people who hit them up offering to do the work for them. Many of them may even be jaded because of past negative experiences, so starting out approaching businesses you know is the lowest barrier to entry.

Online Marketing Consultant

Becoming a marketing consultant online is a bit more advanced than being a local consultant. It's a lot more work to compete against businesses web-wide. There are a LOT more intricacies and knowledge bases you will need. So this path is really only a "get up and go right now" path if you already have some working knowledge of online marketing, SEO, etc.

Many people are working a traditional 9-to-5 job providing these exact services. Those of you with this knowledge can take that experience and establish yourself as an independent online marketing consultant. You can also refer to yourself as a digital marketing consultant. My advice is to start with services and areas you already know well and then slowly branch out from there.

SETTING UP YOUR BRAND AND ONLINE PRESENCE

When starting this type of business, you are your first customer. Many of the services you'll be selling you will want to perform for yourself to get established online in your new endeavor. You don't have to have your own online presence optimized before you can approach business owners, but it will really help you if you do. If you're going the local route, you have a little bit of grace when approaching businesses who already know and trust you. They are less likely to rely so heavily on what they find about you online.

In Chapter 15, "Business and Marketing 101," we talk about the basics of getting your business name and entity set up, so I'm not covering that information in the specific Profit Path chapters of the book. However, one thing you need to keep in mind when you're thinking about becoming a local marketing consultant is that you will be considered a local business because your clients all live in one geographic location. So they will often look to see how you're positioned online to verify that you know your stuff. That said, many businesses have no idea what to look for or how to tell if you are or aren't optimized properly online. (This is part of their problem!)

Obviously, as a digital marketing consultant of any kind, you will be under a certain amount of scrutiny by your potential prospects. However, if you are a traditional digital marketing consultant, you are dealing with businesses that are already online and may be using ecommerce as their only monetization path. Businesses like this are apt to know their stuff a bit better. After all, they had enough know-how to establish a business online. So if you're just starting out at selling SEO services, make sure the SEO on your own website has been done well.

WHAT WILL YOU CONSULT ON?

As a marketing consultant, you will consult on how your clients can gain market share online, increase their online presence and brand recognition, and outrank their competitors for lead acquisition and sales. I realize many of you will resell services you can freelance and provide by doing those services on your own, and that's great. However, I'm including outsourcing options along with basic services you can provide for those of you who don't want to do the fulfillment yourselves. While what you can choose to consult on is limitless, I'm going to highlight three prominent and lucrative areas.

The Bare-Bones Basics

Obviously, in order to be competitive online, you must have an online presence. Many of the businesses, especially local ones, you approach will have a website of some sort, but it will also surprise you how many do not. You can be of great service by helping them get set up with the basics. Remember, you don't have to be a personal expert; you just need to understand enough to sell what your prospects need and have a good outsourcing solution lined up to fulfill the orders.

This can be especially useful to older business owners because during most of their lives, their business was likely run offline. They didn't grow up with the internet, and learning to monetize their online arm might be a completely foreign concept. They're sadly missing out simply because the prospect of getting online is overwhelming, and many of them are skeptical because they've been burned by vendors in the past. Ramping up their online presence is a service you can sell as a consultant. Some of the different bare-bones services you can consult on and sell are:

- Assistance with researching and choosing a domain name
- Domain registration
- Getting a website built
- Assistance with managing the website build
- Logo creation
- Setting up the top three social media sites that make sense for their business

◀ Arranging a press release announcing their new website

Having a website or at least a Facebook business page is the foundation that must be in place before much digital marketing can be done. Even if your prospects already have a website, that doesn't mean you cannot offer these basic services, because often they have reasons to create new websites, and this is something you can assist them with. Two useful resources for creating your website are:

1. *Domain Registration*: GoDaddy (www.godaddy.com/domains/search.aspx?isc=IAPdom4)
2. *Affordable Logo Design*: 99designs (http://99designs.com)

The one caution I would give you is that if you decide to wrap your expertise into what you are selling them, like assistance in choosing a name, or help overseeing the website build, make sure you have the appropriate knowledge to do so because they will hold you accountable for the results. Be sure you understand enough to make professional judgment calls you can stand by.

Social Media

There is one thing social media does for a business that no other form of marketing I've seen can do as well. No amount of SEO or PPC (pay per click) can come close to matching the engagement that social media can create for your client's followers. The big win with social media is getting your client's followers talking to you and each other and interacting with you on a more familiar and personal level.

Social media itself is not much of a tool for conversions, in my opinion. What it does brilliantly is collect your prospects together in an engaging environment and begin to indoctrinate them to your brand, value, and the solutions you provide. It is the responsibility of the business to create monetization paths from its social media following. People get really excited about the thought of 10,000 followers, but if they have no plan in place to convert those prospects into customers, they're of little monetary value.

So when you are selling social media, position it and its power properly so your client doesn't end up with unrealistic expectations that then go unmet. You need to sell social media for what it is, and it's even better when you can sell a monetization strategy along with it. This is something to keep in mind.

Social media is a HUGE buzzword that not everyone understands but wants to incorporate in their business. The thing I love about social media is that you can quickly get beneficial social media platforms set up even if your client doesn't have a website yet. As you will read in Chapter 15, many businesses get up and running on social media platforms long before they ever build a website. Some of the most popular among businesses at the time I'm writing this are:

- *Facebook*: More beneficial for some markets than others, but a universally appealing platform
- *Twitter*: Universally appealing
- *LinkedIn*: Universally appealing
- *Pinterest*: Most beneficial if you have a very visual product, but can be universally appealing
- *Google+*: Less exciting, but makes Google super happy
- *Instagram*: Highly beneficial if you are in the fashion or arts industry or if you have a very young audience

You can sell the service of setting up social media profiles and platforms separately from selling them ongoing social media services. Your outsourced designers will customize the platforms with your client's logo and make it look very professional and sharp. If your client doesn't have a logo yet, this is a good opportunity to upsell them a logo design so they can have a holistic, branded presence across the web.

If you have the right outsourcing solution, this is a GREAT service to sell because no one really wants social media services only one time. These types of services are commonly sold on a recurring, monthly basis. You can break this up and sell platform-specific social media services like Twitter or Facebook campaigns. You can also create more expensive packages where you manage the campaigns across multiple platforms.

Social media services can provide you with so much leverage from one piece of high-quality content. We have a lot of clients who come to us just for weekly spreadsheets full of social media posts that their teams can use at their discretion. They have a capable team to do the work, but they don't have the marketing knowledge to create ongoing content with the right mix of self-promotion, engaging topics, and humor.

Don't just post business stuff. If the only posts on your FB wall are about what sales are going on, people are going to become blind to it. They're not going to share your posts, and you're not likely to get much traction with your followers and fans. When in doubt, our basic formula is 80 percent engagement posts and 20 percent business/sales posts.

If you're a local business, post about other cool things happening in your area. People will share your posts informing the community of events taking place, which is exactly what you want. One of the most popular posts we ever did on an A/C company's Facebook page was "The Top Stories of 2013 in Pensacola, Florida." We posted this right as the new year was rolling in.

> **Ask questions.** Don't just post *at* people, try to engage them. See what type of posts they respond to.

> **Actually look at analytics.** The various platforms have built-in analytics that can show you which of your posts get the most attention. This will dictate the type of content you should post moving forward.

> **Have fun and be interesting.** If you're not interested in what you're saying, why would anyone else be?

Many businesses haven't the time or inclination to do this themselves. In addition, they don't have the expert knowledge to make social media beneficial to their businesses. But right now, almost all business think they need social media services whether or not they actually do.

Here is one basic strategy that has worked well for us:

1. Interview your client on a regular basis (monthly, bimonthly, quarterly, etc.).
2. Transcribe the interview.
3. Create a content calendar based off the content you got from the interview.
4. Leverage that content into multiple social media content pieces.
5. Wash. Rinse. Repeat.

One piece of software I can highly recommend for social media management is Hootsuite (https://hootsuite.com).

SEO and Content Marketing Services

These are likely the most common and most lucrative consulting services you will do. The main objective of SEO and content marketing is to help the business monetize its online presence. To really understand SEO, you need to understand the three basic types of web traffic.

First, there is organic traffic. Organic simply means that when someone types a search term into Google, the results that naturally populate are the organic rankings. It's what Google has decided is the best match for your search term. The statistics vary, as it's become harder and harder to calculate exactly. But it's fair to say that the top five results on the first page of Google get somewhere between 50 to 75 percent of the clicks from organic traffic. By comparison, everything after spot number five is breadcrumbs. (However, a breadcrumb out of two million searches is nothing to sneeze at.)

Next is the direct referral traffic route. Technically, direct referral traffic is under the flag of "organic traffic." However, I separated it because most analytic reporting software does as well. It represents people who land on your website by clicking through a link found somewhere on the internet. Generic organic traffic comes because you've done a good enough job with content marketing and SEO to get your site naturally ranked well in Google. Direct response traffic is a result of properly distributing content across the internet with a link back to your site.

Two companies offering SEO services are:

1. Ember Dragon (www.emberdragon.com)
2. HubSpot (www.hubspot.com)

Then there is paid traffic. Paid traffic is exactly what its name implies: It's traffic you buy. It can be in the form of banner ads on a website, PPC (pay per click) through AdWords, or specialized paid marketing like Facebook or Twitter Ads. On the SERPs (search engine result pages), the organic listings are the ones that populate the main body of the screen when you do a search, and the paid advertisements are down the right-hand side and across the top of the page.

SEO actually helps both organic and paid traffic. By using SEO, you tell Google what your website, products, and services are about so you can hopefully organically rank at the top of page one for the search terms that matter the most to your business. On the paid side, SEO helps you have a better Quality Score. The Quality Score has to do with how relevant your website is to the search terms, ads, etc., you attract and how high-quality your website is. The higher your Quality Score, the lower your PPC costs.

So by default, two of the main reasons people hire SEO consultants are to rank well for their target keywords and to get better pricing on their paid ads. After all, if you're a business and no one can find you online, your website is useless to you as a point of monetization.

All these efforts add up to better branding for your clients, which is another reason people hire consultants: to increase brand awareness of themselves or their company, products, or services. It's one thing to rank well for your target search term. It's even better to become well enough known that people search for you specifically. Branding is very important to every business. It's also one of those words that can encompass a LOT of things. But for a digital marketing consultant, branding usually refers to increasing your client's credibility and authority online. Companies dream of being a household name. Ideally, instead of searching for "workout videos," their target market searches for "Beach Body Videos." See the difference?

POPULAR SERVICES TO SELL

There are many services you can sell via this particular Profit Path. I'm going to focus on a few here, including the website audit, market analysis, keyword research, content marketing, video services, infographics, and independent market consultations. Separately, these services each offer the customer a look into his or her brand and how it performs against its competitors. Together, they can help take a client from small-time player to powerhouse. You can offer these as a la carte items or synergize your model and offer different packages based on the client's needs.

Explore these options to see what might fit your Profit Path model best, starting with the website audit.

Website Audit

Most companies looking to hire an SEO/marketing consultant are not getting the results they are hoping for with their website. This could be because they are not ranking well, or their offers aren't structured properly, or any number of other problems. A very beneficial service you can offer is to perform a website audit. In our company, we refer to these as on-site evaluations.

This is where you take a "look under the hood," so to speak, to figure out what can be improved on their website to help them achieve their goals.

Common on-site optimization areas that you will evaluate are:

- Content pages that should be added or modified to match the intent of their target buyers
- Basic SEO optimization criteria like proper H1 and H2 tags, metadata, and image tags
- Proper compliance factors like a site map, terms of service, privacy, and contact information
- Identifying broken links or improper linking structures
- Irrelevant, low-quality, and duplicate content
- Errors of any kind
- Basic functionality like load speed
- User experience like proper navigation

Market Analysis

I like to sell the on-site evaluation and the market analysis together. It's an easy combination to sell. It's very, very rare for people not to buy both if they are positioned correctly, because how can you properly understand how to optimize your client's website if you don't understand how much market share you own, who your competitors are, and how much market share you could gain? More important, how can you optimize your client's site if you don't understand the intention of the buyers in the market?

There are three basic components I like to package together under the flag of "market analysis": competitive analysis, market intent, and online presence.

When competitive analysis is done right, you don't just learn about who the main competitors are. You learn WHY they are outranking you and what you need to do to dominate them. It's easy to find out who the top competitors are for your target keywords. Once you have that information, some of the valuable data you can glean is:

- What keywords are they paying for? Remember, if they are ranked first for a keyword they are paying for, they are most likely making money with that keyword.
- What do their ads for that keyword look like?
- What do their landing pages look like?
- What are their offers?
- What pages on their website are optimized for that keyword? What message is being sent to the prospects?
- Are they active in social media? What are they doing? Are their followers engaged with them?

People can really miss the boat on how much beneficial information you can learn from looking at your competitors. Depending on your budget, I would even encourage you to pull out your credit card, buy from your competitor, and go through his entire sales funnel process. If he's top-ranked in Google, he's doing something right that your client is not. Often, buying from him and evaluating his process is cheaper than split testing to figure out the magic formula. Don't reinvent the wheel. Learn what the competition is doing right and then figure out how you can make it even better.

Next is market intent. You don't want to rely only on traditional keyword research when you are evaluating a market. You want to get inside the buyers' heads and ask yourself what their pain points are. What solutions are they looking for? What do they care about? A few places to quickly scan to glean market intent are:

- *Related searches at the bottom of the page on Google.* Google doesn't list anything on the first page by accident.

◀ *Market-specific forums.* What conversations are taking place? What questions are your prospects asking?

◀ *Hashtag searches on social media sites.*

Finally, consider online presence. The online presence is all about how prominent your client is online in his market across all areas that matter. Some of the things we look at are:

◀ Do they have a strong social media presence?

◀ Are they ranking well?

◀ Do they have a strong content marketing presence?

Ultimately, after getting all the relevant data, determine how prominent they are in their market compared to their competitors so you can put a plan together to increase their branding, presence, and market share. There are several companies that offer a diagnostic button you can add right to your browser's toolbar:

◀ SEOquake (www.seoquake.com)

◀ Marketing Grader (https://marketing.grader.com)

◀ SEMrush (www.semrush.com)

◀ MozBar (https://moz.com/tools/seo-toolbar)

Keyword Research

Keyword research is a standard service requested and sold by marketing consultants. It is a common belief that keyword research is at the heart of developing an effective online marketing campaign. I don't disagree, but I do think about the topic more than many people. In my experience, keyword research is where you *start*. It's not enough information by itself for many types of effective campaigns in the current search environment.

Yes, I want to know the keywords buyers are typing into Google, but I also want to know the intention behind those searches. I want to know what questions they are asking and why. You can charge double the normal keyword research fees just by including intention-based research with the standard keyword research.

The keyword research will dictate the type of content and optimization you do on your website, but the conversions will be far higher if you combine those with the buyers' intention. Just as a reminder, your clients may know the intention of their buyers, and that is useful, but what is most important is to discover what Google thinks the buyer's intent is. It's Google's opinion that determines who gets the traffic. Below are some useful tools to help you in your research:

- SEMrush (www.semrush.com)
- iSpionage (www.ispionage.com)
- Raven (http://raventools.com)
- Google AdWords Tool (www.google.com/adwords)

Content Marketing

Content marketing is one of those phrases that is thrown around with a lot of different meanings attached to it. As a consultant, you can resell a variety of content marketing services. Popular services include:

- Blogging services
- Content distribution across authority sites like LinkedIn, Facebook, and guest blog posts
- Press releases (Shelby's Favorite: Press Advantage; www.press advantage.com/)
- Newsletters and fliers

Content marketing is currently the driving force behind high-quality SEO. Things change quickly when it comes to marketing online, but one thing that has always remained constant is this: Content is king!

Video Services

Video marketing is a very popular service. People love to use videos on their websites and blogs, but they also love to have video marketing campaigns done for them. Businesses love the idea of having a YouTube channel full of videos that are distributed across the internet. But a lot of power can come from one well-made video.

I don't see the popularity of video going away any time soon, but like most things online, the strategies that provide the most benefit may change. In other words, videos will remain a lucrative service to sell, but the way the videos are used will most likely continue to change and grow as Google does.

People use a wide variety of videos online. The quality, price, and purpose range from low-cost, link-bait videos to professionally made talking-head videos with scripts and hired actors. There really is a vast array of opportunity here. Some of the popular aspects of this service you will want to brush up on are:

- YouTube optimization and marketing strategies
- Vimeo strategies
- Simple video creation tools like Animoto
- Whiteboard videos

One thing people tend to really love about videos is their ability to go viral so quickly. When someone sees a video they like, they share it on Facebook or on their blog, and the next thing you know that video is being passed around all over the internet. A viral video is a dream for any business or brand. Here are some resources to help you create and post online videos:

- YouTube (www.youtube.com)
- Vimeo (https://vimeo.com)
- Animoto (https://animoto.com)
- Animated Whiteboard (www.animatedwhiteboard.com)

Infographics

Infographics are increasing in popularity. The thing I love so much about infographics is the power they have to express a message to the prospect within seconds. The attention span online is short, sometimes measured in seconds. If you write an article, the title has to be alluring enough to get the prospect to at least scan the bold subtitles throughout the piece in hopes that they will stop and read it. But with an infographic, the prospect can grasp a fairly complex message within seconds.

Infographics can also be heavily leveraged in a lot of areas:

- Your client's website and other online platforms like Tumblr, document-sharing sites, and Web 2.0 properties

- Social media platforms (think of the popularity of memes)
- Popular image-sharing sites like Pinterest and Instagram
- Print (I especially like putting infographics on one side of a postcard with information on the other. This is GREAT for local businesses.)

Infographics are nice because they can go viral just like videos. Also, they are images, so you have additional marketing avenues, yet they still have words that tell a story or make a point. I'm not surprised they are becoming such a popular aspect of content marketing strategies. I have a couple of tools I like to use for creating infographics:

1. www.visualcontentcreators.com
2. Infogr.am (https://infogr.am)

Independent Marketing Consultations

If you're really good at marketing online, people will pay a premium price to have strategy days or one-on-one consultations with you to help map out the direction their business should be heading. This is a more advanced service because you have to develop the right skill set and a portfolio of success before you will have much luck selling yourself as qualified to consult for their business. However, it's good to keep in mind for the future, because it's really great to be paid a premium for your brain instead of the services you provide.

SPECIAL SERVICES FOR LOCAL BUSINESSES

While local businesses have a set of unique needs, they also need the same basic services as any business that wants to be competitive online. Early on, I made the mistake of assuming that every local business has a website or at least a Facebook page. I could not have been more wrong.

When I lived in Minnesota, we would frequently attend the farmers' markets and buy fresh produce and locally sourced meat, bread, cheese, etc. At the downtown farmers' market, we would go see "The Cheese Guys." I can't remember their names now, as it's been many years, but they seriously had the most phenomenal cheese. They were so popular that you had to get there early or they would quickly sell out of your favorite cheeses.

One day I asked them how I could continue to buy cheese from them during the frozen months when the farmers' markets weren't running. They told me they get asked that all the time, but they didn't currently have a website. I was shocked. I loved their cheese so much I told them I would create a website for them for FREE. I just needed their email address to send them the information. They looked at each other a little sheepishly and admitted they didn't have an email address and never had. Honestly, I couldn't have looked more surprised had they sprouted horns and grown a tail right in front of me. The point of my story is that you may be shocked how many successful businesses don't even have the basics.

Before we get into the services that are universally appreciated by all businesses with an online presence, I'd like to cover two specific services that are part of what I consider the trifecta of critical services to sell to a local business.

Google My Business Optimization

Many local businesses don't have a clue what they need to do to market themselves online, but most of them know they want to show up on Google Maps. This was always critical for local businesses, but with the popularity of local searches on mobile devices, it's almost marketing suicide not to be optimized for Google Maps.

Here's the deal. Google only wants to list actual, legitimate, brick-and-mortar businesses in its results. So in order for Google to include a business, they must be convinced that it actually is a legitimate business with a real address. This is why Google My Business optimization is in my top three services to sell a local business. Because without a Google My Business page, Google will not list a business on Google Maps.

Google really cares about putting what you're looking for in front of you whenever you use it as a search engine. So if you type in a search term and it determines you are looking for something local, it will give you primarily local results. Any search term you add a geo modifier to is an obvious signal. For instance, if I type in "car insurance," Google will return all kinds of informative websites related to car insurance. However, if I type in "car insurance Austin," it pops up a Google Maps result on the top right and gives me results that are local to Austin.

However, Google is now sophisticated enough that on many search terms, it recognizes you are most likely searching for local results even if you don't specify. For instance, if I type in "dentist," "Baskin Robbins," or even "Honda," it brings up the map box and local listings. Not ranking for local search terms buyers are typing in for your local business is effectively killing any business you might have generated organically online.

Now more than ever, the impact to a local business of not ranking in Google Maps for search terms that matter to their buyers is critical. Here are some possible consequences of not marketing yourself properly on Google Maps:

◀ *Lost real estate*. The Maps results can take up 75 percent of the first page. In the online ranking world, people strive to rank in the first three spots, but anything below the fold is considered less than ideal. So when you know your primary prospects will be searching through the Maps listings and you're not listed there, that's a tough pill to swallow. The chances of your prospects continuing on to the bottom of the page or the second page are slim. Plenty of businesses matching their search within a short distance from their home have already appeared at their fingertips.

◀ *Mobile devices*. Many mobile devices use Google Maps as their map app. So when people are driving and do a search on their map app for a business, if you're not qualified to be listed in Google Maps, you won't come up in that app either. At the time I'm writing this book (early 2015), it is predicted that before the end of the year, local searches on mobile devices will beat out local searches on a PC.

◀ *You won't be found*. When it comes to being found by your target market online, if a local business isn't ranking well in the map search results—or, worse, isn't listed at all—it will find it very difficult to create satisfying lead acquisition online. Its competitors will get most if not all of the potential online prospects.

Google My Business has a snazzy dashboard that walks you through claiming, setting up, and optimizing your Google+ Local page. However, here are some highlights of what you want to pay attention to:

- *Accurate information.* Make sure all the information you list about your business is 100 percent accurate. Inaccurate citations and business information can negatively affect your rankings in Google.
- *Visual content.* Add pictures that show your business. Add pictures of people at your business. Add lots of great pictures. If you have video, you can add that to your page as well.
- *Informative content.* You can now add content like articles that educate your prospects about topics related to your business. If you're good at identifying the topics and keywords that your buyers really care about, writing informative pieces on these topics will be beneficial.
- *Deals, offers, and promotions.* Google+ is primarily business-focused, so many people turn to it to find deals and discounts. Host your promotions here.
- *Interact with your fans.* Think of your Google+ page as an interactive site. The more real people who leave comments or reviews on your site, the better. Reviews are the golden ticket when it comes to your Google+ page.

You can see why selling Google My Business claiming and optimization services can be very lucrative. It's not very difficult to explain why a business needs it. It actually is critical for any sort of organic marketing success online.

All that said, Google isn't the only game in town. I tend to talk about Google a lot because it's the industry leader in search engines, but it's definitely not the only player in the game. You want to take similar steps with Yahoo Local and Bing Places. Each is a little different, but they all serve the same purpose and provide similar benefits. Claiming and optimizing on all three major platforms helps reinforce that the business is indeed a legitimate brick-and-mortar company.

Citations

We already covered how important it is to get ranked in the Maps search results if you're a local business. One of the main reasons Google requires you to fill out a Google My Business profile is to verify that you're a legitimate business in a physical location with an actual address. The first critical step, as we just discussed, is claiming and optimizing a Google My Business page. However, one of the best ways you can send a signal to Google that you are in fact a real, physical business is to build citations. Figure 9.1 shows the top citations sites in the United States, according to Whitespark.

Citations are simply locations online where you list information about your business like its name, address, phone number, hours of

1.	ExpressUpdate	18.	Kudzu	35.	Nokia Here
2.	Localeze	19.	Merchantcircle	36.	Yasabe
3.	Acxiom	20.	Manta	37.	Angieslist
4.	Factual	21.	Mapquest	38.	SaleSpider
5.	D&B	22.	ShowMeLocal	39.	FindTheBest
6.	Citysearch	23.	MojoPages	40.	Yellpedia
7.	Bing Places	24.	HotFrog	41.	MyHuckleberry
8.	Yelp	25.	Brownbook	42.	ZipLocal
9.	Facebook	26.	Cylex-USA	43.	MagicYellow
10.	Yellowpages	27.	InsiderPages	44.	City-Data
11.	Yahoo! Local	28.	EZLocal	45.	Thumbtack
12.	Superpages	29.	eLocal	46.	MyWebYellow
13.	Local.com	30.	Tupalo	47.	B2BYellowPages
14.	Foursquare	31.	ForLocations	48.	Pocketly
15.	Chamberofcommerce	32.	CitySquares	49.	Tuugo
16.	Yellowbot	33.	GetFave	50.	WikiDomo
17.	Yellowbook	34.	2FindLocal		

Source: www.whitespark.ca/top-local-citation-sources-by-country

FIGURE 9.1—**Top Citations**

operation, etc. The more places Google finds this information around the web, the more it believes your business is legitimate and worthy of Google sending local traffic to it.

Keep in mind, though, that not all citations are created equal. I can't even begin to guess how many different places there are to create citations online, from spammy business directories all the way to more authoritative places like Yelp.

Once local businesses understand what citations are and why they need them, they will commonly purchase them. Often, they will purchase a monthly plan to have citations built for them over time. This is a great service to bundle into your offerings as a consultant. Some resources to help you are:

- Moz Local (https://moz.com/local)
- Whitespark www.whitespark.ca)

Local Marketing Intent

One trap that many consultants who cater to local businesses make is to only focus on the keywords that trigger map search results in Google. You can watch two videos I made highlighting the importance of paying attention to the intention behind local searches by visiting the resource section of www.MoonlightingontheInternet.com. I highlight how businesses are regularly missing out on their most profitable prospects simply because they did not understand the intention behind their search patterns. If you can wrap your head around this concept, you will be one step ahead of most of your competitors.

SETTING YOURSELF UP AS AN EXPERT, EVEN IF YOU'RE NOT!

When you're first starting out in this Profit Path, you need to do all you can to brand yourself as an expert, someone who can help people get their own business thriving. There are a few ways to do this without outright fabrication or prevarication.

- *Engineer testimonials.* A great way to demonstrate how competent you are is to rank either your own site or someone else's as a test case study. You might need to do this one pro bono, or as an exchange of services, but this can pay off handsomely when prospective customers see what you can do.

◀ *Trust seals/badges for your site.* Apply for any trust seals or badges you can to append to your site.

◀ *Videos.* Make a video detailing your services. Make it available on your site and your YouTube channel, and send it to anyone interested in your services.

◀ *Webinars.* Use free webinars to reach a large audience, some of whom are looking for your services. Offer a webinar-only discount.

◀ *Joint ventures.* You might team up with a web designer (or any other useful service provider) to cross-promote each other's services.

◀ *Press releases.* Sending out a press release announcing your launch or successes can get you noticed favorably.

Authority Jacking

When you're starting out as a consultant/reseller of quality service providers, your outsourcing solutions become your team "behind the curtain." Most of these companies will have case studies and testimonials you can leverage toward the success of their strategies. This is great to rely on while you are first getting started. As a side note, many of these companies will also supply you with literature and information designed to help you sell their services.

HOW TO FIND NEW LEADS

New, fresh leads are the lifeblood of your consulting business. Without them, you will soon run out of services you can sell to your existing clients. You need to ensure there is always an influx of new leads pouring into your business daily. Many will not pan out, and others will want something for free. Resist the temptation to give your services away for the promise of a larger payday down the road. This almost never pans out, and they will only keep asking for more.

This is not to say you should never help someone out, but be selective and remember this is your business! Treat it as such. (Trust me: Been there. Done that. Have the T-shirt.)

There are a large number of ways to generate consulting leads. Remember to pre-qualify your leads according to the parameters you want to work within. You don't have to take each and every person who comes along. Many will be very hard to work with or want guarantees you simply can't make, and while it can be hard to decline business, particularly when starting out, in the long run you'll be better served if you do.

12 Great Ways to Generate Leads for Your Consulting Business

1. *Ranking your own site*. Perhaps the best way to generate targeted leads is to have your consulting site come up at the top of Google's search results when your keywords are searched for. If you're consulting specifically for local businesses and your consulting business in Carlsbad, California, ranks in the top three in a search for "internet marketing Carlsbad," you'll be sitting pretty in the pole position.

2. *Blog*. Your site should have a blog where you regularly post useful content that genuinely helps people in some aspect of their business. When they see your expertise and how much great content you're willing to give away for free, you'll get some calls.

3. *Targeted paid ads*. Running precisely targeted ads, especially on Facebook where you can really zero in on your demographics, makes a lot of sense. This can be a very cost-effective method of lead generation.

4. *Google+ communities and Facebook groups*. Each of these can yield large numbers of leads, but be careful to geo-target your services.

5. *Video*. Making a promotional video(s) is a great way to help target your presence for consulting keyword terms. These videos will likely show up in Google's search results and bring a good amount of direct traffic as well.

6. *Strategic partnerships*. Striking deals with other service providers can work wonders for both of you. Perhaps they offer something

you don't and vice versa. You can work out a deal whereby each of you benefits and effectively get more of the available market share.

7. *Retargeting.* Investigate retargeting as a way to follow interested parties around the web in the hope that they will succumb to your persistence. While some may think retargeting smacks of stalking, it has been proved that most people need to see your offers seven times before buying, and retargeting works very well—and it's fairly inexpensive to boot!

8. *Email marketing.* Building and marketing to a targeted list will ensure that your business lasts for many years to come.

9. *Social media.* Using your social media channels as a way to market and engage with your audience, announce events, and highlight your services gives you yet another lead generation tool.

10. *Meetups and local events.* If there are local business groups in your area, make sure you get in front of them. Ask to speak at a local chamber of commerce meeting, and join any Meetups or similar groups trying to promote business in your area. These people are your audience!

11. *Referrals.* Don't just solicit those you've worked with for referrals, but consider asking highly trafficked establishments in your area if they wouldn't mind referring your services to anyone asking, and be sure to incentivize this.

12. *Brochures, business cards, and fliers.* Don't be afraid to go old school and distribute your printed materials. Be strategic about where you leave these, and you will find that there's a reason they've worked for a long time.

PRACTICAL CONSIDERATIONS

There will come a point at which you simply need to get the work done. And if you are the sole provider of services for your business, there are only so many hours in the day. Moreover, you can't be an expert at everything you may want to sell as a service. This is where outsourcing comes into play. Ideally you'll have several subcontractors you are comfortable working with who can help you deliver the work well done and on time. I've given you some suggestions of my favorite outsource solutions to get you started, but ask around and do a little digging so you know your options.

This is how you will scale your business over time: by effectively becoming the expert who sells the services and manages a team of outsourcers who actually perform the work. Don't worry; this is not as hard as it might sound. Also, you may end up using a few tools that help you automate part of your business and create reports and spreadsheets that will leave clients wondering how you had time to do all that!

At first, however, you may be doing the lion's share of the work, and that is good. You'll then attain an intimate understanding of what it takes to actually do the job and will be in a better position to run your business. It will also give you a clear view of which services are most profitable and which ones simply aren't a good fit.

IS THE CONSULTANT PROFIT PATH FOR YOU?

Becoming a marketing consultant may be the right choice for you if you are not afraid to seek out and engage new clients, and do the work for them that they can't do for themselves. In many ways it can be very gratifying to help these clients make a positive impact on their businesses. You need to be comfortable with selling, because at least at first, that will be entirely on you.

It also helps if you are the type of person who can study the digital marketing world and retain enough of the information and strategy to have intelligent conversations with your prospects and identify which of the services you provide are the solutions to their problems.

PART III

DIGITAL AND INFORMATION PRODUCTS PROFIT PATHS

We're going to shift gears into exploring Profit Paths that are product based. All of the Profit Paths in this section center around models that sell products. Something to keep in mind is that products aren't always physical. You're going to read about selling both physical products and digital/information products. Before getting into the details, let's first take a look at why these paths might be right for you.

PROFIT PATH PREVIEW

These paths are ideal for people who resonate more with "Create my own business" over "Be my own boss." These paths center around information products and are great for people who find ecommerce appealing, but don't have their own products.

Top Level Pros

- No physical products to store or ship
- You do not need your own products
- Nearly unlimited markets to choose from

Top Level Cons

- High competition
- You really should know a thing or two about marketing
- Easy to get copied

DIGITAL AND INFORMATION MARKETING EXPLAINED

You will hear me use the phrase "digital marketing" two different ways, so I feel like it's important to clarify the definitions right from the beginning. I own a digital marketing agency called Ember Dragon, and people hire me for digital marketing services. So when I refer to this, I'm talking about marketing products, services, or businesses online. It's really an advertising agency in the digital, online world.

Businessdictionary.com defines it like this: "The promotion of products or brands via one or more forms of electronic media . . ."

Products Instead of Services

All of the Profit Paths in this book will be powered by digital marketing. However, this chapter is about selling digital and information products as your business. There are a wide range of products that fall into this category, everything from ebooks to software as a service. I consider having software or technology built to be a more advanced track that takes longer to get off the ground, so for this book we are going to primarily focus on two specific paths in order to stay true to the intention of providing paths that have realistic, low-barrier entry points. However, if you're interested in creating software or other technologies online, there is more information about that on our website, and the information in this chapter should make it easier to research online as well.

You're going to have to shift your mindset a bit because we are moving on from service-based paths into product-based paths. There are things that are similar between all the Profit Paths, but product-based businesses are definitely a different beast than service-based businesses. Each of those categories have their own specific benefits and unique pain points.

DIGITAL AND INFORMATION MARKETING PROS AND CONS
Pros

- *Lack of manual labor.* You are no longer monetizing your manual labor processes. This doesn't mean you won't work; you definitely will have to work to be successful with digital products, but your income is not dependent on services that you can consistently perform in exchange for money.

- *No inventory or shipping.* Because all of your products are digital, there is no physical inventory that you have to send. Some people do choose to add a physical component to their offerings, like sending out printed material or USB sticks, etc., but it is not required.

- *Decent scalability.* You can sell as many copies of digital products as you want. There is no limit outside of what you might set for yourself. With freelancing, your scalability is controlled by your personal limitations. This is not such a strong issue with digital products.

- *Huge income potential.* Because there is no limit to how much you can sell and any buyer is a potential repeat buyer, the income potential is nearly unlimited too. (Don't get too excited—if it was that easy, everyone would be rich, right?)

◀ *Nearly unlimited premade audiences.* Honestly, if you know of a niche that has buyers in it, then there is room for digital products in the space. So the great thing about digital marketing is the huge breadth of variety available to focus in.

◀ *Ready-made products.* There are massive amounts of products already in existence that you can sell. Selling digital products doesn't mean you have to create your own. This helps this to be a quick-start option.

◀ *Ready-made marketing.* Some forms of digital marketing, like affiliate marketing, often come with all the marketing materials laid out for you to work with. So this can be beneficial when you're not prepared to develop everything from scratch.

◀ *Can be low client interaction.* It is possible to successfully sell digital marketing products and never speak to your buyers.

Cons

◀ *High competition.* Have you ever been on the internet? It's a HUGE space with a gazillion people, products, and offers on it. You have to figure out the most strategic way to jump in there and carve out a small corner of the web for yourself.

◀ *Marketing.* While I listed as a pro that you don't always need to be super marketing savvy because some programs come with marketing help, that does not eliminate the importance of understanding how to get your product not only to in front of your prospects, but also to stand out in the sea of products.

◀ *Lower perceived value.* People tend to naturally value a digital product lower than they might value a physical product. Also, with the competitive space, many people sell products for dirt cheap which drives the average pricing down.

◄ *Shorter shelf life.* It depends on the topic of the product and the market, but a lot of digital products have a short shelf life.

◄ *Easy to copy.* People can and will rip off your products. No matter how careful you are, if someone wants to copy your product, it's not very difficult to do.

CHAPTER 10

AFFILIATE MARKETING

A ffiliate marketing can be a highly lucrative Profit Path and has been a staple in the internet marketing world for years. In this chapter, we'll delve into what affiliate marketing is, how to get started, and the different avenues you can take when joining the ranks.

WHAT IS AFFILIATE MARKETING?

As far as Profit Paths on the internet go, affiliate marketing is one of the fastest and easiest to get started in. Depending on the path you choose, the investment to get up and running can be minimal. It's all dependent on your preferred marketing model and how much you need to outsource as opposed to doing it yourself. Once you get your foundation in place, your main ongoing costs are associated with advertising and promoting the products you sell, and you get to choose how much or how little you would like to put into the process.

MEET THE EXPERTS
JAY KUBASSEK AND STUART ROSS

Jay Kubassek and Stuart Ross run a really innovative company called Digital Experts Academy (http://digitalexpertsacademy.com/). Digital Experts Academy (DEA) has courses that teach their members how to do affiliate marketing as well as other entrepreneurial trainings. They also happen to be amazing human beings!

Affiliate marketing is essentially a way for you to earn cash for promoting and selling items or services without ever having to be responsible for the product, shipping, or fulfillment of the order. You strike a deal with a business, company, or individual that you will promote their products, and in return, when an item is sold through your affiliate account, you get a commission—a certain percentage or dollar amount for that sale. It's a win/win situation for you and the business: They get free advertising and customers they might not have otherwise reached, and you are compensated for the work you've put in. The commission they pay you is essentially part of their marketing budget. For some companies, it is their exclusive form of marketing.

For the business owner you work with, the pros far outweigh any drawbacks. They decide how much they want to compensate the affiliate, and the cost of the commission is much lower than the costs of traditional advertising. Even the customer comes out a winner in this scenario: Since affiliates and businesses are extremely motivated to sell, sales and coupons are becoming a big part of the affiliate marketing world. It's a low-risk, high-reward setup if you're willing to put in the time and effort.

A Real-World Example

Let's take a look at this scenario: At Moonlighting on the Internet (www.MoonlightingontheInternet.com), we sell courses, training, and classes designed to help people successfully create Profit Paths online. We, like many companies, have an affiliate program. If you are one of our affiliates, every time a customer makes a purchase with your affiliate link or ID, you get a commission. So if the course or product costs $100 and the commission structure is 30 percent, you get paid $30 just for leading the horse to water, so to speak. It is a win-win process that opens an easy sales channel for the business, the affiliate, and the customer. If you can drive buyers there, you get paid.

Personalized Affiliate Links and Cookies

This is an extremely simplified explanation, but basically there are two ways an affiliate program will track the prospects you send them:

1. *Personalized affiliate links.* If your affiliate program uses links to track sales, you'll be given a login and a link associated with your account, which you will send to customers so the purchase can be traced back to you.
2. *Cookies (and not the yummy chocolate chip kind).* Some programs use cookies instead of personalized links. Cookies are tiny pieces of data the internet uses to track someone's online habits. It's a way to see where a customer came from and what they bought— think of it like a trail of breadcrumbs showing where customers originated and how they arrived on the site. (If you're the type of person who is uncomfortable with "Big Brother Is Watching You" scenarios, you probably don't like cookies.)

Different programs have different duration policies. Some companies will pay you for life any time a prospect you have sent them buys something. Other programs pay only on the initial sale. There are even some programs that have specified time ranges—30, 60, or 90 days—during which they will pay you on purchases made by the prospect you sent them. It is advantageous for you to choose affiliate programs that have cookies that last for at least 30 days so you get credit for all the purchases your leads may make. You should find out this information before you move forward with an affiliate program.

A FEW POINTS OF CONSIDERATION BEFORE YOU GET STARTED

As with anything, there are a few drawbacks. If you're not willing to learn and adapt, you will most likely not be a very successful affiliate, but that's true for most things in life. You have to be willing to invest your time, energy, and patience into making it work for you. Small sales here and there are great, but if you want to make this your main Profit Path, you have to be able to land a lot of sales to make a significant amount of money. You need to think about your efforts as building a business. Two considerations in that vein are creating systems that are set up to get consistent new lead acquisition and choosing higher-margin offers. (Same amount of work, more money.)

For this to be sustainable as a long-term Profit Path, you need to create promotion strategies that will lead to consistent sales. Just like any business worth getting off the ground, it takes commitment, time, and dedication. This path will be easier for those of you who have some experience with SEO or paid traffic generation.

And finally, you really need to choose who you are an affiliate for wisely. If the merchant's site is not up to par, slow, buggy, full of errors, and not geared toward making the sale, you will lose out as well. Customers don't have faith or confidence in an online retailer who can't properly run its website. This issue is out of your hands, which is why it's important to take it into account before becoming an affiliate. Take a look around the site and ask yourself, "Would I feel comfortable buying from here?" If the answer is "no," you may want to reconsider becoming an affiliate for that business. When you're an affiliate, you are at the mercy of the merchant/business that is selling the actual product.

TYPES OF AFFILIATE OFFERS

In reality, any business can create an affiliate program and recruit affiliates as part of their marketing strategy. However, most offers you will be exposed to can be lumped into three categories: products, services, and stores. We'll briefly explore the differences that will help you identify which options might be the best fit for you.

Products

There are two types of products online you can be an affiliate for: physical products and digital products. The marketing strategies you will employ won't really change either way, but they do each come with their own sets of pros and cons.

PHYSICAL PRODUCTS

Pros: Not all consumers buy digital products, but pretty much all consumers buy physical products. If you choose a product that is in demand, made by a trusted brand, and sold through a credible online store, the selling is really already done for you.

Cons: The biggest cons to physical products are the shipping cost and the fact that it takes some time for the product to arrive. Also, there are certain products that consumers want to be able to touch and experience before they buy. That can sometimes hamper an online purchase.

DIGITAL PRODUCTS

Pros: One of the biggest advantages of a digital product is instant gratification. The consumer can immediately dig in and enjoy the product they purchased while they are excited about it. If you are really in tune with your prospects' problems and have a digital product that gives them the solution to that problem, conversions can be really high. No shipping costs are another plus.

Cons: Digital products are often swimming among a lot of competition that you need to stand out from. Also, you're at the mercy of the retailer when it comes to making sure the product downloads properly. Sometimes digital products are so complicated they overwhelm the consumer, which can hinder additional sales from that prospect.

Services

When most people think of affiliate marketing, the first thing that usually comes to mind is selling products. However, there are also many services people pay for online that have affiliate programs. Some examples are:

- ◖ Financial services like tax preparation
- ◖ Social media and digital marketing services
- ◖ Professional services (hosting, payment processing, etc.)
- ◖ Travel-related services like Hotels.com and Travelocity

Storewide Programs

There are tons of stores that will give you commissions on the entire purchase made by a consumer you send to their site. This is great because it gives you the flexibility to market just one product they sell and still get credit for anything else your prospect adds to their cart, or you can just promote the entire store in general.

Where to Find Affiliate Products and Services to Promote

When you're first getting started, I recommend trying your hand at some of the proven affiliate marketing networks before tackling the smaller markets. They are all fairly similar in intent, but each one has its own processes, requirements, and restrictions. It's very important that you take the time to read through how their program works to make sure it's the best choice for you.

Some aspects to research:

- ◖ *Sign-up criteria.* Each network or program will have its own sign-up criteria for you to be accepted as an affiliate. You may not initially qualify for some, but keep trying, as others will take you straight off.
- ◖ *Payment arrangements.* The payment policies for each program can differ. You might get instant, seven-day, two-week, or

monthly payments, and in some cases these won't start until 60 days have passed. Understand your terms so you won't be left holding the bag for advertising costs you've incurred.

◖ *Restrictions.* Make sure you understand the rules and restrictions and that they will fit into your business model.

If you have any questions or concerns, the time to ask them is before you sign up, because after that you're bound to the terms and services you agreed to.

Some Popular Programs

There are a lot of programs out there for you to research, explore, and experiment with. I can't emphasize enough how important it is for you to take some time to research these sites and figure out which one will be best for you. I could give you a list of pros and cons for each one, but your situation and your Profit Path are unique, so only you can decide which resource makes the most sense. Here are a few that are currently popular:

◖ DealGuardian (http://dealguardian.com)

◖ JVZoo (www.jvzoo.com)

◖ ClickBank (www.clickbank.com)

◖ CJ Affiliate (www.cj.com)

◖ ShareASale (www.shareasale.com)

◖ PeerFly (https://peerfly.com)

◖ Amazon Associates (https://affiliate-program.amazon.com)

The great thing about people who play in this space is that they are very vocal about what they like and don't like. You can do a search for each of these programs and find a lot of aspects that people love and dislike about each one. If you take the time to do a little research, you should be able to identify which one will be the right fit for you and the direction you want to take your business.

A QUICK NOTE ABOUT HIGH-END SALES

If you know a little about affiliate marketing already, you have probably heard about "high ticket item sales." The dollar amount that is

MOONLIGHTING ON THE INTERNET, AMAZING.COM, AND DIGITAL EXPERTS ACADEMY

Digital Experts Academy (DEA) is worth mentioning because they have a unique model that is similar to mine. Because both DEA and Moonlighting on the Internet are focused on teaching people how to make money online through various training courses and products, we structured our affiliate program to be more aligned with creating a sustainable Profit Path as an affiliate.

Because we are selling education, people often buy courses off and on for years, and we pay commissions on any prospect sent to us for life. So if one of our affiliates sends us a prospect, we will pay them on anything that prospect buys for as long as they are our customer. This is great because if you're going to put time and money into driving traffic, it's nice to know you have the potential for ongoing income from one successful lead acquisition. We really tried to make our program as beneficial as possible for our students, members, and affiliates.

I want to call attention to Amazing.com because they are . . . well, amazing! They are a sister company to ours, and our values and educational platforms are aligned. The thing I love best about Amazing.com is that they are in 100 percent alignment with our vision, standards, and goals. It's a company full of great people, great strategies, and great students. Amazing!

If you like to shop online, think about the products, services, and businesses you like to buy from. Now that you know what affiliate marketing is, you can go to their website and find out if they have an affiliate program. One of the best things about affiliate marketing is that you can promote the businesses and products you love and are passionate about. You might be surprised how many options are out there that you don't even realize exist.

You can also consider giving weight to the occasional random, one-off offer. Every once in a while opportunities will pop up that make a lot of sense for you to promote in your chosen market. A good example are events and conferences that your target market would be interested in attending. For instance, if you're in the marketing niche like I am, you would likely do well to promote a couple of the popular marketing seminars that take place throughout the year. Even if only a few people buy it, the commissions are often on the higher end of the pay scale and can add a nice little boost to your bottom line. In addition, it helps position you as a well-informed authority in the market they can return to in the future.

considered "high end" is different to different people, so for the sake of making things easy, let's call a high-end commission any sale where you earn $1,000 or more.

People are often intimidated by getting into a high-end market, especially when starting out. I just want to take a minute to talk about it because I want you to keep yourself open to all potential options and not self-disqualify just because the dollar amount is daunting. There are many benefits to being a high-ticket affiliate:

1. It's a high-cost item that you, as an affiliate, don't have to put into production yourself but still get the benefit of the price by way of commission.
2. You put in the same amount of work with a MUCH bigger pay-off.
3. You only need to persuade one or two customers to make it a good day, as opposed to dozens or hundreds with lower-cost items.

But keep in mind that some high-ticket items may not be continuous—you may make a lot of money off a $10,000 summer workshop, but once that workshop is over, it's over. So it's important to have more than one avenue and strategy. Even so, market experts will tell you it's typically far better to sell a few high-ticket items than a lot of low-cost items. If you sell 100 $1 items, you've made $100. If you sell 10 $100 items, you've made $1,000. Which of those scenarios piques your interest more?

This doesn't mean that low-cost items don't have their place in affiliate marketing; they can be huge lead generators for you in the future! If you sell a small item to a customer today, they are more likely to come back to you in the future for a big-ticket item. The key is to strike a balance between low-, medium-, and high-cost sales—that's how you achieve the best of both worlds in marketing.

HOW TO EVALUATE WHICH AFFILIATE PROGRAMS ARE RIGHT FOR YOU

Which programs are best for you has a lot to do with the type of industry you are marketing in. Who is your target market? You want to pick programs and offers that make sense for your market. The very first thing you want to think about is whether the offer fits the needs of your target market. Outside that, it's really about choosing a program that has processes and guidelines you feel in alignment with. I don't really have a magic pill to give you regarding selection. Now that you know the important criteria, you just need to be sure to do your due diligence.

There are lots of affiliate marketing programs out there and more are coming online every day, but as mentioned above, not all are created equal. There's no way to go through all of them and tell you which ones are legitimate and which ones are a scam, but here are a few things you should look out for.

If an affiliate program is asking you for money upfront: SCAM. Never hand over money to become an affiliate; it's a mutually beneficial arrangement and no one should be paying for it.

If the site is filled with pop-up ads and banner advertisements, it's best to steer clear. Legitimate affiliate marketing programs do not need to market themselves so heavily.

If an affiliate program begs you to bring other affiliates into the mix, that is not affiliate marketing, it's multilevel marketing (MLM), which is a completely different beast.

HOW TO CHOOSE AN AFFILIATE OFFER

Choosing the right offer is critical to your success. Here are some tips from successful affiliate marketers I know:

- *Product and service quality*. Choose offers you would be proud to have your name behind. You want your prospects to consider you a credible source to return to for suggestions of things to buy.
- *The merchant website*. I may be a little jaded after so many years involved with digital marketing, but I wouldn't trust the statistics the merchant's website claims at face value. Take a look around the website and observe what your experience would be if you were visiting there as a first-time buyer. Is it laid out well?

Are you able to find what you're looking for? Are you having a good experience? Would you return?

◖ *Commissions*. I'm sure it goes without saying, but the better the commissions, the more enticing the offer. This could be in margins or longer cookie durations.

◖ *EPC*. This stands for earnings per click and represents how much on average the affiliates make from the sale.

◖ *Return percentage*. Choose offers that have low return percentages.

◖ *Deep linking*. Sites that don't allow deep linking hinder an affiliate's conversions. You want to promote offers that allow you to link directly to the offer landing page.

◖ *Create marketing content*. Don't just rely on the content the merchant provides you with. Create high-quality content your competitors can't compete with.

◖ *Traffic variations*. Don't rely on only one traffic source.

Do You Need Mad Skills to Make Money with Affiliate Marketing?

Your job is to drive interested traffic to these offers, and the more you do that, the more money everyone makes. There are many, many ways to go about that. So while marketing skills are essential, they can be learned. You don't even need to have a website. Many people successfully sell affiliate offers through social media platforms and Web 2.0 sites. It really just depends on what your chosen business model is.

There are a number of ways you can effectively market affiliate products, but here we're going to talk about the most common and accessible methods for those just getting going. As you gain more skills in promoting products on the internet, you'll be able to scale your efforts and create larger paydays. Let's look at several methods successful affiliates use to promote their offers.

Blogging

If you have a blog or want to go this route, it's important to understand that in order for this method to work, you'll have to be consistent when it comes to posting and building your audience. Simply showing up once a week to post some random affiliate links won't yield many results. You won't be a trusted voice recommending anything. On the other hand, if you build an engaged, interested blog community that is used to receiving quality content and the occasional offer from you, you will do well.

If you're managing a blog and building a list in a specific market, you have the flexibility to mix up the type of content you are putting on it. It's great to write content about your offers, but you can also actually place the affiliate ads right on the page of your blog. You can even add navigation that clumps different offers by topics and categories. This is especially useful for those of you who want to build out an authority site in your chosen industry.

Email Marketing

Affiliate marketing via email is one of the oldest and most effective methods to make money in this Profit Path. This of course assumes you have a relevant email list you can market to. Having a list of several thousand trusted followers can be akin to having an affiliate annuity: mail and make money. That said, you have to constantly grow and nurture that list and regularly deliver value that is not an affiliate offer. Do that, and you'll succeed. If you employ a "churn and burn" email marketing campaign, you'll eventually lose your list and your income, and you could get blacklisted in Google so that all your emails get filtered into the spam section of your prospects' email accounts.

If you don't have a list yet, it's definitely worth the time and effort to build one. The ability to send out one email to multiple people promoting the product(s) you are interested in selling is an easy and effective way to make good money for little effort. Experts in the field estimate you could expect at least $1 per month from each subscriber on a well-put-together list of clients. What other type of marketing tool can provide that? Not many.

Many people buy email lists. This is not something I would advise when you're first starting out. Buying email lists can be really great or really terrible. It takes some experience to get a handle on quality resources you can trust vs. ones you shouldn't touch with a barge pole.

You might feel tempted to purchase a "Targeted Email list of 50,000 subscribers for $99." That is an actual ad I just saw, and what this likely entails is a list of scraped email addresses that even if they are still good are not connected to a live person, may reside in different countries, and most certainly aren't eager to hear from you. Until you have a bit more experience, I wouldn't suggest chasing shortcuts: Build it the old-fashioned way!

PAID ADVERTISING

I'll repeat what digital marketer Ryan Deiss often says: "If you want traffic, you go to the traffic store and you buy it." Paid traffic is really efficient, but it's also overwhelming when you are first starting out, and mistakes can be costly. I would suggest finding outsourced solutions you trust, putting some time and money into taking a course, or learning the ins and outs of any of the paid traffic platforms you might want to use. The good news is that most of them have their own tutorials and training videos because they want you to use them. They make money whether you do or not! Some of my favorite paid traffic platforms are:

- *Google AdWords* (www.google.com/adwords)
- *Google Display Network* (www.google.com/ads/displaynetwork)
- *Facebook Ads* (www.facebook.com/business/products/ads)
- *LinkedIn Ads* (www.linkedin.com/ads)
- *Twitter Ads* (https://biz.twitter.com/ad-products)
- *Pinterest Promoted Pins* (https://business.pinterest.com/en/promoted -pins)
- *Banner ads on relevant websites*

FREE ADVERTISING OPTIONS

Paid ads are not your only option. However, you need to keep in mind that the old adage "You get what you pay for" often rings true when it comes to paid vs. free ads online.

- *Free ads*. Ads on free sites like Craigslist (www.craigslist.org/about/sites) and USFreeads (www.usfreeads.com), among many others, are indeed free but require a constant investment of time. Not recommended as your primary advertising avenue.

◀ *Video marketing.* Many affiliates who have some video skills are making healthy incomes creating short promotional videos, uploading them to YouTube, and then promoting the video. This can work well if you are skilled at getting your videos to rank highly in YouTube's results.

◀ *YouTube partner program.* This is connected to your Google AdSense account; the basic premise is that YouTube shares the ad revenue they collect from viewers who see the ads that have been placed on your video. As an affiliate marketer, in essence it gives you the opportunity to double dip:

1. Your video is promoting an offer you are an affiliate for.
2. You're getting paid for people who view the ads YouTube placed on your video.

◀ *Social media marketing.* Marketing your affiliate links on social media networks through organic engagement, as opposed to paid advertising platforms, is a great way to build a list and make sales. The most important thing to remember is that if you build a list on a social media platform, you need to also make a plan to monetize that list. Often when people are first starting out they create a great following but don't understand how to monetize it. The most popular social media platforms right now are:

- Facebook (www.facebook.com)
- Twitter (https://twitter.com)
- Pinterest (www.pinterest.com)
- Instagram (https://instagram.com)
- LinkedIn (www.linkedin.com)
- Tumblr (www.tumblr.com)

Social media audiences are very attuned to when they are being marketed to, so seller beware. Strive to regularly engage your followers with interesting information that isn't selling anything. A side note: If you are a member of large Facebook groups that are related to the topic of your offer, you might be able to post a link if you have been a valuable contributor to the group. You can even offer to share commissions with the group owner. On the front-runners like Facebook, the key is to be aboveboard and as transparent as possible and carefully adhere to their rules to stay compliant.

Which platform makes the most sense for you has a lot to do with the market you're in. You'll want to do some research and find out

A WORD FROM SUPER AFFILIATE PAT FLYNN

Super affiliate Pat Flynn talks about how affiliates basically fall into one of three categories: Unattached, Related, and Involved.

◀ *Unattached affiliates.* Unattached affiliates have no authority or presence in a market other than sending out an affiliate link. This can work, but it requires a lot of traffic. Most often you see this in CPA (cost per action) marketing. CPA affiliate marketing is where you send out your affiliate link via email, paid ads, or social media as far and wide as you can, hoping for that click. Many times in CPA marketing all you need to do is get an email submitted, and you've earned a commission.

◀ *Related affiliates.* Related affiliates promote products related to their own presence online. For instance, if you have a health blog with active readers and followers, you would choose offers that coordinate well with the subjects you write about.

◀ *Involved affiliates.* An Involved affiliate may or may not have a specific niche, but they always recommend products and services they have used before so they can make a personal recommendation.

There are a lot of ways to succeed in affiliate marketing—far more than we have room for in this book. Some people set up one authority-level presence in a market and build a strong following over time that they can regularly sell to. Others frequently distribute offers across the internet and strategically drive targeted buyers to those offers.

It's hard to make a recommendation to you in a book without knowing your situation, market, and preferred business model. However, deciding which approach suits you best will help you with focus and advertising costs.

where your target buyers hang out and which communication channels they use most.

HOW MUCH MONEY CAN I MAKE?

It shouldn't surprise you that, just like most other business models, the amount of money you can and will make is variable. Some days, weeks, and months will be better than others; you'll need a long-term average to really gauge how much you're making. Holidays are usually a big time for sales, and summer is usually when a slump occurs (unless you're selling swim gear!). A 2013 survey by Finch Sells (http://finchsells. com/2013/10/10/how-much-can-you-earn-from-affiliate-marketing/) estimates that about 18.8 percent of affiliate marketers make less than $20,000 per year and 6 percent make more than $2 million; where you fall on this scale mostly depends on you, your skills, and a little luck! As with anything, what you put in is what you get out—it's a Profit Path, not a get-rich-quick scheme, but if you stick with it and make the right choices, you could bring in a significant amount of money in no time.

I probably sound like a broken record, but once again, your odds of success will be much higher if you are really in tune with the intention of the buyers in your chosen market. Whether you already have some experience with marketing and driving traffic or whether you'll be learning it for the first time, keep your eye on their intention. Understanding intention will help you not just get in front of your target buyers, but also get in front of them with messaging that speaks to the heart of what they are looking for.

In the end, affiliate marketing is not particularly difficult, but it's also not an easy, quick, or even painless process. If it were, everybody would be doing it! If you're looking for a fast, get-rich-quick scheme, this probably isn't it. But if you're willing to put in the effort, time, and dedication, the benefits can be substantial for you, your brand, and your financial future.

CHAPTER 11

KINDLE PUBLISHING PROFIT PATH

I personally believe that everyone has a book inside them just waiting to be written. Some people know it and some people don't. The good news is that whether or not you feel that way, you can create a solid Profit Path publishing books on Amazon Kindle. It helps, especially your first time, if you're writing about a topic you are interested in or passionate about, but it's not required. If you have the ability to research a topic and write comprehensibly on that subject, this Profit Path could be a great option for you.

If you've looked into publishing books before, it's possible you got discouraged and overwhelmed by all the logistics of actually getting the book written, edited, and accepted by a publishing house. Countless writing and publishing dreams die due to logistical intimidation. Well, the good news is that the dream is alive again in the form of Amazon Kindle publishing!

Amazon Kindle Direct Publishing (https://kdp.amazon.com/) is a self-serve publishing platform that has forever changed the landscape for independent publishing. Now anyone with an idea and a computer can create a digital ebook and sell it on Amazon's platform for minimal production costs.

Here are three amazing statistics that can begin to give you a glimpse of why Kindle, and ebook publishing, is here to stay:

- eBook sales are expected to reach $9.7 billion by 2016.
- Kindle titles account for more than 20 percent of all books published in the U.S.
- Amazon now sells more Kindle books than print books.

Of all the Profit Paths I am writing about in this book, this may have the absolute lowest barrier to entry. The platform and model are pretty straightforward and easy to understand. Here are some of the benefits Kindle publishers love the most:

- *You control the timeline and costs.* If you're doing the research and writing yourself, the timeline from inception to publishing is completely in your hands and the costs are almost nonexistent. One of the reasons people love this Profit Path is that you really do get to set your own pace. As long as you understand the Kindle Direct Publishing (KDP) guidelines and stay compliant, there are very few hoops you have to jump through to reach your first sale.
- *The answer is yes.* One of the main reasons Kindle is so attractive is that no one can tell you no. There are no arbiters of taste who will tell you to go back to the drawing board, start over, or get a day job. You are the captain of your ship, and it will sail any direction you wish. That said, I suggest you find an editor or good friend to offer honest feedback and critiques. Trust me, it's much better to receive the message that your book sucks from your editor than from your sales figures.
- *Wealth is realistically attainable.* But without doubt the best part is that you are entirely capable of creating an income stream that in time can seriously augment or replace a traditional full-time income. Stories abound of authors who are pulling six figures a

month from Kindle titles. Of course these are the top end, but it's not an unrealistic possibility if you apply yourself with some degree of consistency. The real income comes from creating a process to consistently publish titles that sell. Success depends on many other factors as well, which we will cover.

Kindle publishing is one of the many new forms of online passive income; that is, you do the work once, and the asset will pay off for you for some time to come. All right, let's dive in!

FICTION OR NONFICTION?

This of course is a question only you can answer, but there are a few things to consider. First, if you have a seven-part bodice-ripping romance just dying to get out of your head and into print, there is nothing that can stop you. (And if you do, you'll likely be positioned very well, as series fiction is where the big money is!)

But let's face it, an endeavor like that takes some time to put together, and if you're like most people, you're not entering the market solely with a long play in mind. Most people have short-term cash infusion needs in the beginning. That doesn't mean you have to put your long-term goals on hold. I like to build my Profit Paths with short-term and long-term initiatives in mind. For instance, if you're leaning toward gaining experience publishing fiction, Kindle has other opportunities for you to consider.

Kindle Singles are shorter and therefore quicker to publish. While they won't make you as much money, they could be a launching pad, as well as a place to publish stories that may not have the legs for an entire book.

Many new authors start out publishing nonfiction titles because they're easier and faster to write and very lucrative. If you possess expertise in a particular subject, this could be a perfect vehicle for your first nonfiction title. However, you don't need specialized expertise to excel. Like any of the Profit Paths in this book, you'll need to know how to discover which niches, topics, and markets will be most profitable to write on.

In addition, nonfiction titles don't need to be a particular length to satisfy the reader: If you give the information you promise, you're done! For the purposes of this chapter, we're going to assume you're going to take the nonfiction route and talk mostly about that.

DECIDING ON YOUR NICHE

Have you ever heard anyone say that marketing is more important than the product you're marketing? It holds true in publishing: It doesn't matter if you have the greatest book in the world if no one knows about it and no one is buying it. When it comes to hitting or exceeding your financial goals with Kindle publishing, choosing your niche is half the battle. If you're going to dominate a niche, pick one that has a LOT of buyers.

One of the best indicators of a healthy, thriving market is the Best Sellers Ranking of the top books in that category. So if you have an idea of the topic you want to write on, you need to look through Amazon and Kindle stores for other books on that topic and evaluate their Amazon Best Sellers Ranking. There are some common estimates that people use to determine the approximate number of books sold each day based on their Best Sellers Rank. But remember that it is only an estimate because Amazon keeps its data proprietary.

At the time of this writing, the chart that most people consider a good approximation is one created in December 2013 by Theresa Ragan, an author (www.theresaragan.com/salesrankingchart.html), based on her own experience.

Amazon Best Sellers Rank	Approximate Number of Books Sold Daily
50,000 to 100,000	close to 1 book a day
10,000 to 50,000	5 to 15 books a day
5,500 to 10,000	15 to 25 books a day
3,000 to 5,500	25 to 70 books a day
1,500 to 3,000	70 to 100 books a day
750 to 1,500	100 to 120 books a day
500 to 750	120 to 175 books a day
350 to 500	175 to 250 books a day
200 to 350	250 to 500 books a day

Amazon Best Sellers Rank	Approximate Number of Books Sold Daily
35 to 200	500 to 2,000 books a day
20 to 35	2,000 to 3,000 books a day
5 to 20	3,000 to 4,000 books a day
1 to 5	4,000+ books a day

You can see the Amazon Best Sellers Rank on each book's listing page in the Product Details section in Figure 11.1.

This picture is a great example. As you can see, Stephen Covey's *The 7 Habits of Highly Effective People* is No. 1 in the Business and Money: Processes & Infrastructure, Management and Leadership, and Skills categories as well as No. 56 overall in Books. This information will help you get an idea of what you can expect your sales to be if you dominate that category with your book. Remember, competition is a good thing! If no one is making any money in this niche, run away!

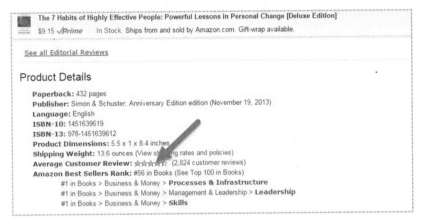

FIGURE 11.1—**Amazon Best Sellers Rank**

Titles and Cover Research

While you're doing your research, also notice titles and covers. You're looking for two things for opposite reasons:

1. You want to notice the covers and titles of the bestsellers because obviously they are doing something right.

2. You don't want to unwittingly duplicate or come too close to another title, as you want your book to stand out. That said, titles aren't copyrightable, so if you must name your book *The Secret*, go ahead, but know you have a marketing battle ahead of you and hope the buyers will figure it out.

Reviews

You can glean data about market intent from the reviews just as you do in Google SERPs. When you read the reviews, is there a common type of question1 that keeps popping up from readers? Is this an area of opportunity? Digesting questions the readers are asking and feedback they are giving can really help you understand what your target market is looking for. This may even help you strike a vein others have missed!

To recap, here are the steps you should take to choose a lucrative niche:

- Choose a few niches you are interested in publishing in.
- Browse the Amazon and Kindle Stores and look at the Best Sellers Ranking for the top books to verify the niche has the level of sales you desire.
- Take notes on the covers and titles of books to help you design yours.
- Read the reviews the books are getting and compile a list about what your target buyers are looking for to help you write a book that will dominate the market.
- Make your choice, get embedded into your chosen niche, and start writing.

GETTING THE BOOK WRITTEN

Let's assume you have found a profitable niche and chosen a title you could publish that would be a big win. Now we get down to the nitty-gritty: getting the work done. This is often where the dream gets stuck in the mud and is never realized. So your task, should you choose to accept it, is to make sure that doesn't happen to your book. Do not get intimidated; you have options.

Write the Book Yourself

This is obviously the least expensive option and one that offers you ultimate control. One of the pluses of writing it yourself is that you can roll along at a breakneck pace if you so desire and have a publishable manuscript in a very short time. You can also make revisions on the fly and change direction easily if the muse strikes you.

If you're someone who struggles with writing, then setting yourself up for success is very important. You will want to set goals and a schedule for yourself to make sure you are producing a consistent number of pages daily. This book isn't about writing productivity tactics, but this Profit Path can't start until you have a manuscript ready to publish. So whatever you need to do to keep yourself accountable and get the writing done, do it. However you choose to manage yourself, realize that it is essential to do so!

One tip I can give you, from one writer to another, is not to research and edit at the same time you're writing. You use a different part of your brain to research than you do to write. It takes a lot longer, and it's not efficient at all. One method that works for many writers is to write the first draft as a sort of mind dump, not worrying about mistakes or editing anything until the draft is complete. Once that is done, and you've managed to catch your breath and regenerate some brain cells, you can go back and make your changes, with the whole manuscript in mind.

Also, if you choose to write the manuscript yourself, you might find it useful to read through the freelance writing section of this book; while you're not writing for a client, there is still a lot of great information in there that might help you out. Writing is a solo journey and can be exciting and daunting at the same time. It's most important to do your prep work really well, take a deep breath, and believe in yourself.

Outsource the Writing

If you simply don't have the time, skill, or inclination to write the book yourself, you can find someone to write it for you. Depending on the situation, hiring a decent ghostwriter might be out of your budget.

This is especially true for a Kindle title that you will likely be pricing anywhere from $2.99 to $9.99. Paying a ghostwriter on top of that (in fact, in ADVANCE of that!) may not make financial sense.

If you don't have the funds to hire a ghostwriter but it really is the ideal route for you, you could consider partnering with someone on the first book, perhaps someone who is already a specialist on your chosen topic. You may also be able to find a college intern who would be willing to do the writing for free or for very little in exchange for learning the Kindle Publishing Profit Path information.

Outsourcing does have its caveats, one of which is that you should not outsource to overseas writers, regardless of your budget constraints. The pricing for this type of work varies wildly, usually depending on the time and scope of the work. I've owned a content company since 2007, and I can tell you that outsourcing writing overseas, especially content as important as a book, rarely ends well.

First, the outsourced writer's first language may not be English, and this could present you with a host of problems you don't need. Even if they have a technically sound command of the language, the verbiage used will tend to be stilted and mechanical and lack any colloquial flavor. Also be aware that work schedules and deadlines may mean something entirely different to them, and you being half a world away won't help. But really, all that is a moot point compared to the fact that it will be difficult to get people to buy your books if they're poorly written.

If you do engage someone to write your book, make sure you have a written agreement that details the scope of the work to be done, as well as payment arrangements and deadlines. Ask to see samples of their writing before you hire anyone, and don't be afraid to keep interviewing until you find a suitable candidate. You need to be able to work closely with them, so you want to do all you can to ensure a good fit. In the section on the Freelance Writing Profit Path, you can glean some great tips on hiring a freelance writer.

Below are a couple of outsourcing solutions to aid you in finding a freelance writer:

1. Content Divas (http://contentdivas.com)
2. Upwork (www.upwork.com)

Determining Book Length

A common saying in the writing world is "as many words as it takes, and not one more." Once you've said what you need to say, you're done. No one likes to read filler you wrote just to fill space and make your book more substantial. On Kindle we see many "books" that are but a few pages, many as little as 10 to 15, but these are not usually great sellers. The short answer here is to make a valuable but not overstuffed book you can be proud to have your name on. Creating your book in this fashion will result in far better sales than adhering to some random page count.

Recording or Dictating Your Book

One easy way to make the creation process simpler is to either record yourself speaking your book and have it transcribed or dictate your book using a software program like Dragon NaturallySpeaking (www.nuance.com/dragon/index.htm). This can save you a lot of time and works surprisingly well.

Ditch the Perfection Standard

Many times writers agonize over every word as if the fate of the planet hangs in the balance. Unless that happens to be true, cut yourself a little slack and do your best, and let it go at that. That's not to say we should turn out subpar work, but getting it done is more important than getting it perfect.

EDITING YOUR BOOK

None of us can see it all. In fact, it's nearly impossible for a writer to edit their own work well. Your brain tends to read the sentences how they were supposed to be written, regardless of what's actually on the page. Have a fresh set of eyes, preferably ones with at least a passing acquaintance with proper English—or, better yet, a professional editor—take a pass at your book. They will inevitably find mistakes you may have looked at a thousand times and missed. It's a worthwhile expense.

Hiring an editor can be tricky. Like most freelance positions, there are a lot of scammers out there. You can minimize your risk by choosing trusted resources. Start by asking for referrals from people you trust. If you don't find an editor that way, the next step is to go to some of the job boards listed in this book and only hire an editor with a lot of positive reviews and extensive number of successful editing jobs under her belt. Obviously, there are no guarantees, but you can save yourself some pain and wasted money by doing your due diligence and being smart about who you hire.

PROTECTING YOUR WORK

I wish I didn't have to write this, but horror stories still come along of some poor soul who lost hundreds of manuscript pages to carelessness. The very first time I was hired as a freelancer to write an actual book on hedge funds, one of my babies got on my laptop while I was away from my computer on a break and deleted the manuscript. I cried for hours as though someone had died! Lest this should happen to you, make sure you have redundant backups of your work, and not all on the same system. Hopefully, that is enough said. Because trust me, if you learn from experience, it's a lesson you will NEVER forget. It's like the writer's version of PTSD.

FORMATTING YOUR BOOK FOR KINDLE

This used to trip everyone up, as prior to the implementation of Kindle Direct Publishing you had to resort to technical gymnastics to get your book to look good on the Kindle platform or hire a tech whiz to compile the book for you in some obscure format. Not anymore. Kindle heard the cries of the oppressed, and now you can get your book to render by simply uploading a Microsoft Word document. Just make sure to use simple formatting, and you'll be fine. If your book is image-heavy, you'll need to ensure the images are optimized well. Kindle has very helpful guidelines for you to follow in this regard.

Shelby's Formatting Tips

The formatting requirements for publishing through CreateSpace are different from the formatting requirements for Kindle. Even if you are only intending to publish the book on the Kindle platform and never offer a print version, we still advise you to format your book for both Amazon and Kindle. The reason is that there are additional promotional options and benefits just in having the book formatted for CreateSpace, regardless of whether you ever list it as a print option. By formatting for both platforms, you can reap the most advantages and benefits. I will cover CreateSpace in more detail shortly.

Don't be tempted to go the cheap route by publishing as a PDF without the KDP or CreateSpace formatting requirements. The final ebook version will be a much lower-quality product and provide a subpar user experience for the reader.

When you choose images for your manuscript, to get the highest image quality possible, you, or the person you are paying to format your book, will need to save the images separately in a file in addition to placing them inside your working document.

Amazon provides comprehensive instructions on this topic. You can read more about it here: https://kdp.amazon.com/help?topicId=A3R2IZDC42DJW6.

YOUR BOOK COVER

The cover of your book may not have the most impact on your success with Kindle publishing, but it is very important. It's no secret that attractive covers sell far better than unattractive ones, so unless you have design skills, don't attempt this at home! Commission someone who knows how to craft a winner. One tip is to make your title a bit larger than you might think it needs to be, as it will show up far better in the thumbnail shots Amazon uses to show off your book.

You have a lot of flexibility when it comes to creating a title, but there are a few nuggets of wisdom to keep in mind. If you have a nonfiction book and want to do well in search engine results, at least consider using a primary keyword in the title and/or subtitle. This can make a marked difference in how well your book gets indexed and ranked in Google, and how well it shows up in Amazon's search results also. This may be one of the most important pieces of writing you do for your book!

Second, don't forget all the harping I'm doing in this book about market intent. You want to create a title that will not only grab your prospect's attention, but that also sends the message that this book IS what they are looking for. Titles are important. Don't skimp on this aspect.

CREATESPACE

We are primarily discussing Kindle in this chapter, but some of what we cover about uploading to Kindle in the next section will make more sense to you if you have a basic understanding of CreateSpace. CreateSpace is another arm of the Amazon publishing system where you can easily create print-on-demand (POD) books. The setup is similar to Kindle, and it is connected to the same Amazon account. There are many reasons you might want a physical copy of your book, such as events, signings, seminars, and more. (And perhaps for Mom, who just can't seem to get used to this online thing!)

Royalty arrangements are close to Kindle's, but Amazon takes a bigger piece of the pie, as there are hard costs associated with printing physical copies of your book. You can check out CreateSpace here: www.createspace.com.

UPLOADING YOUR BOOK TO KINDLE

Once your manuscript is ready for publication, the hardest part is done! Now it's time to actually get the book live on Kindle. Fortunately, this is not difficult. Kindle Direct Publishing (KDP) has you complete 11 simple steps, and within 24 hours, your book will be live.

Prior to starting this process, you need to have a working Amazon Kindle account. You can sign up at https://kdp.amazon.com/help?topicId=A1OYOT0ESBAU69.

Once your account is live, you can upload your book. The 11 steps you'll need to complete are:

1. *Enter your book details.* This is where you enter your book's title, description, and a few other details. Pay particular attention to the description, as this is basically the Kindle version of a sales letter.

2. *Verify your publishing rights*. This is where you declare that you have the right to publish this book.

3. *Target your book to customers*. Choose your book's categories—very important. You can only select two, so you need to take the time to go through a rather exhaustive list they've provided and choose the two that best represent your book. You can also enter up to seven keywords for search. Make sure you've identified the best seven keywords you can, as this will have a large effect on which segments of the Amazon audience see your listing.

4. *Select your book release option*. Choose whether you want to publish now or set up for pre-order.

5. *Upload or create a book cover*. Here you can either upload or create a book cover.

6. *Upload your book file*. Digitally upload your book manuscript.

7. *Preview your book*. Once uploaded, you can review how it will look before you actually publish.

8. *Verify your publishing territories*. This is where you choose which countries you'd like to sell your book in.

9. *Set your pricing and royalty*. You have the freedom to sell your book at whatever price you want, but understand that Amazon has a predefined royalty structure in place:
   - Books priced below $2.99 pay out 35 percent to the author.
   - Books priced between $2.99 and $9.99 pay out 70 percent.
   - Books priced above $9.99 pay out 35 percent.
   - It's popular opinion that the sweet spot for Kindle books seems to be at $2.99.

10. *Kindle MatchBook*. If you create and sell print versions of your book in CreateSpace, the Kindle MatchBook program allows you to offer those customers the Kindle digital version of that book for free. (Note: Not just any print version of your book qualifies for this program. It has to be published through CreateSpace.)

11. *Kindle book lending*. This allows users who have purchased your book to lend it to friends for up to 14 days.

Once you've completed these steps, your book will go into the review hopper, where assuming there are no issues or glitches, you will get an email from Kindle when it goes live for sale, usually in less than a day.

MARKETING YOUR BOOK LAUNCH

Remember, it doesn't matter if you wrote the greatest book of all time if no one ever finds it or buys it. This is where you shape the success or failure of your book. Simply getting it up on Kindle is only the foundation of the process; now you have to actively market your book if you hope to crack Amazon Best Seller status. Let's go over several of the essential ways in which you can help your book get noticed.

Amazon allows you to publish a page on Amazon Author Central (https://authorcentral.amazon.com/) to showcase yourself and your work. Take full advantage of this!

Then you can focus on getting great reviews. This will be the linchpin that determines whether your book is successful. Everyone selling on Amazon pays close attention to the reviews their products get because your prospects actually read them, and those reviews heavily influence whether they purchase from you or from one of your competitors. Obviously, the more great reviews (preferably 5 stars) you have, the better. Anyone can leave a review on a product whether or not they have purchased it. This is a value-add for the consumers because they can get additional feedback and information that will help them choose the right products.

While this is universally great for the consumer, it is a mixed bag for the sellers. Just as you can get the benefits of raving fans of the products you're selling posting reviews on your listings, you can also reap the pain of people posting negative "buyer beware" reviews due to experiences they have had with the items. In addition, a "verified purchase" review, meaning the person reviewing the product actually bought it, carries more weight. Simply encourage your readers to review your book. The worst that can happen is they don't do it. The best that can happen is you quickly build up a collection of positive verified purchase reviews.

WARNING: Do not, under any circumstances, generate fake reviews. Ethics aside, Amazon is actively seeking out and punishing people who do this to keep their marketplace clean.

KDP Select

This program allows you to earn royalties from the people who read your book by lending or otherwise accessing your book, as in Kindle Unlimited. Easy money! One downside is that you can't have your book for sale on any other digital platform, such as Nook or iTunes, and take advantage of this program.

Amazon Free Promotion Days

One cool feature of publishing through KDP Select is that when you first publish your book, you can offer it for free to consumers for up to five days. This can be helpful in building a buzz around your book and generating some initial reviews. However, if you have a version of your book also formatted for CreateSpace (whether or not you actually intend to sell a print version), you also have this same option every 90 days.

Amazon segments its best seller lists by Top 100 Paid and Top 100 Free. During any period during which your book is being offered for free, it will have a sales rank in the free list instead of the paid list. Then once the promotion period is over, its ranking falls back under the paid Best Sellers Ranking criteria. This is especially advantageous if you are in a highly competitive category where it takes time to rise to the top of the paid ranks. The exposure you gain from having the extra free promo period every 90 days could be invaluable.

Kindle eBook Announcement Sites

There are a large number of sites dedicated to announcing your ebook to the world. Here is a short list of just five to get you started:

- Pixel of Ink (www.pixelofink.com)
- Ereader News Today (http://ereadernewstoday.com)
- KBoards (www.kboards.com)

- Goodreads (www.goodreads.com)
- Amazon's Top Customer Reviewers (www.amazon.com/review/top-reviewers)

Facebook and LinkedIn Groups

There are countless pages dedicated to ebooks and Kindle titles in particular on both of these websites. Make a Facebook business page for your book, and explore the vast reach these two sites can provide.

Email Your List

If you already have an email list, you'll want to announce your book to them. This is also a terrific way to get some good reviews from people who may already be inclined to like you.

Press Releases

You can write and publish a press release announcing your new book. There are sites where you can do this for free, but you may want to opt for a paid version, as these get far wider distribution and usually include submitting it to Google News.

YouTube Videos

Making a short promo video about your book and submitting it to YouTube is a great way to get noticed on the world's second-largest search engine!

Wattpad

Another terrific way to get people to notice your book is by sharing some of it on a site called Wattpad (www.wattpad.com). This site is a marvel, where you can get loads of reads on your work, sometimes numbering in the tens and hundreds of thousands—and even millions—very quickly. It's an awesome way to get feedback buzz and create an audience.

Covers to Instagram and Pinterest

Make sure to upload your book covers to appropriate spots on these image-sharing sites. You can realize a large number of visits this way.

Announce on Social Media Channels

Assuming you have social media sites set up and flourishing (and if you don't, start now!), you should announce your book to your followers when it is almost ready for publication (thus creating some anticipation) and when it goes live, of course posting a link to help them get to the sales listing. Be sure to implore your audience to kindly review your book. These are, after all, your fans! Unless you have a huge following on another site, these three will suffice to start:

- Facebook (www.facebook.com)
- Twitter (https://twitter.com)
- LinkedIn (www.linkedin.com)

These marketing tasks will help you make more sales, plain and simple. These aren't the only promotional tactics you can use, but it is a solid list of options. Don't make the mistake many Kindle authors do in thinking the work is done when the book is listed for sale. That's actually only the beginning!

RINSE AND REPEAT!

The foregoing is a brief summary of what's involved with publishing on Kindle. Many authors have made this into a significant income stream they might have missed by opting to go the traditional publishing route. Remember, you are the boss here: No one can tell you no!

Two of the primary keys to making money in this Profit Path are to create more than one title and to effectively promote those titles. Do this, and you'll soon find the sales racking up and the income streaming in!

eCOMMERCE PROFIT PATHS

eCommerce Profit Paths are ideal for people who resonate with the idea of creating their own business centered on selling physical products online. These paths are great whether you already have a product but aren't sure how to go about selling it online or are just getting started and do not yet have a product.

As with any Profit Path, there are pros and cons. In ecommerce, the top-level pros include:

- No physical storefront
- Familiar business model
- Most of the heavy lifting is on the front end

The ecommerce top-level cons include:

- High competition
- Need for inventory
- Lack of instant gratification

MEET THE EXPERT
EZRA FIRESTONE

Ezra Firestone is a marketer who believes in serving the world unselfishly. I consider him the leading expert at ecommerce. The information and courses he offers at his website (http://smartmarketer.com) are second to none.

I'll discuss more detailed pros and cons later in this chapter.

eCOMMERCE EXPLAINED

eCommerce has a fairly broad definition. Dictionary.com defines it like this: "Business that is transacted by transferring data electronically, especially over the internet." By those terms, most businesses online could be considered ecommerce, including the digital and information product-based businesses we covered in the previous chapters. While technically most, if not all, the Profit Paths I'm covering can be considered ecommerce, for the purpose of this book, I'm defining it as selling physical products online.

How This Differs from Affiliate Marketing

In Chapter 10, we briefly talked about how you can sell other people's physical products as an affiliate. In this chapter, we are also going to talk about selling other people's physical products, so I'd like to clarify how ecommerce is different from affiliate marketing. In simplified terms, your primary objective in an affiliate marketing model is to drive targeted prospects to landing pages and websites with offers you have signed up for as an affiliate. When the prospects you sent there make a purchase, you get paid a commission. In essence, you are part of the marketing arm for that merchant and are being paid for your valuable service.

With these ecommerce Profit Paths, you will be selling physical products directly, even if the products you are selling are not yours. You won't be driving customers to someone else's landing page or website. You'll be selling products from a platform of your choice. Whether you're actually the one who fulfills the order and ships it to your customers depends on which model you choose. Regardless of the platform you choose to sell from or your fulfillment arrangement, you are selling the items directly to the consumer and reaping the profits. Those buyers are your customers.

Two Giants

There are a lot of different platforms you can use to run an ecommerce business. In this chapter, I am going to lump them into two categories: Amazon and everything else. First we will explore the basics of ecommerce and various platforms you can sell from independently. Then we will specifically address using Amazon as your primary sales vehicle.

I promised we'd delve into more pros and cons, and here they are. Weigh these carefully before you jump into the ecommerce fray. First, the pros:

- *No need for a physical store.* Sometimes for real-world retailers, needing a physical location is the biggest hurdle.
- *Flexible hours.* You can make sales 24/7. The internet never sleeps.
- *Low overhead.* Because many of the processes in an ecommerce business are automated, it requires less staff to run your business than a traditional retail store.
- *Overcome geographical limitations.* Business owners can sell on a global level with relative ease, when before something like that would be an overwhelming feat.
- *Familiar shopping model.* Unless you're living under a rock, everyone knows what online shopping is. You don't have to educate your audience that you exist.

Next, keep the cons in mind. They include:

- *Inventory.* eCommerce businesses require inventory. If you're drop-shipping, this may not fall on your shoulders, but products need to be stored somewhere.
- *Price matching.* Brick-and-mortar stores like Fry's have price-matching programs that will give their shoppers the online price. This allows the buyer to have their item as soon as possible.
- *Lack of instant gratification.* Consumers don't receive your product until it arrives at their door days later. This sometimes makes them feel empty-handed for some time after making an online purchase.
- *Chargebacks.* Credit cards can be quite liberal when it comes to approving chargebacks for consumers. In my experience, the credit card companies favor the consumer FAR more than the sellers.
- *Good, old-fashioned competition.* eCommerce is a popular business model. (That's why I'm writing about it!) So you will find you have a LOT of competition.

Think on these, choose the direction of your eCommerce Profit Path, and start selling!

WHY CHOOSE eCOMMERCE AS A PROFIT PATH?

Have you ever bought anything online? Once upon a time that was a legitimate question that produced mixed responses. Now, in most of society, that is like asking if someone has ever bought anything from a grocery store. The majority of consumers who shop also shop online. I could dig up current statistics about exactly how many people shop online and how the growth has been increasing each year, etc. However, I feel that's a waste of both of our time because if you didn't recognize the opportunity online shopping presents, you likely would not be reading this book.

EZRA'S BIG SIX

Ezra has six reasons he prefers ecommerce as a Profit Path, which he refers to as the Big Six. To wit:

1. *There is a higher barrier to entry.* Because of this, many people choosing a business model get intimidated and choose other models with lower barriers to entry.

2. *There is more work upfront.* He really likes that the lion's share of the work of getting a proper foundation laid takes place upfront. After that, the main focus tends to be on driving traffic, optimizing for conversions, and providing an excellent customer experience.

3. *A high percentage of your competitors are "mom and pop" businesses.* There are not a ton of sophisticated players in the markets doing less than $1 million in revenue. This makes it much easier to dominate.

4. *Selling physical products online does not require a lot of persuasion techniques.* If people go to a website to buy a dog bowl, it doesn't take a lot of psychology to close the sale.

5. *You enjoy a higher-than-average dollar-per-visitor value.*

6. *Given the fact that people come to your website to buy a specific item and you don't have to do a lot to persuade them to buy it, the conversion rates, on average, are high with ecommerce.*

When the average person thinks about having a business online, most of the time what they picture probably falls into the eCommerce Profit Paths. They think of online stores and platforms where they can shop and buy something they are looking for. Because shopping online is now such a commonly understood concept, it can be wildly profitable. It has a lot of moving parts and there can be a lot to manage, but at least you don't have to start out educating the public that shopping online is even an option in the first place. You will not be a pioneer; instead you are walking into a lucrative and established model.

In this section we will focus on the foundation of ecommerce and how to get set up as an independent website and online store. Then, after learning the basics, we will apply that knowledge to exploring the option of selling your products on the ecommerce king known as Amazon.

SOLO WEBSITE VS. MULTIVENDOR STOREFRONT

There are some great authority multivendor storefronts you can use as opposed to going the solo ecommerce route. As I mentioned, I've created a Profit Path that is exclusively selling on Amazon. So you might ask why you would ever create your own ecommerce store when you can instead sell from one of the online giants like Amazon, Etsy, and eBay, which already have substantial credibility and millions of shoppers. You'll learn in this chapter and the next that both the solo and the multivendor storefront routes are viable options, and both come with their own sets of benefits and pain points.

Benefits of Being a Stand-Alone eCommerce Store

It is awesome when your products are featured in an active, thriving marketplace like Amazon or eBay. However, there are most definitely some benefits to being a stand-alone ecommerce store. Here are a few that are commonly appreciated:

1. *You maintain full control.* When you are solo, you maintain full control of your business. You can sell what you want to sell and how you want to sell it. You don't have additional compliance

regulations or restrictions beyond the standard ones any online store would have to be aware of.

2. *You keep your customers.* Your customers are YOURS. You get every bit of data they are willing to give you, including their name, email address, phone number, address, and permission to contact them. No one else gets to have your clients or tell you how you can and cannot communicate with them or whether you can sell more items to them.

3. *More profit.* You are not sharing the profit from your sales with any other organizations like you will on platforms like Amazon, Etsy, and eBay.

4. *Brand clarity.* When you're on a site like Amazon, someone may purchase from you because you sell an item they were searching for. But the impression that sticks with them is that they bought the item on Amazon. When someone buys from your own ecommerce site, the only association they can attach to the item is your brand, because there aren't any other vendors or brands selling on your website.

Whether your ecommerce site is an extension of a business you already have or an independent Profit Path, understanding your options will help you pick the best route for you, your business, and your unique situation. The biggest benefit by far of the solo route is your ability to maintain maximum control of your business, the direction it goes, and the factors that impact your success.

TYPES OF eCOMMERCE

There are several types of ecommerce business models to choose from. Since this book focuses on Profit Path models that can easily get up and running quickly, we are going to explore only three of the many options out there: drop-shipping, wholesaling and warehousing, and white labeling and manufacturing.

It is not by accident that I gave them in that order. In my opinion, those options are listed in order of complexity. Each is a legitimate, solid choice. However, if people getting started in ecommerce for the first time are looking to start with the easiest model and progress from there, they would start with drop-shipping. That said, Jason Katzenback and Matt Clark have many success stories from students using their popular course "Amazing Selling Machine" to learn the ins and outs of selling on Amazon through white labeling and manufacturing techniques. So just because I'm telling you drop-shipping is the easiest way to get up and running quickly doesn't mean you have to start there.

Drop-Shipping

Drop-shipping is when you sell items on your website that are manufactured, fulfilled, and shipped to your customers by someone else. Generally these relationships are established between you and a manufacturer or a wholesaler who has a warehouse full of the items you would like to sell. Once the proper agreements are in place, the manufacturer or wholesaler will send you images of the products you wish to sell along with pricing. You will then place those items for sale in your ecommerce store. Your job is to sell the items, and the manufacturer or wholesaler will fulfill the orders and ship them to your customers.

Here is a quick drop-shipping example. My family and I run a nonprofit reptile rescue out of our home. Because I have a passion for bearded dragons, I happen to know that people who own beardies are so crazy about them that they put women who carry little dogs around in their purses to shame. Bearded dragon owners go nuts for items for their health care and habitats and even frequently buy costumes and clothing for their animals. So for the sake of this example, let's pretend I opened an ecommerce store that sells items for bearded dragon lovers using the drop-shipping model.

If my supplier can sell me a 40-gallon breeder tank (a common enclosure for bearded dragons) for $50, I would list it on my website for $100. Then I would market my product through my awesome online store. Once a customer placed an order for one of these tanks, I would turn around and pay my supplier $50 of the $100 I collected and supply them with the order and shipping information. They would then ship that tank to my customer as if it came straight from my ecommerce business.

Some of the benefits people love most about the drop-shipping model is that there is very little upfront investment to be made. You don't buy any of the products until one is ordered from you and paid for. Once your foundation is set up with the platform you're selling from, and your relationship with your drop-shipping partner is in place, your primary focus is driving targeted buyers to your store and providing an amazing customer experience. Once the sale is made, that is when you pull money out of your pocket to pay for the item sold. This is a low-risk, high-reward model. You don't have to stock any inventory or deal with the headache of order fulfillment.

Some of the drawbacks are that you have no control over the shipping and fulfillment, and sometimes your suppliers let you down. If a supplier is running behind or forgets to provide you with a tracking number, that increases your customer service responsibilities. Also, since you're not keeping any of the inventory, you don't always know if an item is running low. You could end up unknowingly selling something that is out of stock. Then you have to deal with the customer service and reputation ramifications.

The good news is that if you don't feel the supplier you have chosen is living up to your standards, it is pretty easy to get out of a drop-shipping contract. Your assets are entirely digital. It's much easier to transition an ecommerce business that uses drop-shipping as its fulfillment model than it is if you have a warehouse full of items that have already been manufactured for you.

Wholesaling and Warehousing

This model is when you buy products in bulk and store them in a warehouse somewhere. Usually people who prefer this model are selling product in volume. People most commonly use this in a B2B market as opposed to a B2C model. Using my previous example of an ecommerce store selling bearded dragon supplies, in this case I would be the wholesaler who sold the tank to a B2C business owner for $50, and they would sell it individually on their website for $100. Whether or not I would also fulfill the order would depend on the type of business I'm in.

With this model, you get better pricing because you're buying in bulk instead of making one-off purchases, as in a drop-shipping business. If you're buying in bulk and selling the items individually on your website to consumers, you also have better margins than you do with drop-shipping.

However, if you're like most people using this model, you are selling in bulk to businesses who are selling to consumers, which has lower margins. In most wholesale businesses, you need to create enough sales volume to make up for the smaller margins. This model also requires high upfront investments for purchasing and housing the product.

(Ezra makes a really great point about scaling. If you start out using the drop-shipping model to sell to consumers and ramp up your business to the point where you're selling several hundred items per month, you can transition into the warehousing model and increase the margins on your already awesome sales volume.)

White Labeling and Manufacturing

Manufacturing is when you are actually paying to have the items created for you. In white labeling, you aren't manufacturing the product, but your licensing contract allows you to put your name or brand on it as if you are the manufacturer. So with this scenario you are either manufacturing products overseas or importing them from overseas and putting your brand on them. You are the top of the product chain at this point.

When you are importing or manufacturing overseas, your margins are much higher. You get to create the product for a very low price and then sell it online for a much higher price. You also control all the shipping and fulfillment yourself; while it's more work, it has a lot of benefits too. You get to control the entire cycle and always know what's going on with the product. Also, at this point, you can take advantage of wholesalers and drop-shippers to retail your products for you.

This model is not for the commitment-phobe. There is no easy way to end a manufacturing contract. You had the products made, you've imported them into your country, and you have them sitting in a warehouse somewhere. You also have to develop a process to monitor and maintain quality control. This is definitely an advanced model. There is almost always a large cash investment required upfront, so you need to have a financial plan.

eCOMMERCE PLATFORMS

Regardless of which ecommerce business model you choose to go with, you have to create an online storefront, and you have some options to choose from. Since we're saving multivendor storefronts for Chapter 13, that leaves you with three options for independent sites I feel comfortable recommending to you:

- Custom website
- Hosted solutions
- Self-hosted solutions

Which platform is right for you really depends on your situation, knowledge, and finances.

Custom Website

I actually hesitated to put this option in here because while you can build your own ecommerce website from the ground up, I honestly do not know why anyone would. Even if you have the capital, resources, and intelligence to do it, I would be hard-pressed to believe that what you would create would be better than one of the many solutions already out there. That said, I would feel remiss if I didn't at least state that you can in fact build your own site and do not have to go with one of the other solutions I am going to write about.

Hosted Solutions

These are often referred to as "hosting for ecommerce," but it's not actually just a hosting service. Ecommerce hosted solutions are actually considered software as a service (SaaS) because they are literally designed to be ecommerce stores in a box. I hesitate to say that a hosted solution has everything you need as a store owner, but if it doesn't, it will come pretty close.

I like to advise people starting out to go with a hosted solution simply because it makes the process of going from zero to profitability much quicker. Unless you're already an ecommerce expert, it can take quite a while before you know enough to optimize your store for the highest results. By going with a hosted solution, a lot of the heavy lifting is done for you.

Here are my top reasons for choosing a hosted solution:

1. *Better security.* Hosted solutions would go out of business quickly if they weren't able to protect the stores using their platforms. Therefore they tend to have decent security built in.

2. *Backup systems.* Backup and data recovery are usually included as part of what you get with a hosted solution.

3. *Hands-off maintenance and upgrades.* When you go with a hosted solution, maintaining the technology behind your storefront is not your responsibility. If they want to remain competitive, they will strive to always be upgrading with features that benefit you.

4. *Quick and easy installation.* Hosted solutions are meant to have a "business in a box" feel to them. So installation is generally a nonissue.

5. *Support.* Hosted solutions will come with support; most of the time you get unlimited access.

You're entering this game at the right time. When the first generation of hosted and nonhosted solutions first came to market, they made a lot of mistakes. The good news is that the newest wave of them really learned from those mistakes, and I feel I can put my name behind recommending several of them. Remember, all platforms have their own pros and cons, so it's important you do your due diligence and find the solution that works for you. Here are a few I like:

First up is *Bigcommerce* (www.bigcommerce.com). Bigcommerce is the preferred platform choice of Ezra Firestone, one of the leading experts in ecommerce strategy. That is a pretty heavy endorsement all by itself. But here are a few more benefits that make this platform an excellent choice:

- Affordable pricing starts at $29.95 for almost every feature and caps out at only $79.95 per month for unlimited everything

- Google Trusted Stores certification assistance
- Assisted setup to increase sales
- Easy to integrate with eBay, Google Shopping, and more
- Excellent customer service
- Real-time quotes, gift cards, and 24/7 phone/email/chat support are included in the base plan
- Popular with small to medium web stores
- Unlimited products, storage, and bandwidth

Next is *Shopify* (www.shopify.com). It's got some great things going for it, including:

- Affordable plans start at $14 per month
- Popular with small web stores
- Innovative app store to expand your default web store
- Includes unlimited products and bandwidth
- Easy to integrate with shipping carriers, fulfillment centers, and drop-shipping companies
- Manage store and payments via a mobile app
- Point-of-sale option to take payments in person
- Assistance in setting up your store

Finally, consider *Volusion* (www.volusion.com), another wonderful option. Its features include:

- Affordable plans start at $15 per month with enough features to legitimately test the waters
- Popular among all business sizes
- Offers abandoned cart recovery services at the cheapest price point
- Built-in loyalty program
- Built-in deal of the day option
- eBay and Amazon integration

Self-Hosted Solutions

Self-hosted solutions are a good option for those of you who are tech-savvy enough to build your own website but still want the convenience of having the built-in core features ecommerce businesses care about. Self-hosted solutions trade convenience for full control and customization capabilities. They do not fall in the SaaS category. Think of it more like a customized shopping cart with some special features that cater to ecommerce.

Self-hosted solutions focus on the basic functionality that matters to ecommerce sites. Some of this functionality includes:

- Catalog features
- Shopping cart
- Checkout flow

They may not have all the bells and whistles of a fully hosted solution, but the basics are covered, and those of you who are tech-savvy might enjoy the ability to customize your store on your own. There isn't really a wrong answer; it's all about preference and what's right for your specific situation.

If having the ability to fully customize the look and feel of your web store is important to you and you really want to build your own site, I would suggest a self-hosted solution. That way you have some basic functionality to work with and yet can still make the changes that are most important to you.

Here are a couple of self-hosted solutions I would suggest looking into further:

WooCommerce (www.woothemes.com/woocommerce)

- Free to download
- Runs on WordPress
- Light application that does not tax your server
- Basic functionality is above average with hundreds of plugins to enhance it
- Makes use of most free and paid WP plugins
- Easy to set up and customize
- If you're already familiar with WordPress, it will feel easy to navigate
- Huge library of gorgeous themes available for affordable prices

Magento (http://magento.com)

- Free download of community edition
- Boasts 11 percent of the market uses it
- Most integration options in the industry
- Hundreds of high-quality templates to choose from
- No need to upgrade to a better solution in the future
- Can easily set up different storefronts with one shared product base
- Feature heavy

Magento has the most bells and whistles in the self-hosted solutions world, but it is also a beast on your server. Once you're large enough, it's commonly suggested you host your back end on a separate server.

FURTHER CONCERNS

Remember, even with hosted solutions or self-hosted solutions, you will still have some important aspects you will need to take care of before your web store will be complete.

Payment Solution

You will still need to set up a way to take money. This can be as simple as using PayPal, or you can apply for your own merchant account. While all the solutions mentioned above come with shopping carts, they don't come with a payment processing solution. Honestly, you should keep the money collection in your hands anyway.

Analytics

The platforms likely have integration options to make this easy, but if you want to track your results and be able to split test for conversions (and if you don't, then don't choose this Profit Path), you will need to hook your ecommerce site up to analytics.

Images and Design

Depending on what you want to do, you may still have need of some design work to make your web store complete. It's possible you may be able to get by without this, but it's something to keep in mind.

Content

Every website needs content. Whether you write it yourself or hire a ghostwriter, one way or the other you need to factor this into your process.

EVERYTHING YOU NEED TO KNOW IS ON THE INTERNET

You really don't have to reinvent the wheel when you are trying to figure out which market you would like to play in. Go to the popular websites like Amazon and eBay, and look at the different categories and subcategories listed. Type your target keywords into Google, and look at the top-ranking sites. How do they categorize their products and websites? Sites like Amazon and eBay aren't casually organized—there is a purpose behind the way they are structured. This also shows you how the prospects in this market are used to finding the products they are looking for.

When doing market research for a new ecommerce business, there are a couple of tools that will help you. First is WatchCount. com (http://www.watchcount.com). This is a great tool! You can go there and type in your keywords and see the most-sold items on eBay. You can also search by categories to see the top-selling offers per category. I love this tool because it not only tells you the amount of past sales, but also how many people are watching that auction right that moment.

Another great place to look is Internet Retailer (www.internetretailer. com). This is a FABULOUS resource for anyone in the ecommerce space. They also put out two books called *The Top 500 Guide* and *The Second 500 Guide*. They rank the top 500 ecommerce businesses and show you the main reasons they are at the top of their industry.

CHOOSING A PROFITABLE MARKET

There is a lot of information out there about how to choose a profitable market. The simplest explanation I have found from a resource I trust is the "Market Criteria Checklist" by Ezra Firestone in Figure 12.1. (You can download it from his website, www.smartmarketer.com.) He has created a list of 15 criteria and assigned a point value to them. Not

MARKET CRITERIA CHECKLIST

POINTS	CRITERIA: FOR EACH QUESTION ANSWERED "YES", ADD THE SPECIFIED POINTS TO THE LEFT COLUMN.
	A. AVERAGE ORDER VALUE $75-$200? (+5 PTS)
	B. GROSS MARGIN 20% OR MORE? (+5 PTS)
	C. FRAGMENTED MARKET? (+2 PTS)
	D. LENDS ITSELF TO RETURN CUSTOMERS? (+3 PTS)
	E. LENDS ITSELF TO MULTIPLE ITEM ORDERS? (+1 PT)
	F. CAN YOU ADD VALUE TO THE MARKET? (+5 PTS)
	G. PRODUCTS DIFFICULT TO BUY LOCALLY? (+4 PTS)
	H. SEASONAL BUSINESS? (+3 PTS)
	I. GOOGLE TRENDS US DOMINATED? (+4 PTS)
	J. NON-COMMODITIZED PRODUCTS? (+5 PTS)
	K. AT LEAST 70 SKU's? (+3 PTS)
	L. IS THERE COMPETITION? (+4 PTS)
	M. AVERAGE PRODUCT WEIGHT UNDER 10 LBS? (+1 PT)
	N. TOP 3 KEYWORDS HAVE COMBINED 15K EXACT MATCH SEARCHES (+3 PTS)
	O. TARGET MARKET IS WOMEN? (+2 PTS)
	← TOTAL POINTS FOR ALL QUESTIONS ANSWERED YES

ANSWER KEY	POOR	FAIR	GOOD	EXCELLENT
	0–20 POINTS	20–30 POINTS	30–40 POINTS	40–50 POINTS

FIGURE 12.1—**Market Criteria Checklist**

every question is assigned equal points because not every criterion is created equal. At the end, you add up the points, and the score gives you a reasonable idea whether you should move forward in that market.

Ezra has a transcript on his website from a video where he walks you through his thought process around each of the 15 criteria. I've excerpted parts of it with his permission and am reprinting them here.

THE MARKETING CRITERIA CHECKLIST
BY EZRA FIRESTONE

Keep these tips in mind when you are thinking about your ecommerce business in relation to profit margin, risk, and income potential:

1. *Average order value $75 to $200?* You want your average order value to be between $75 and $200. This is different from the average profit per order. You don't really know yet what your margins or profit per order are going to be, but you can be pretty sure if the average order value is $75 to $200, you are not going to be making less than $20 in profit on each order. As a general rule of thumb, you never want to earn less than $20 in profit per order because you can't make enough money to build a successful business on less than that.

2. *Gross margin 20 percent or more?* If your order is $100, you want to make at least $20 in profit. You don't always know the margins upfront on products, but if you are considering two niches and they both have the same average order value, you should go with the one that has the higher profit margins.

3. *Fragmented market?* A quick and easy way to evaluate this is to type the top 15 or 20 content page keywords into Google. If it's always the same ten companies that populate the first page of Google, it is not a fragmented market and instead has a handful of entities dominating the market share.

    You'll notice I only gave this one two points because competition is not a huge deal. You can break in no matter how competitive the market is. But it is something you want to look at. And a fragmented market is better because it's easier to break in. So check and see if you've got a fragmented market.

4. *Lends itself to return customers?* Do you have the opportunity to resell to your past customers, or is it one and done? An electric fireplace is kind of a one-and-done sale.

It's a high-dollar sale, so it's not super bad. But people aren't going to come back and buy another electric fireplace from you. With gift baskets, on the other hand, you have the opportunity to sell to those people every single holiday.

5. *Lends itself to multiple-item orders?* This one is pretty self-explanatory. Multiple-item orders are fantastic. Let's think about costumes. You take a niche like dance costumes. Most of the time, when people are purchasing dance costumes, they are buying them for an entire dance team. They purchase something like 15 at a time. It's a huge benefit when people order more than one item at a time. Again, if your product line has a bunch of accessories, this is fantastic because you'll sell the main product and you'll sell a bunch of accessories as well.

6. *Can you add value to the market?* This one is huge. This is where you really stand out. You are going to want to choose a product line you can add value to—something you are willing to learn and talk about. The days of ecommerce stores just being stores where there's no face, there's no person, there's no name behind it are going away in our hypersocial society. It's becoming more about connecting with your customers and creating a community. There are a lot of ways to add value to a marketplace. Educational content is a fantastic one. So are buyer's guides: stuff that solves the purchaser's problem.

7. *Products difficult to buy locally?* If you don't live in, say, New York City, can you buy it down the street? Fire pits are a good example. Walgreens, Costco, and Home Depot might have one or two fire pits, but they don't really have a large selection. The only place you can find a really good selection of fire pits is online.

8. *Seasonal business?* Are the products seasonal? Most markets are somewhat seasonal. I love seasonal product lines—toys, Halloween costumes, Valentine's gifts. I just love the craziness it brings out in people. They don't think twice about purchasing something when they are buying a gift for someone or when they need a costume for their kid.

9. *Google Trends U.S. dominated?* You can use Google Trends to find out all kinds of valuable information. Google Trends is a tool that analyzes how often certain keywords are searched for, who is searching for them, and when. It's great for highlighting trends in your market that could be beneficial for you to align your marketing strategy with. For instance, is your product seasonal? Are most people searching for your products in the United States? You can use Google Trends to find out. In the United States, I look for a score of 100 or so. If you are in Canada or the U.K., you are not going to have a search volume index of 100 because right now there is just more ecommerce happening in

the United States. So it's no big deal if you're not in the U.S., but definitely worth looking at.

10. *Noncommoditized products?* Never sell a commodity. Seriously, write that down. You don't want to be competing against Walgreens. In economics, a commodity is a generic term for any marketable item produced to satisfy wants or needs. For example, if I open an ecommerce store selling Toms shoes, people will shop purely on price. They will scour the internet for other people selling the exact same shoes for a lower price. That is a position you hope to never be in. That's a simplified explanation, but really, commoditization occurs when goods or services lose their differentiation across the supply base. Basically, what that means is that anyone can produce it. It doesn't cost a lot. It doesn't require a lot of capital to produce it efficiently. You just don't want to sell anything that's readily available that anyone can produce anywhere.

11. *At least 70 SKUs?* SKU (stock keeping unit) is a fancy term for a company's catalog system. Books all have SKU codes on them, for example. Does your ecommerce store have at least 70 different items? It should be pretty easy for you to figure out. If you are selling a product line that has accessories, you can clearly tell there are a lot of products in your product line. The reason I say at least 70 is because when you have a store that sells 50 items or fewer, it's pretty hard to grow that business up to six and seven figures. You just don't have enough products to sell unless you are building a brand. But when you are doing a drop-ship store, you want to have a larger fishnet. My best stores have between 500 and 1,000 SKUs. I think that's a really good number of products to shoot for.

12. *Is there competition?* Take your top five keywords and type them into Google. You should see a full page of ads for each one. You probably all know this: If there's no one buying ads on your keywords in the market you're evaluating, no one is making money on those keywords. So make sure there are people actually paying for advertising in your market.

13. *Average product weight under ten pounds?* If you have heavy products, it just makes things more complicated. Shipping hassles can be a big nightmare. I've dealt with this. It's not a deal breaker. As you see, I only gave this criterion one point. But if you can find lighter products, that's better for the most part.

14. *Top three keywords have combined 15K exact match searches?* Do your top three keywords have at least 15,000 exact match searches per month on the Google AdWords Keyword Planner (https://adwords.google.com/KeywordPlanner)? If you're new to this topic, exact match means when someone types in that exact phrase. Most

people freak out about keyword volume. They just go nuts on this subject. It's not a huge deal, to be honest. Most markets you'll find have a bigger long tail. You'll make more money from your long tail than just about anything else. Most markets have a huge long tail if you know where to look.

15. *Target market is women?* I really like to sell to women. They're just better buyers. They are more willing to engage and comment on the products and talk to you about them. It's not a huge deal because products geared toward men are great too. It's only worth two points on the checklist. But you'd be surprised what women are buying. They are buying the furniture for the house. They are buying the costumes for the kids. They are ordering gifts more often. A lot of markets are female-oriented if you think about it.

I'm giving you guys my personal market criteria checklist. I made this fancy PDF, but this is the same checklist I go through when I'm picking markets. A lot of these aren't deal breakers on their own. That's the point of the checklist: Overall you have to score in a good or excellent bracket. But if you are missing one, two, or three of these things it's not going to kill your market. I really want to stress that.

FINDING AND WORKING WITH SUPPLIERS

Perhaps the number-one obstacle for people thinking of getting into this type of business is the often bewildering world of finding reputable and trustworthy drop-shippers and wholesalers. There are networks like Alibaba and others that serve as middlemen here, but if you're looking to get the best deals you can and wring the maximum profit from a deal, you'll need to learn to find and work with them yourself.

There are a lot of ways to find these suppliers, but the easiest is to purchase a wholesale directory that contains current listings and information about wholesalers. This can save you loads of time in searching out prospective product suppliers. Here are four of the top wholesale directories:

- Worldwide Brands (www.worldwidebrands.com)
- SaleHoo (www.salehoo.com)
- Doba (www.doba.com)
- Wholesale Central (www.wholesalecentral.com; this one is free!)

Before approaching a supplier, make sure your business is set up to enable you to work with them. Each has different requirements, but for the most part you'll need a business license, incorporation or other business structure, EIN from the IRS, a business checking account, and a business credit card, which can be helpful to pay for your products (at least for your first smaller orders). Make sure these ducks are all in a row before approaching a supplier, to give your business an air of legitimacy.

CREATING THE PERFECT PRODUCT PAGE

Since you'll be the one creating your product pages, you need to have a clear understanding of what exactly goes into the perfect product page. Unlike a listing on Amazon, where it is all essentially laid out for you, now you have to do it. (Though it's a very good idea to study Amazon pages, as no one does it better as far as getting the sale. Some aspects of their situation and yours are wildly different, however.)

Here are seven crucial aspects to a product page you'll want to make sure you incorporate into yours:

1. *Get as many terms on the page as possible*. You want to have common concerns that many customers will have addressed right on the product page. For instance, this can mean having shipping, return, and FAQs there so they don't have to leave the page, where they may not return. This can be done in many clever ways, including question mark popups. You've probably encountered those before. It's when something on a website has a little question mark over it, and when you click on it or hover over it, it opens up a content box to give you information about the term or item in question.

2. *Use images to avoid duplicate content issues*. Many times your product information and specifications will be the same information you can find on other pages of your site. Solve this by making these sections images, which aren't read as text by the Googlebot, thus avoiding any duplicate content issues.

3. *No left navigation*. Many times this can distract the viewer from the action you are hoping they will make: to stay on the page

and eventually buy. Avoid adding anything to your page, such as left-hand navigation bars to the rest of your site, that might lead them elsewhere.

4. *Everything happens above the fold.* The "fold" is the part of the web page that appears on the browser screen before the user scrolls down. It's important to get as much content in this as you can, leading them to read on.

5. *Suggested products.* "You might also like . . ." One thing Amazon does particularly well is to cross-sell other products. You will want this farther down the page, and perhaps on the checkout page as well. (More on that later.)

6. *Product reviews.* Another staple of a great product page is as many great reviews as will fit. (That's an exaggeration: Use your best with a pop-up link to more if they want them, but keep them on the page!) This is often the social proof that will tip the sale in your favor, so be sure to actively solicit and use great reviews.

7. *Security trust badges.* Another social proof element. If you can legitimately display security and trust certifications, such as BBB and website trust seals, it adds to your site's trustworthiness and gives you a few more points in your favor when it comes to decision-making time. Don't discount this!

INCREASING CONVERSIONS ON YOUR eCOMMERCE SITE

Increasing the rate at which you convert a prospect to a sale is by far one of the easier ways to make a large addition to your bottom line. Conversions are becoming more and more a science and involve several elements of customer interaction. Here are a few simple ways to increase conversions on your ecommerce pages.

1. *Simplify the checkout process.* Make sure your checkout process is as simple as you can make it, requiring customers to jump through the fewest hoops possible. Requiring endless information (much of it needless) is a major cause of shopping cart abandonment, so be ruthless in your quest to make the customer checkout experience as easy and seamless as possible.

2. *Use lots of visual content.* Use as much visual content as you can, as this reduces confusion about what they are buying and increases buyer confidence.

3. *Display trust certifications and badges.* Having trusted social proof on your checkout page many times can help sway the sale in your favor.

4. *Offer several payment options.* Make sure you are offering more than one way to pay. Don't limit your sales. Even PayPal offers the ability to pay with several different methods.

5. *Include free shipping if possible.* If you can swing it at all, try to include free shipping. Shipping costs are the number-one reason for shopping cart abandonment. Two other eye-opening stats: 47 percent of all online orders now include free shipping, and 93 percent of online buyers are encouraged to buy more products if free shipping is included. Food for thought!

A NOTE ABOUT TRAFFIC

Once you choose your market and products and build your ecommerce site, the remainder of your tasks center on driving targeted buyers to your site, testing and tweaking for conversions, and providing an amazing customer experience. I didn't include specific traffic generation strategies in this section because they are so similar to what you will find in the other Profit Path chapters and in Chapter 15. One word of caution: Ecommerce sites are notorious for being too thin on content. This will get you in trouble with Google, so make sure, even though you are an ecommerce website, to still add decent content to your site.

TIP OF THE ICEBERG

While I've given you a TON of great information, there is so much more to be learned. You can find a lot of great, affordable training courses to learn more about how to set up and optimize your ecommerce site. Ezra has a ton of great information at his website, www.smartmarketer.com, and we also offer training material at www.MoonlightingontheInternet.com.

CHAPTER 13

SELLING ON MULTIVENDOR STOREFRONTS

Now that you have a basic understanding of ecommerce and how to build a foundation, I want to take some time to discuss multivendor storefronts. Essentially, these are platforms you can sell your products on, as opposed to running a solo ecommerce store. The most popular three at the time of this writing are:

- Amazon (www.amazon.com)
- Etsy (www.etsy.com)
- eBay (www.ebay.com)

I'm going to primarily focus on Amazon, as it is the world's largest ecommerce platform, but much of what you will learn here will be useful to marketing on other platforms as well.

AMAZON

Amazon is a beast! It's the world's largest ecommerce platform, projected to make $100 billion in sales in 2015. They have nearly 245

MEET THE EXPERTS
JASON KATZENBACK AND MATT CLARK

Jason Katzenback and Matt Clark are two of the greatest guys I have the pleasure of knowing. They also have the world's best training about winning on Amazon, called the Amazing Selling Machine. Their course is a bit more advanced than what I write about in this book, but it is the very best information about selling successfully on Amazon. Check them out at www.amazing.com.

million customers, many who have their credit cards on file who've made a purchase within the last year, and they are expanding into more and more categories all the time. Amazon strives to provide the greatest selection at the best price, with the easiest repeat shopping experience. Getting the products you're selling into such a successful platform with such a vast and ready-to-buy market is an online seller's dream.

However, like most things, selling on Amazon has its pros and cons. It's important that you understand what these are so you can make informed decisions. Here are a few of the benefits that vendors selling on Amazon like most:

◀ *Trust and credibility*. Have you heard of "trust jacking" or "authority jacking"? This refers to benefiting from the established authority or trust someone has created in the market by being associated with them. Selling on Amazon definitely lends you a level of trust and authority that doesn't come naturally when you first start out on the solo ecommerce path. You're interjecting yourself into the Amazon ecoverse, and the average consumer is not going to think of you as autonomous from them. Hence, authority jacking.

- *Huge customer base.* As I already mentioned, Amazon IS the world's largest ecommerce site, so your target market is likely shopping there regularly. When you're first starting out, have no prospects of your own, and are still learning the ropes of traffic generation and list building, Amazon's ready-made shoppers can give a jump start to your ecommerce business.

- *Amazon FBA.* With the addition of Fulfilled by Amazon (FBA) service, you can ship your merchandise to Amazon's warehouse, and they will fulfill your orders and handle any returns and customer service needs on your behalf—for a fee, of course. Amazon also makes it easy to ship internationally.

- *Internal recommends.* Amazon product pages have some built-in social proof that can refer more sales to you without any additional efforts on your part. Three of these types of services are: 1) recommended purchases; 2) related products; and 3) "customers who bought this also viewed." When your products attract frequent views and sales, they can show up on many pages that aren't related to you, but you can benefit from the sales all the same.

- *A perfect extra income stream.* One great thing about Amazon is that you do not have to make it your main Profit Path vehicle. Don't get me wrong: Using Amazon as your primary selling platform is an excellent choice. However, it can also be a great addition to a solo ecommerce website. This is also the type of opportunity that lends itself to being a perfect add-on for a traditional brick-and-mortar business. If you have your own products you sell offline, Amazon is a great platform for making additional sales online without a ton of extra effort.

Cons of Selling on Amazon

As with anything else, there are downsides to selling on Amazon. It's a behemoth of a site, and it can be easy to get lost in the retailer shuffle. Beware of these caveats when you go big with the big dog:

- *Fees.* The fee structure you pay has to do with which aspects of the Amazon platform you choose to take advantage of. Either way, Amazon is taking a cut of all your sales in exchange for allowing you to sell on their platform. One article I read recently claimed that after adding up the seller fees, warehousing fees, and other transactional costs, they pay 26 cents of every dollar to Amazon.

- *Commodity is a real issue.* When you're on Amazon, you are mostly a commodity. You are on a platform with lots of other vendors selling the same products you are, and at any point they can lower their prices and change the current market value of your products.

- *Branding.* In general, no one comes to Amazon looking for you. They come looking for something you happen to sell. As I mentioned in the pro section under authority jacking, most consumers won't remember you as anything other than Amazon. So there are next to no branding benefits by selling on Amazon. This also impacts customer loyalty, as they are loyal to "Amazon," which to them includes you.

- *You can't capture buyer information.* When you sell on Amazon, the buyers are Amazon's customers, not yours. Amazon does not give you your buyer's email address. So if you're wanting to build a long-term business, selling on Amazon makes that a bit more complicated. However, I do have some great strategies I'm going to share to help combat this.

SOME PRACTICAL INFORMATION

Since there are so many places you can go online to get quality information about selling successfully on Amazon, I'll just share a few practical tips for you to keep in mind.

Unless you don't plan on selling more than 40 items a month on Amazon, you'll want to sign up for a Seller Central account (https://sellercentral.amazon.com/gp/homepage.html). This costs $39.99 a month, plus you get a one-month free trial to get you going.

Once you have an account and have established a relationship with a supplier, you'll be ready to have your supplier ship the products directly to a Fulfillment by Amazon (FBA) warehouse. You never see or touch the product! One caveat, though: I would definitely order a couple and check out the quality of the product and packaging before committing money. Once your products are in stock at the warehouse, you can begin making sales.

Make sure the products you choose to sell have a profit built in for you. Many FBA sellers adopt the 3X rule when it comes to deciding on a product. This is a rough estimate, of course, and there are variables, but it can suffice to start.

What Does It Cost? The Money Details . . .

Selling on Amazon via the FBA program can be quite lucrative if you can learn to manage costs. Let's look at a few of the expenditures you'll be making so you can begin to plan how to make this work for you as a Profit Path.

- *Seller central account.* This will run you $39.99 a month after your free trial.
- *FBA fees.* There are several fees associated with product storage, shipping, handling, and package labeling. In general they amount to 15 percent of the purchase price, but Amazon has numerous calculators on the site to help you determine if a product you are thinking of selling is actually going to be profitable.
- *Cost of goods sold.* These are the hard costs you pay for buying the products from the supplier, white labeling, and shipping to FBA warehouses.
- *What's left is profit!* Most of the time, if you carefully watch costs, this turns out to be 40 to 50 percent of the retail price. If your numbers are significantly less than this, there could be a few

reasons. Either the cost of the item is too high, you're not selling it high enough, or some of the other ancillary costs are out of whack. This is where you really need to be on top of your game to maximize your profits.

MAKE YOUR PRODUCT LISTINGS STAND OUT!

Your product listing is essentially your sales page on Amazon. It's therefore vital that you give this a lot of attention. Take advantage of every available inch of space, and employ your best sales skills to make your products rise above the rest. We're going to cover the key components of your product listing now and give you a running start to beating the competition.

The Product Listing Title

There are several important elements in your title. At least your primary keyword should be present, and possibly a couple more if you can do this and still have it make sense. Having a key benefit woven into the title as a sales enticement can't hurt. You have roughly 80 characters that will show in your listing, so don't make the title overly long, but attempt to convey the essence of the product and what it can do for them.

Product Description

This is where you get to sell all the benefits (not features!) of your product and what it can do for the consumer. Sell the benefit the consumer is hoping to get from your product. They want to know how it can help them; save the features for the product information box.

Make sure you use bullet points, pointing out the many ways in which this product will make their lives easier and why they need to get theirs today. Use strong calls to action in your listing; in other words, tell them what to do. Buy it now, get yours today, and other similarly worded sales copy. Don't be afraid to sell. Far too many Amazon product descriptions are as dry as any desert, which contributes to their lack of success.

Make Your Product Images Pop!

Your product images are among your best-selling tools, and you simply have to do the best you can here. Getting professional-looking photos will make a huge difference in your sales. Here are several key points to remember that are vital to having excellent imagery in your product listings:

- Amazon images offer a hover enlarge feature, so your images need to be large—at least 1,001 pixels by 1,001 pixels.
- Image backgrounds must be white and well-lit, and the image must be a good representation of the product.
- Each product is allowed up to ten images: one main, one swatch, and eight other images.

GETTING PRODUCT REVIEWS

If you've ever shopped for anything on Amazon, you will no doubt have at least browsed the customer reviews for a product you were interested in purchasing. This is normal; in fact, 90 percent of consumers say that reading online reviews impacts their buying decisions. They assure consumers of the quality of your product, as well as push those who may have been on the fence into the checkout cart. They are the online equivalent of word-of-mouth advertising.

So if this is the case, as a seller we want to get great reviews, as many and as fast as we can. How to get your product to rise in the product pages on Amazon isn't really a mystery; it's tied intimately to sales, and sales are tied to reviews. Your seller reputation matters as well, but let's assume you're going to be an aboveboard seller.

You need to encourage reviews from your buyers, and you can use Amazon to do this by sending an email to them. Do this shortly after the product has arrived, and politely ask for an honest review, and whether they have any questions or concerns.

One way to generate some initial reviews is to ask for a review from your friends and family. Since Amazon usually only publishes reviews from verified purchasers, you'll need to supply them with a promo code that covers all or most of the purchase price. Consider this a cost of doing business. This tactic is a bit edgy, and Amazon may not like it, but it's done every day. Use this technique to get over the initial hump and to start generating sales.

Never stop soliciting reviews from your buyers, as this will only help you as time goes on. You've undoubtedly seen many products with literally thousands of good customer reviews, and in all likelihood, you've seen them on the first page of the product listings!

GETTING TRAFFIC TO YOUR AMAZON PRODUCT PAGES

It seems almost unseemly to talk about driving traffic to a site like Amazon, which gets more buyer traffic than any other site around, but it's a question that comes up all the time, so let's address it. There aren't any huge surprises here, just good solid marketing skills that can help you make money with your product listings.

- *Optimize your product pages.* The very first thing to do to increase traffic to your page is to optimize your product listing all you can. This means all the product listing detail we talked about previously, as well as making sure your product is in the proper categories and is using the best search keywords. Rising in the Amazon Best Seller rank is the best way to get more organic traffic, and a side benefit is that if you manage to do this, Google will likely rank you well in general search.
- *Get reviews.* Closely associated with optimization is your success in getting reviews. This is a key ingredient in Amazon's product ranking algorithm and delivers awesome social proof you can use as well.
- *Amazon-sponsored products.* This is Amazon's pay-per-click ad platform for your products. These show up on keyword searches for your product and really couldn't be easier. You simply pick your keywords, Amazon builds your ad using your own product listing, and you show up when Amazon searchers type in that keyword. Prices are competitive, meaning that whoever bids the most will show up most often. You only pay when someone clicks on your ad. It's great for long tail terms. Another great plus

is that you can choose a mobile option, which now accounts for roughly half of all web traffic.

- *Social media.* Talking up your listings on your social media channels can be a good no-cost method of spreading the word. If you have a popular Facebook page or Twitter following, this can bring you a lot of free traffic. Other good options here include Instagram and especially Pinterest.
- *Paid advertising.* Taking out ads on Facebook, Google, or other paid ad platforms can be effective if you know how to precisely target and manage your costs.

GREETING CALLS

If you're serious about building a sustainable ecommerce business but plan on starting out primarily selling your products on Amazon, then create a plan to build your business outside Amazon as well. There is a great company called ECustomerSolutions (www.ecustomersolutions.com) that is an expert at this. Here is one of the strategies they use that is worthy of duplication:

It is against Amazon's terms of service to call your Amazon customers and try to sell them something on a platform other than Amazon. However, it is completely fine to call your customers and thank them for purchasing from you. In addition to thanking them, it's completely acceptable to offer to send them a coupon to use on their next purchase at your store on Amazon. You just need to get their email while you're talking to them on the phone so you can send them the coupon.

Once you have their email address, you can now consider them a prospect on your list and begin providing value through email communication. Also, while you have them on the phone, be sure to encourage them to leave a review for your product. This strategy consistently:

- Increases sales
- Reduces negative reviews and increases positive reviews
- Helps establish brand awareness outside Amazon

As I mentioned, you can find a TON of information online about selling successfully online, but Jason Katzenback and Matt Clark in particular are experts whose strategies are creating success stories like wildfire right now. You can check them out at www.amazing.com or www.amazingsellingmachine.com.

While I'm not going to cover details about optimizing for eBay and Etsy, much of the information regarding Amazon does cross over to these multivendor storefronts as well. Below are some good-to-know pros and cons about each.

eBAY

One of the best things about eBay is that its tools make it really easy to quickly list and sell your products to millions of customers. It has more than 155 million active users around the world. So, like Amazon, eBay comes with a premade audience buying from a trusted source. Keep in mind this reach isn't just within the States. The auction site is one of the easiest ways to get your products in front of a large, global audience.

That said, like Amazon, you have to pay to play. If you're not paying attention, the fees can really add up. You will always pay at least 10 percent, up to a maximum fee of $250, with advanced listing upgrade fees adding to the costs. There can also be hidden costs in the form of nonpayment by customers. Bidders/buyers that don't pay are a huge problem on eBay. Not all auctions require a payment to make a purchase, so you need to factor this in. The site most definitely favors the buyers over the sellers. Should there be a dispute between you and a buyer, even if you are not in the wrong, eBay leans toward keeping the buyers happy over the sellers.

ETSY

Etsy is especially popular among vendors who make products in the arts and crafts niche. Just like any other multivendor platform, they have their pluses and minuses:

On the upside, Etsy has a targeted audience. You're probably beginning to see a trend here. Etsy, like Amazon and eBay, comes with a large pool of buyers. One thing to keep in mind about Etsy is that it tends to attract buyers looking to buy handmade items. It's ideal for sellers who are marketing their own handmade products.

It's also a low-tech startup. It is very easy to set up a storefront and payment options and generate shipping labels on Etsy without needing to know HTML or CSS. In addition, Etsy has cornered the market on community building. Etsy has a fun community amongst the sellers that is unique to them. It breeds a "family" feel, and the sellers tend to really enjoy supporting one another.

However, it's not all handmade satin rose petals at Etsy. There are, as with any site, downsides. The biggie at Etsy is the crush of fees. Big surprise, right? There are three layers of potential fees with Etsy:

◖ Listing fees
◖ Final sales fees
◖ PayPal processing fees

These add up quickly and can eat up your profits in no time.

Look and feel is another issue with Etsy. You have very little ability to personalize your pages and customer experience, which makes it difficult to stand out among the other sellers and storefronts. And low-category selection and high competition can create issues for your store. Because Etsy specializes in only a handful of categories, there is a ton of competition in each category.

All in all, though, Etsy—along with the other multivendor sites—can provide you with the diversification for your brand that will help you reach multiple audiences at a variety of price points. What are you waiting for? Get out there and start selling!

CHAPTER 14

HYBRID— THE AGENCY MODEL

This Profit Path is an advanced path. I included it in this book because a lot of people who start working for themselves online quickly want to scale into an agency. This chapter is different from any of the other Profit Path chapters because most of the information you would need to run an agency is already in this book. So instead, I wrote this section to ring in some of the realities of running an agency so that you only go down this path if it really is the best choice for you.

THE AGENCY MODEL EXPLAINED

So far we have covered some excellent service-oriented Profit Paths and product-oriented Profit Paths. The agency model will draw on a lot of the knowledge we have already covered throughout this book. I consider it a hybrid model because the services you are selling ARE your products. This is an advanced Profit Path and something you ascend to over time, as opposed to starting with right out of the gates.

To offer some clarity, let's talk through the differences between freelancing, consulting, and an agency. A freelancer is someone who sells services that they themselves provide. This is a solo gig. A consultant is primarily being paid for their brain, but also commonly bundles services they are reselling to their clients. The key word here is "reselling," meaning they are primarily not fulfilling the services themselves. Ideally, they have gathered outsourcing solutions to make fulfillment of the work simple and reliable. An agency, by contrast, is an establishment that gets paid for consulting and services. However, instead of outsourcing the work through reliable vendors, you build up an internal team and bring the fulfillment in-house.

Types of Agencies

There are no limits to the type of agency you can create. You can build a full-scale digital marketing agency like mine that provides most services a company needs for marketing their business online. You can also specialize in one area and have a graphic design agency or a social media agency. I'm not going to list all the different types of agencies; the point is to recognize that the agency model is available as an advanced Profit Path in many areas.

I am also not going to give you a list of pros and cons, as I did with the other Profit Paths. Deciding to scale up into an agency is a HUGE undertaking, and you will only know if it's right for you by experiencing the journey that leads you in that direction. A ton of the logistics I might give you about running an agency are spread throughout this book. I could write a book twice as long as this one just on how to start, maintain, and scale a digital marketing agency. Since this is an advanced path and not an entry-level option, I'm simply going to brain dump some of my thoughts and hope they will offer you some clarity and value.

DON'T START AN AGENCY

Seriously, you should write that down. Because of how I'm positioned in my market, every once in a while I get asked to be interviewed for a web show, podcast, or popular blog. One of the typical questions they ask is, "If you lost everything and had to start over with the knowledge you have now, what would you do?" My answer, although I'm not always comfortable enough to say it out loud, is "I DEFINITELY WOULD NOT START AN AGENCY."

You might be asking yourself why I'm even writing this section if I feel so strongly about this, so let me explain. The truth is that running an agency is hard work. Sincerely, it's really hard work. If it wasn't for my passion to supply moms and other individuals with legitimate work-from-home opportunities, I might have ditched this model a long time ago. Don't get me wrong: Having an agency can be a lucrative and rewarding Profit Path. It's just that services, especially on the scale of an agency, take way more work and have smaller margins. Your overhead is really high simply due to payroll.

Common Agency Pain Points

Before I get into all the wonderful aspects of owning and running an agency, I'm going to list out some of the primary pain points. Starting an agency is not something you should enter with your eyes closed.

Do You Love Business?

You need to ask yourself if you love the business of business. Many times people start an agency because they are passionate about a specific Profit Path. For instance, it was natural for me to start a business outsourcing moms as writers because I loved being a freelance writer myself. Guess how much writing I did once my business got off the ground? Next to none. There was no time. In addition, writing, which had always been a pleasurable hobby for me, became a chore. To give you a realistic idea of what I'm talking about, I started my business in 2007, and this book, in 2015, is the first time since then that I've actually written something for myself.

It's really fortunate that I love the business of business. Because owning an agency is about creating and running a business. It's high-stress, people-driven, and takes a lot of trial and error to get right. The point I'm trying to make is that if you're thinking you want to

MOONLIGHTING ON THE INTERNET

create a technical agency outsourcing web dev teams because you love programming, don't. Do it because you love business and are fortunate enough to have a topic you're passionate about that you can successfully monetize.

Do You Love People?

When you run an agency, your most valuable assets are the people who work for you. The majority of your success and your failures ride on your ability to recruit, hire, and retain the best talent with personalities that fit your culture. If you're familiar with Myers-Briggs, I am an ENFP. I am the ultimate people person, and even I find the people-driven aspect of agencies challenging. You have to patiently nurture and train your staff to perform to the standards that you and your customers have for your company.

The Buck Starts and Stops With You

You will sometimes find yourself in highly frustrating situations that make you just want to rage at your teams. But if you sit back and evaluate things from a neutral perspective, chances are you'll discover that things didn't go the way you wanted them to because you didn't have proper processes and procedures in place. It's true, sometimes people let you down, and that's an unfortunate pain point of having a large staff. But often you let yourself and your staff down by not creating systems that allow you to scale with the demand of your client base.

At the end of the day, you don't have anyone to blame. Even when your teams screw up, you're the one who has to talk to the client, own it, fix it, and move forward. You get the credit and accolades when your team does well, and you get the reputation hit when they fail. With agencies, SOPs, systematization, and processes are not optional—they are critical.

You Get the Last Buck

Speaking of bucks, when you have an agency, you have a lot of people on staff. So everyone gets paid before you do. I'm sure that's probably

248   ◀   PART III / DIGITAL AND INFORMATION PRODUCTS PROFIT PATHS

a universal truth in most businesses, but it's especially true with an agency. If you don't pay your people on time and lose them, your "product" just walked out the door. You will always get paid last; it's just a reality of this model.

Constantly Playing Defense

One frustrating component of owning an agency is that it seems you are in a never-ending cycle of defending your value and your company. This would be understandable if you were putting out subpar work. But when you're an agency, especially in the marketing industry, people depend on you to make them money, and once the money starts rolling in they mistakenly think they can continue on that successful path without you. It is very common to lose clients simply because they generate enough income and learned enough of what you do by working with you to hire someone in-house to replace you.

Also, when you're providing a service, there is so much room for error. Often clients have a vision of what they want but don't know how to accurately communicate it. So even though you did exactly what they asked you to, their perception is that they clearly explained what they wanted and you failed them. The only way to avoid this scenario is to get very, very good at the new project intake process.

This Is Not a Work-Less-Overtime Path

If you're looking for a Profit Path where you can put a lot of hard work into the front end and then sit back and relax while the money rolls in, this is definitely not the right Profit Path for you. With an agency, you can definitely position yourself in your company to not always have to work so hard, but only if you get the right people under you, and good people—especially driven, proactive thinkers—are tough to come by. Depending on the type of agency, stepping back will be easier in some cases than in others. Usually when you're providing services, you need to stay on top of the hottest trends, technologies, and strategies. I have yet to meet an agency owner who is not still working more hours than they consider ideal.

I could list out more pain points, but I think I'll stop there. If you have read all that and still feel like it might be a great path for you, read on!

WHAT I LOVE ABOUT BEING AN AGENCY

Now that I've gotten some of the "buyer beware" out of the way, I'll tell you a few things I truly love about being an agency. If you put the time in and struggle through the really hard years of getting yourself established, you will get to reap the fruits of your labor.

I love . . .

- getting to only work with clients I love.
- that I can charge a premium for my services and my clients still feel my value is greater than the amount they paid for it.
- that my brain and knowledge are the most valuable assets I have and people are willing to pay for my strategy and thoughts alone.
- that I'm supplying legitimate work-from-home jobs to 200+ people at any given time.
- having a large in-house staff I can use at cost to help nurture other business initiatives I take on. This asset is invaluable to me.
- my teams. I really have the greatest people working for me.
- my clients! I attract the best clients.
- waking up every day proud of the empire I'm building.

Don't get me wrong: Having an agency is a beautiful thing, but it is an especially challenging business model. It takes a lot of work and dedication. However, if it's the right model for you, you may just build something exceptionally special.

GETTING STARTED

Do you already know what type of agency you want to be? You might have a good idea of the type of services you are interested in providing, but there are a few other aspects to consider.

How many people do you ideally want working for you? Will you focus on one area, or will you diversify and provide services across multiple areas? What will be special and unique about your agency to help you stand out from the herd? As branding expert Sally Hogshead says, "Different is better than better."

Seed Funding

Many people look to attract investors when they decide to take on a project like starting an agency. It's great to accumulate investment money, but honestly, an agency is something you can scale into over time and bootstrap along the way. I'm not saying that method doesn't have its ups and downs; every method does. The thing to consider is that if you bootstrap the financing, then you hold 100 percent of the company and can make 100 percent of the decisions. Also, I feel this is a realistic option because developing an agency is rarely something you wake up one day and just randomly decide to do. It's usually something your business ascends to naturally.

Lead Acquisition

The time to create a lead acquisition strategy is not after you put the time, energy, and money into getting an agency up and running. Clients are the lifeblood of your business, and you need to have a strong plan for lead acquisition, optimization, and retention in place from the start. Believe me, chasing clients to put food on the table is a really lame way to run a business. As a side note, you really have no business transitioning to the agency model until your current business is in such demand that by doing so you will have a base of clients to launch with.

If you're not good at sales and marketing, then the ideal solution is for you to put serious effort into getting comfortable and excelling at it anyway. Outside salespeople will never sell your business as passionately as you will. In addition, people are buying you as much as if not more than what you are selling. YOU are an amazing asset for your agency, and you should put time and energy into developing yourself as a resource.

If you do hire outside sales team members, be very picky. This is NOT the area of your business to skimp on. Hire people you trust to not only sell well, but also to represent you and your brand well. It is more important that your sales staff really connect with your clients and give the impression that they sincerely care about their business than it is for them to have the greatest closing rates on paper. True sales is an art, not a science. I would even consider it a gift to be grateful for.

BEEN THERE, DONE THAT, TRUST ME TIPS

There are so many tips I can share on this topic. The first one you need to know is that you should work ON your business, not IN your business. Cliché? I know. But while it's a cliché, it is absolutely true. If you are not careful, as an agency owner you will constantly get sucked into putting out fires or filling in for an employee who got sick or dropped the ball. As a business owner, you do what needs to get done to serve your clients well and succeed as a company. But along the way you have to put processes and procedures in place to fix black holes that suck you into your business, which takes you away from growing your business. Eye on the prize!

Next, raise your prices. It is so tempting when you are first starting out to place your prices toward the low end of average. You really want to do well and attract as many clients as possible, but when it comes to services, trust me on this: Raise your prices. You do not want the headaches that come from people looking for the best, lowest-cost deal. In the end, even if you get more clients, you will often make less money. Charge fairly, but charge on the high end of fair. I'm thoroughly convinced that for the agency model, this is the only winning path.

You should also feel free to turn work away and fire clients. I can't stress enough how important it is to develop your ideal client profile and be brave enough to turn work away from clients who don't seem like a good fit for you and your agency. Every time my intuition tells me I shouldn't take a client but I do it anyway for the money, I get burned. Not just some of the time or most of the time—EVERY TIME. You have to be comfortable saying no to clients and turning work down. Also, if you do take on a client and it's not working out, you have to be willing to fire them. One high-maintenance, horrible client can overtax your entire team, and then your other clients suffer too. This is a rough lesson to learn but an absolute must when growing an agency.

Hire the best people you can afford. Because your success is so dependent on your staff, you really have to put serious effort into hiring and retaining the best talent you can. I'm not going to give you suggestions on what to look for in terms of specific talent, because I assume you will do your due diligence and hire people with the skills you need. Instead, I'm going to give you advice on things to look for that I have found invaluable regardless of their role in my company. Here are some tips:

- *Drivers, not trackers.* I want to hire people who own their positions or divisions of my company. This one factor is so important to me that I am seriously willing to pay double for someone who is truly a driver, not just a tracker. These employees don't just track things to make sure projects are on task—they drive the projects to success.

- *Hire people smarter than you.* Don't let ego get in the way. I really hope that when you're at team meetings you feel a little intimidated by how smart and driven the people on your teams are.

- *Don't hire interns as cheap labor.* I always hear people talking about the beauty of hiring college students as interns to get work done at a low cost. It sounds good in theory, but in my experience, training anyone to do a job well takes a lot of time and energy, and frankly, I have no interest in putting that time and energy into someone who is going to be a short-timer for my business. I'm interested in bringing on interns to inspire and educate them because I care, but not as a cheap labor solution. My time and the cost to get someone up to speed is more valuable than the higher wage due to someone who is already qualified for the job.

- *ONLY hire ethical and moral people.* I know there is no way to know for sure if someone is ethical and moral, but in my experience ethics aren't something you can teach someone—skills are. For me, this is non-negotiable.

- *Now get out of the way!* Your job now is to be the best business owner and leader your industry has ever seen. Hire people you trust to be the best at their jobs, and get out of their way. Being the boss doesn't mean being the best at everything. Build an amazing business. Hire well. Inspire well. Get the hell out of their way.

NOTES FROM LESLIE

I asked our operations manager, Leslie, if she would write up her thoughts on what she would tell people considering the agency model as a Profit Path. She's been with us from when the agency was just a few years old, and she has a clear understanding of the realities of running an agency, both good and bad. Here are her notes:

Know What You Are Getting Into When Running an Agency

Be sure you know what you're getting into, and be confident. Know whom you can rely on for help. An agency has to have a great team to thrive.

It's All About Economics

No matter how much you love people and have a vision and want to change the world, you're still in business to make money, not just break even. Don't discount yourself or your services—those people asking for deep discounts can often afford you, and there's a reason they are where they are. They don't give their products/services/ideas/help/work away for free or for cost, and neither should you.

Speaking of costs, one of the most important lessons I always think about in my personal and professional life is the opportunity/cost equation. The cost of a decision is not necessarily money—in fact, often the cost is something much more important than your paycheck. Don't be naive, be realistic. Build in margins that make sense. You can't help anyone if you are stressed out all the time and can't pay the bills.

Be Honest and Manage Expectations

Be open, honest, and upfront about services, delivery, and fixed and variable costs. Get contracts signed. It's unlikely you'll want to pay to take someone to court, since it will likely cost you more than you'll get in return, but making people sign a contract sets the tone for a level of responsibility and accountability for both sides.

Know Your Limits

Don't take on more than you can handle unless you're willing to work 70+ hours a week. Decide what's most important before you start: Is it money, power, prestige, being your own boss, family, being financially independent? Never take on a 70+-hour week unless you know the reason you're doing it is worth the sacrifice you're making. Family is much more important than money for some, so really—really—be realistic about what you can and will sacrifice to make money for yourself and your clients.

Be Committed and Stay Committed

Your clients are people, and your reputation is the center of your business success. If you start dropping the ball on your clients, they will notice, and word will get around. Running an agency is not something you can just stop doing when it stops being fun.

Outsourcing Is More Than Having a Reliable Vendor

Outsourcing is another major component that isn't just about handing off work—it's more management, assessing skills, tracking, documenting, making sure cost is covered and profit is made. Building lasting relationships with outsourcers. Having real expectations. Providing support to the outsourced teams. Making sure they're paid and feel valued (morale is hugely important, and people will screw you if you treat them like crap).

Business Is Business

Don't forget, business is business. You're not in business to make friends—really, you're not. You're in business to make money, otherwise it's called a hobby, and people don't give hundreds of thousands of dollars to others for hobbies unless they're loaded. As a startup, you're likely not dealing with people who want to hand you money with nothing promised in return.

Don't Forget Your People

Don't forget that the people on your team are extremely valuable and that the synergy of a team is much greater than a single person. You can't (and didn't) grow to become an agency without help; don't forget who, what, and how things helped you get where you are. Your people may include:

- Family
- Friends
- Coworkers
- Employees
- God
- Church

- Crisis

- Love of money

- Fear of loss

- Legacy

- Drive to succeed

- People pushing you forward

- People knocking you down

When you have an agency, your people are critical to your success. When it comes to people, it's not always the knowledge they have that matters the most—it's how they use the tools they have and build on their strengths and those around them, pulling the best qualities out of others, knowing and respecting people's strengths and weaknesses, and not faulting them for it. I've found both you and Heather are so successful and inspiring as bosses because you really want people to do what they are passionate about and good at and you both do the same and respect people for being who they are.

Thanks, Leslie!

TOOLS I CAN'T LIVE WITHOUT

This section details some of the agency model tools I simply can't live without—and neither should you! Think of these as your deal-breaker tools for getting an agency up and running.

- *Project management platforms.* I've come to the conclusion that at some point I'll need to have my own CMS built for me to meet the exact needs of my agency. While none of these meet our needs 100 percent, they get the job done:
    - Teamwork.com (www.teamwork.com)
    - Asana (https://asana.com)
    - Basecamp (https://basecamp.com)
- *Time tracker for staff.* When you have an agency, tracking the time your staff works is non-negotiable. There is so much data to be had from time tracking, including the ability to export reports

for time that should be billed back to a client. Our favorite time-tracking tool is Toggl (www.toggl.com).

◖ *Invoicing.* There are a lot of different ways to invoice clients, but our favorite tool is FreshBooks (http://www.freshbooks.com/).

◖ *Communication.* When you're running a company that is people-driven, communication is key. There are many platforms to aid this; our two favorites are:

– Skype (www.skype.com/en/)
– Slack (https://slack.com/)

◖ *Merchant account.* I have a difficult time giving you my suggestions on which merchant account to use. There are a lot of options, ranging from your favorite banks to specific merchant accounts designed for businesses. I've used a lot of them and don't love any of them, but my favorite at this point is Braintree (www.braintreegateway.com).

◖ *Accountant.* I don't have a recommendation for a specific accountant—I can only tell you that you had better get one. Between payroll and taxes, no agency should live without one.

We use a ton of tools, and I could probably publish a small Kindle book just going over my favorite tools to help entrepreneurs run their business. However, the few listed above are core tools that I rely on daily to run my agency.

PART IV

TAKE ACTION 101

Alright, you have made it through all the Profit Paths! Good job! Hopefully you have a better idea of which paths will be the best match for you. There are some things you need to understand regardless of which Profit Path you choose. The remainder of the book will cover some of those important topics.

CHAPTER 15

BUSINESS AND MARKETING 101

As much as I would LOVE to dump all my marketing brilliance into this book, we just don't have the room, nor is it the primary focus. However, I do cover some fundamental knowledge in this chapter and list some of my favorite free or dirt-cheap tools.

FIRST THINGS FIRST

If you're going to create a Profit Path, you will need a business name and website or some other online property to use as your home base.

Picking a name is always a fun and frustrating process. Here is mine:

1. Brainstorm lots of names.
2. Check GoDaddy (www.godaddy.com/) to see if various names are available.
3. When I find one I like and the domain is available, I do a search online and on Facebook to see if anything else pops up.

4. If there doesn't seem to be anyone out there operating with the same name, I register the domain with GoDaddy. At that point, I am the proud owner of a domain! (As a side note, I definitely do a search for a coupon code first. There tends to be one floating around somewhere, and you can commonly buy a domain for less than $3.)

Next, you need to determine your legal structure. I am not an attorney, so I am not qualified to tell you how to structure your business. This is really just here as a reminder for you to research your entity structure options and make sure you're legally structured and protected.

Building Your Web Presence

There are a lot of ways to have an online presence. A lot of people actually even operate their business from a Facebook page. Depending on which Profit Path you choose, this could potentially work for you at first. However, if you want other people to take your business seriously, you really do need a website. This can be done a lot of ways, but if you're looking for a basic website, have it built in WordPress. It's the most user-friendly way to go when you're starting out.

These days, most of my clients run websites built on WordPress. This is usually the case until you start getting into websites that are near enterprise-level or above. I love WordPress themes—they make building and scaling websites a lot easier. My two very favorite themes are X Theme and Genesis.

If you choose one of those two, you can easily create something you can live with until you have a bit of experience under your belt and know better what you want. Two things are important: Make sure your website is responsive and optimized for mobile.

To get a website up and running, you will need to buy hosting. Buy web hosting for your site from a different company than your domain registrar. This makes it a lot simpler should you ever have to change web hosts down the line.

Solid hosting options include:

◀ Pure Speed Hosting (http://purespeedhosting.com; preferred)

◀ HostMonster (www.hostmonster.com)

Graphics

You are most likely going to want some minimal graphic design done to develop a logo and perhaps some professional images. Here are some options:

Cost-Effective Graphic Design Work
◀ Fiverr (www.fiverr.com)
◀ 99designs (http://99designs.com)

Pre-Made Graphics
◀ Bigstock (www.bigstockphoto.com)
◀ iStock (www.istockphoto.com)

Email and Autoresponders

Create a company email account, and don't use Gmail, Yahoo! Mail, or Hotmail. It should read something like YourName@yourwebsite.com. You'll have to create these when you set your site up, but it offers a far more professional appearance than a free mail account. You can use Gmail for this; I do. Just use their business apps to have it go out as a custom email address for your company. Whoever sets up your website should know how to do this for you. If not, you can find information on how to do it here: www.google.com/work/apps/business.

As you scale up, you will need to set up an autoresponder service to manage your email lists. If you want to start out economically, use MailChimp (http://mailchimp.com), which is free for up to 2,000 names. This type of service makes it simple to connect with your customer and prospect lists and effectively market your services.

PayPal

You need to be able to take payments online. There are lots of merchant accounts you can explore, but many people starting out run their business from PayPal. There are a lot of things I don't love about PayPal, but it is really friendly to new businesses and easy to get going. You can even set up a merchant account through them. Another option I like is

Braintree (www.braintreegateway.com), which ironically is now owned by PayPal.

MARKETING BASICS

I can give you a basic knowledge of the marketing aspects you'll most commonly encounter. You should also read through Chapter 4 on the Freelance Writing Profit Path. I give additional information there because writers have to understand the rules in order to stay compliant and effective for their clients. For additional information on this topic, visit the resource section of www.MoonlightingontheInternet.com.

Intentional Marketing

If you're going to put money into marketing, you want to get the most benefits from each dollar, right? A lot of what you are going to read in this marketing section you can Google to find the same information and more. It's not that the information isn't out there; it's that there are a MILLION pieces of information, and it's hard to know what is accurate and what is not. But by having this book as a foundation along with the resources we suggest, you will have a much easier time navigating. That said, what I'm about to share with you regarding intention is not something you can find everywhere because a lot of marketers, even great marketers, don't get it. At least not to the extent I do. So if you can wrap your head around how critically important intent is to Google, you will honestly have a leg up on the majority of your competitors.

Algorithm Changes

I'm going to divert away from intention for a minute because to fully understand it, you have to understand how Google works. Really this applies to all search engines, but Google is the industry leader, so let's focus on them. Have any of you ever joined any online membership site? The basic structure is usually that you pay a monthly or annual fee in exchange for information, services, or whatever else the value proposition is of the membership. When you're the site owner, your biggest challenge is always figuring out what upcoming feature the members are excited about that makes them want to stay. The membership site is a great model, but you are always striving to keep retention as high as possible.

As an oversimplification, think of Google as a giant membership site, and anyone who searches on it is a member. Google makes a lot of money from people searching. A LOT. So it's a top priority to make sure that searchers quickly find what they are looking for. If Google were to become unreliable, at some point people would start using another search engine that gives them better results. Pretty basic, right?

Algorithms are simply the way Google filters through the billions of web pages to get the best answer to the questions their searchers are asking. They need to get the right content in front of their searchers, and algorithms are how they do that. People get really upset at algorithm changes, and I understand why. They aren't perfect, and often there is a lot of collateral damage, but at the heart of it, they are trying to keep the search results as high quality as possible.

Here is a list of the algorithm changes in the past couple of years you need to be aware of. These are quick explanations, and you can check Google for more details. It's important to understand these so you can keep yourself compliant and not end up with a penalty. Recovering from a penalty is challenging, a lot of work, and no fun at all.

PANDA

First up is *Panda*. Panda rolled out in February 2011, and man did it rock the internet boats. Seriously, if we had a medieval interpretation of it, I'm pretty sure it would involve angry mobs with pitchforks and torches. Ultimately the intention behind this algorithm was to set a higher standard for website content. It was a way to weed out thin, spammy websites that offered the searcher little to no value. In the real world, those of us who use Google as a search engine cheer such improvements to our experience. But for those who were making tons of money off thin sites that were easy to rank, it was a sad, sad day!

Primary Takeaways

- Always provide high-quality content on your site.
- Don't keyword stuff. (This means jamming your buying keyword into the content as many times as possible hoping to rank well. Old-school tactic.)
- Manage the balance of ads on your site vs. quality, informative content.
- Avoid duplicate content pages on your website. This often comes into play with landing pages that are optimized for specific keywords. A simple fix is to block indexing and crawling of low-value pages or duplicate pages like landing page clones.

PENGUIN

Next came *Penguin*. Penguin was released in April 2012. While not entirely accurate, you could think of Panda as an algorithm designed to police what's on your website, while Penguin was designed to police the tactics being used to get your website to rank well. The Penguin algorithm has a huge focus on the link profiles of your site, something referred to as "over-optimization." The ultimate goal was to try to rein in people using spammy, "black hat" techniques to game the system.

Penguin is the only algorithm change that negatively impacted me or my clients. When Panda came out, all our clients skyrocketed because we have always focused on high-quality content. However, when Penguin was released, it took the backlink strategy that was considered appropriate and made it toxic overnight. So it took us some time and research to figure out what was happening and adjust our strategies. This is also the algorithm change that went after blog networks. About 50 percent of a blog network I owned with one of my businesses was de-indexed.

Primary Takeaways

- Limit your buying keyword to 40 percent or less of your anchor text link. (These may be technical terms you are not familiar with, but it gives you great information to go research so you can understand what I'm talking about.)

- Make an effort to have good trust flow by keeping the content that is linking to and from your site relevant to whatever the page you're linking to is about. In other words, if you have a page on your website about iPhone accessories, don't link to it from a site about pet grooming.
- Keep your tactics clean. Don't use questionable shortcuts to try to rank your website.

A word of caution: Another change that came with Penguin is the ability to hurt your site through negative SEO tactics. Before, the worst thing you could do is waste your time and money getting little to no results. Now you can get your website penalized and even shut down. Or, worse, you could get your client's website penalized or shut down. The stakes are definitely higher now than they were before.

PIGEON

Pigeon was the next big thing to fly in. In July 2014 Google rolled out the Pigeon algorithm, which is all about local search. Before, searching in Google Search vs. Google Maps would often yield very different results. This was Google's attempt to meld them together in a more cohesive way. Unlike the other updates, this algorithm doesn't seem to have upset people as much. It really has just streamlined local search with maps.

Primary Takeaways

- Stop focusing on city search modifiers and start focusing on neighborhoods.
- Optimize your directory placement for the top-ranking local business directories only.
- Content marketing and link building are becoming as important as reviews, so you need to have a solid plan for this in your local search strategies.

Forget the animal names for a minute. *Mobilegeddon* is coming! I absolutely love that name! I'm sure it will get an official name from Google soon, but in the meantime it's being referred to as "Mobilegeddon."

As I'm writing this, a brand-new algorithm is releasing soon that has everyone on high alert. I don't know enough about it yet to give you much information or takeaways except this: As you're building websites, make sure they are always mobile-optimized and have a mobile-friendly dynamic interface. The word on the street is that websites that don't have this will not rank as well as those that do. Mobile search is so prominent that even without knowing how this latest algorithm will shake out, you should always make it part of your planning. Most modern WordPress sites come this way now.

HUMMINGBIRD

Some of the changes Google has made were more drastic than mere tweaks to its algorithms. When Google rolled out *Hummingbird* in August 2013, what it did was rebuild its search engine for the first time since 2001. You will find sites all over the internet listing Hummingbird as an algorithm change alongside Panda, Penguin, and Pigeon. However, it's not really an algorithm change at all. If you think of Google as an engine, you can think of algorithm changes as parts of that engine. Hummingbird IS Google search, and all the other algorithms are parts in the Hummingbird engine. This is where we begin to circle back to intention, because Hummingbird (i.e., the direction Google is headed and the future of search) is all about intention.

In the Resources section of the Moonlighting on the Internet website there is a video I made for you that shows the power of Hummingbird and intention in a way I could never express as well through writing, so be sure to go watch that. Essentially, Google is trying to figure out what the intention is behind the questions searchers are asking. As you'll see in my video, Google is trying to create an environment where it can string together a user's searches to figure out their intention and what they are really looking for. Buyer's intent has always been an important part of marketing, but in the current search environment, understanding what Google thinks your searchers' intent is is the most important piece of information for you to know.

I get asked to teach on this topic frequently because right now, it is possible to attain 50 percent or more of your rankings just by structuring content correctly on your website. It won't be this easy forever, but right now you can save yourself thousands of dollars in your ongoing marketing budget just by understanding intention and what Google thinks about it. The number-one thing I hope you take away from this chapter is to always think about the buyer's intent for your market and structure everything around that. EVERYTHING. Content, products, offers, sales funnels, email sequences. Absolutely everything.

Primary Takeaways

- Intent of the searcher is everything.
- See the first bullet point.

Keyword Research

There is a lot of great information online about keyword research. But there are a couple of things I wanted you to know about it so you would understand why you need it. Keywords are at the heart of every advertising campaign, online and off. In essence, the research is to find out what your target prospects are typing into Google. This will help you know which terms to optimize your websites, content, and offers around.

To be really successful with keyword research, you need to pay attention to intention. While it's nice to get in front of your prospects any way you can, you especially want to know what terms they are typing into Google when they have their credit card out and are ready to buy what you have for sale. Not every click is created equal. You want to get in front of the buyers in your market as much as possible. This is also where intention comes into play. It's not just about what they want to buy, but WHY they want to buy. Keywords are not always single words; they can be full phrases or even sentences. Ask yourself these questions:

- Why do they want to buy your product?
- What problems or pain points are they experiencing?
- What solutions does your product offer?
- What are the desired end results that your target market really wants?

Answering these questions will lead you to keywords that will not only get you in front of your buyers, but will also get you in front of them with the information they actually care about. That is where the money is.

Generating Traffic

There are two primary ways to get traffic to your website:

1. Buy it (PPC, display ads, sponsored posts, retargeting)
2. Earn it (SEO, PR, viral content)

That may sound oversimplified, but that's what it all boils down to. You're either going to pay for traffic through some program, or you're going to do some great content marketing and SEO and get the rankings you need to get the traffic naturally through search. Let's explore this a bit.

Digital marketer Ryan Deiss says it better than anyone I know: "If you want traffic, then you go to the traffic store and you buy it!" I love that! Buying traffic is a mainstream part of marketing, and more and more people are turning to it as the organic traffic route has gotten increasingly difficult over time. The problem is that people tend to be very intimidated by paid traffic, which is understandable. If you don't know what you're doing, you can burn through a lot of money quickly with very little to show for it. You definitely want to hire traffic experts or take some training courses through us or someone else so you can really get the hang of it. It's a skill that will serve you well for life.

One thing you need to know about is pay per click (PPC) advertising. PPC is exactly what it sounds like: You are paying for clicks. You pay authority websites like Google, Bing, Yahoo!, and even some of the bigger social platforms like Facebook to run ad campaigns, and then you get charged each time someone clicks on your ad. Here are some popular paid traffic platforms:

GOOGLE ADWORDS (www.google.com/adwords)

Pros: Massive traffic volume, and you can be at the top of page one of Google instantly.

Cons: The clicks can be very expensive, and there is a steep learning curve.

YAHOO! BING NETWORK
(http://advertise.bingads.microsoft.com/en-us/home)

Pros: Keywords are often more affordable than on Google, and they are known for having excellent customer service.

Cons: Search volume is lower than on Google, which can limit the growth of your advertising campaign.

FACEBOOK ADVERTISING (www.facebook.com/business)

Pros: Really customizable targeting, which helps you get your ad in front of your ideal prospects, and it is the largest consumer database this type of advertising is available on.

Cons: The clickthrough rate (CTR) is typically much lower than paid ads on the SERPs, and you often have to change your ads more frequently to keep conversions where you want them.

NEWER BUT POWERFUL PROGRAMS

- Twitter Ads (https://biz.twitter.com/ad-products)
- Pinterest Promoted Pins (https://business.pinterest.com/en/promoted-pins)
- LinkedIn Ads (www.linkedin.com/ads)

Display Ads, Retargeting, and Other Traffic Drivers

Display ads. These ads appear on other websites instead of in the search results. You might be on a website reading an interesting article and notice ads alongside the text of the article. Those are display ads. If you are paying for display advertising, your ads will show up on websites related to the topic of your ad. Display advertising is growing in popularity, especially in combination with retargeting campaigns.

Retargeting. Retargeting campaigns are not new, but they might seem that way because they're a popular topic right now. The basic concept is that you enable a technology that places a cookie, sometimes referred to as a pixel, on your website. This is not noticeable to anyone visiting your site, but as a prospect browses the internet, your ads will populate different sites they visit on the web. Even if this is the first time you have heard about retargeting, I'm sure you have experienced it before.

For instance, if you went to Zappos.com to look at a pair of shoes, you might start seeing ads for those shoes on Facebook and other websites. It can feel a little like "Big Brother is watching you," but it is very effective. They say the average consumer needs to see your ad seven times before they buy, and this definitely helps inject your product, service, or brand into their awareness. Almost all our favorite marketing strategies include retargeting.

Sponsored posts. Sponsored posts usually appear on community-driven websites. Facebook is probably the most prominent example. You can pay to have your posts populate inside people's newsfeeds. However, you can also pay for sponsored posts on popular blogs in your industry. This could fall under "guest blogging." If there is a credible or authoritative website in your niche that attracts your target market, it's awesome if you can pay for a sponsored blog post. Guest blogging doesn't technically fall under the official category of "sponsored post," but for a simplified explanation, it's OK.

Organic traffic. Organic traffic means that instead of paying money to get the click, you used tactics to get people there organically. "Organically" is just a fancy term that means when people typed in a search term, your website, or some other piece of content you published online, appeared in the search results and the searcher clicked on your site. Awesome, right? That's why everyone loves SEO. This is what I meant by buy it vs. earn it. You either pay for it with your money or you pay for it with your time. Either way, you're paying for it.

Search engine optimization (SEO). SEO is a massive topic with a long history. I thought a lot about what to put in this book about SEO that would actually help you. You can Google SEO and get plenty of excellent explanations of what it is and why it's important. There is no shortage of information out there. So I'm just going to highlight my favorite aspects of SEO that I feel you should pay attention to first.

On-Site optimization. When you are having your website built, make sure it is properly optimized. No one should be taking your money to build your website without understanding how to properly optimize it for you. However, tons of people build websites without understanding anything about SEO. I wasn't kidding when I said earlier that onsite optimization has a huge impact on your results. Definitely put some time and energy into hiring people to do this for you or learn to do it yourself.

Content. Once you have done some research and know the buying keywords and the buyer intent of your market, produce good content. Remember, content doesn't have to be written. It can be social media, blogs, videos, podcasts, infographics, etc. The point is, you want to produce lots of high-quality content around your buying keywords and the intention behind them. As simple as this sounds, it is a powerful mechanism toward getting you the rankings and traffic you want.

Google likes fresh content. Take the dates off your blog posts immediately.

Content Distribution

Look for quality places to publish your content across the internet. Some of my favorite places to distribute content are:

- Social media sites
- LinkedIn (www.linkedin.com)
- Document-sharing sites
- YouTube (www.youtube.com)
- Press release distribution sites
- Images
- Web 2.0 sites
- Q&A sites
- Forums

You can look at Chapter 4 on the Freelance Writing Profit Path for some good tips on how to structure content with SEO in mind.

Social media. Social media is a HUGE buzzword in the marketing world, and it deserves to be. It's definitely worth putting your time into researching effective social media strategies to help support your brand, create engagement, and enable lead acquisition. Here are my favorite social media sites:

- ◀ Facebook (www.facebook.com)
- ◀ Twitter (https://twitter.com)
- ◀ Google+ (https://plus.google.com)
- ◀ Pinterest (www.pinterest.com)
- ◀ LinkedIn (www.linkedin.com)

Remember, social media can do one thing better than almost any other strategy I can think of, and that's engagement. You can create real-time conversations with your fans, followers, prospects, and brand advocates. Think of social media as your avenue for getting into the conversations your target market is having.

Sales funnels and specific strategies. Creating sales funnels is one of my personal specialties and the service I'm personally most sought for. The topic is a little advanced for this, but I have filled up the Resources section of the Moonlighting on the Internet site with additional information on marketing, specific traffic strategies and tactics, and so on. But I tried to cover the basics so that when you are researching, you will have some familiarity with the terms. Visit the resource section of www.MoonlightingontheInternet.com for these resources.

TOOLS YOU NEED

Here is a list of a few more of my favorite tools I think will help you out as you're getting started:

- ◀ *Asana* (www.asana.com). This is a free project management plat-form that lets you sign up using your Google login.
- ◀ *Canva* (www.canva.com). If you don't have a designer or can't afford one, this gives you a lot of flexibility to create visual con-tent. Use it!
- ◀ *CloudConvert* (www.cloudconvert.com). This converts pretty much any type of document into any other type. I most frequently use it to convert PDFs to Word docs.

- *Compfight* (www.compfight.com). Free stock images you are allowed to use any way you want.
- *Evernote* (www.evernote.com). I especially love the Evernote moleskin notebooks. You can take a picture of your handwritten notes and upload it to your electronic Evernote notebook, and your handwritten page becomes a searchable document. You can do this with Post-it notes too. This rocked my world and is my new favorite discovery.
- *FreeConferenceCall.com* (www.freeconferencecall.com). It's exactly what it says it is. I especially love that it can record conversations, which is immensely helpful when discussing projects.
- *FreshBooks* (www.freshbooks.com). We use this to invoice our clients.
- *infogr.am* (www.infogr.am). This allows you to make quick and easy infographics.
- *Jing* (www.techsmith.com/jing.html). A free screen recording desktop software that you can make up to five-minute videos or take screenshots with one-click options to host it on screencast.
- *join.me* (www.join.me). This gives you screen-sharing capabilities for free.
- *Lucidchart* (www.lucidchart.com). I design all my sales funnels in here. Fabulous!
- *MerchantWords* (www.merchantwords.com). Monitors trends on Amazon. Great for research purposes.
- *SEMrush* (www.semrush.com). A suite of useful SEO tools.
- *Share Tally* (www.sharetally.co). This is free and tells you how many social shares your site is getting.
- *SimilarWeb* (www.similarweb.com). This is great for competitive analysis.
- *Skype* (www.skype.com/en). I run my whole business from Skype!
- *Snagit* (www.techsmith.com/snagit.html). Jing is free, but I prefer Snagit. Snagit is free for 30 days and then costs $49.95 one time.
- *WatchCount.com* (www.watchcount.com). This follows the top trends on eBay and is fabulous for research purposes.

CHAPTER 16

PROFIT PATH
MINDSET

Creating a successful Profit Path takes time and energy and requires you to juggle one more thing and keep balanced while doing it. I wanted to include a chapter that talks about some of my favorite tips about creating and maintaining a profitable mindset. I'm going to share with you my personal daily routine that has changed my life. I've never publicly shared it before.

Each of the Profit Paths in this book gives you a lot of great information designed to help you understand its logistics so you can choose the right path for you and your specific situation. However, it really doesn't matter how much information you consume if you don't have a Profit Path Mindset. How you think and how you view the world around you has an enormous influence on your success.

SHELBY'S DAILY ROUTINE

I started my business in 2007 not even fully realizing I was starting a business. I am 100 percent positive that my journey to success would have been much quicker and less bumpy had I started out with the type of mindset I have now. However, I'm thankful my journey has unfolded the way it has, and each moment created who I am now. A few years ago I went through a particularly difficult time in my life. I would go as far as saying it was the hardest, most painful period of my life so far. (And I hope ever!)

I don't really talk about what the crisis was that knocked me down so thoroughly, but it doesn't really matter what the catalyst was, because all of us will have a "most difficult time of our lives." It could be caused by a gazillion different things. The point isn't to focus on what the hardship is; it's to focus on how you rise back up and recover. You may never experience something so difficult, and I hope you don't.

This chapter isn't focused on recovery. Recovery was just the catalyst that began my focus on changing how I think and feel and view the world. It was out of sheer desperation to do anything and everything I could to keep my mind and heart full of positivity and my head above water that I began developing a daily routine that will most likely be part of my life forever. A big part of that was journaling. I use The Five Minute Journal (www.fiveminutejournal.com/).

I've always loved the thought of journaling and have done it off and on throughout my life, but when you're a mom of five who runs a business, time is a rare commodity. I hadn't been very successful in years at journaling every day, even though I really wanted to. Discovering The Five Minute Journal is one of the best things that has happened to me! In case you're one of those people who feel stressed out just by the thought of trying to journal every day, let alone whether you think doing so will have any real benefits, then keep reading.

The Five Minute Journal does not take long (hence its name). Here is how it works. You wake up in the morning and write three things:

1. You write down three things you are grateful for.
2. You write down three things that would make today great.

3. You complete an "I am" statement.

That's it. It helps you set your intentions for the day in a positive way. Then in the evening before you go to bed you write two things:

1. You list three amazing things that happened that day.
2. You write one thing you could have done to make the day better.

Aside from all the amazing benefits this new daily practice has had on my life, it is so cool to flip through this journal and read what's happened in my life—to see all the amazing things I'm grateful for and scroll to the bottom and see the pattern around the things I want to do better. It's like my own personal archive of what happened in my life each day, but quick and sort of perfect.

I try to keep a focus on gratitude. I gave myself the extra challenge of doing the first 100 days without repeating something I'm grateful for. This is MUCH more difficult than it sounds. However, it requires you to dig deep and really acknowledge things in your life you are grateful for because you run out of your standard list pretty quickly.

I wish I had a way to express to you the true power that harnessing and acknowledging gratitude has had in my life. If I could wave a magic wand and somehow give us the ability to see emotions and how they impact the world, I'm positive we would see that gratitude shapes and betters the world around us. I don't know how to explain it to you, but shifting my focus toward gratitude is without a doubt one of the single most powerful things I have ever done.

I also don't buy the actual journal, which I feel guilty about because I love supporting the creator, but I can't journal on crisp, white, sterile pages. I'm a creative type, and I need pages with color and design. Either way, the process is pretty great. The journal also comes with some fairly decent information about the science behind journaling and how it can help you. (For those of you who are into those types of statistics.)

You can see their website here: www.fiveminutejournal.com. Also, there is a cool video on YouTube in which Tim Ferriss reviews it (www.youtube.com/watch?v=7_dUSGfsQZg). It's only a couple of minutes long and worth watching.

Meditation

I had hardly ever meditated before I started the processes on the app. I had heard and read all about the amazing benefits, but I just CANNOT turn my brain off. So any previous attempts at meditation were frustrating at best and a waste of time at worst. I was surprised to learn how wrong all my assumptions were about meditation. First, mindfulness doesn't mean turning your brain off. Plus, there are all different types of meditation. Transcendental Meditation, which people refer to as TM, uses repetitive affirmations during meditation.

I can honestly say that meditation has changed my life. Even just five minutes of it changes my whole day. To be frank, I spent most of my life thinking that meditation was sort of "woo-woo" and not something to be taken seriously. I was so wrong. There are some GREAT articles about the very real and powerful effects meditation can have on your life, so I encourage you to research it.

The thing that helped me start down the meditation path in a realistic and nonfrustrating way was an app called Headspace. I LOVE it and highly recommend it. It really taught me a lot about how to meditate, and it has a great process that moves you through it in baby steps. You start out only meditating five or ten minutes per day. I played music as well because I feel really connected to music and prefer it to silence when meditating.

You can find the Headspace app in the Play Store for Android, on iTunes for iPhone, and at www.headspace.com on the internet. I get my favorite meditation music at www.live365.com in the Meditation genre; my favorite station is called Musical Spa.

Stop Creating Meaning

Everyone does it. If you say you don't, I suspect you're either lying or less self-aware than you think you are. Humans naturally attach meaning to things people say or don't say or do or don't do. When something happens to us, our brains naturally spiral down a thought tunnel of why it happened and what it means. It's not wrong as long as you're aware you're exploring what it might mean and not internalizing it as fact. Some of us are worse at that than others, and unfortunately, I was the QUEEN of doing that.

This might be the single hardest habit I've ever tried breaking. I had no idea how ingrained this process was inside me, and shifting it has been no small feat. I think it might take intentional work the rest of my life, but it's worth the effort. I went to a Tony Robbins event a few years back, which was the first personal development event I had ever attended, and he addressed this point well. I don't agree with 100 percent of the things Robbins says, and not all his methods resonate with me, but the things I did agree with changed me for the better. One thing I employ is, for lack of a better term, something I call the Crazy Person Method. I'm going to tell you how I overcame the worst of this, and on rough days, I have to revert to this process still. But you might want to lock yourself in the bathroom or something because if anyone sees you, they will think you are a crazy person! My Crazy Person Method is a three-step process.

1. *Let the crazy out.* The first thing I do is let it all out. I spend one minute (one minute only, otherwise it might turn into an angry rant, which defeats the purpose) saying out loud what has me so frustrated/angry/hurt/upset. I rattle off my thoughts with all the self-torturous meanings attached to them that may or may not be true. For me, this is a really important step. Sometimes you just need to verbalize things and hear them out loud.

2. *Just the facts.* The second thing I do is take a few seconds to regroup and then state only the facts without any emotion attached to them. I literally (again out loud) talk through exactly what took place as if I were giving a police statement. Facts only—no assumptions, opinions, or theorizing.

3. *The positive benefit of the doubt.* The last thing I do after taking a few seconds is restate the facts with emotions and assumptions attached. I talk through what most likely happened, giving the person/situation the benefit of the doubt. I make a conscious choice that I want to assume the best of everyone and every situation unless I know from experience that it's not smart or safe to do so. So I restate the issue with a positive slant on it. I'm not asking you to lie to yourself. I'm not even asking you to assume

the best. I'm only asking you to place a slightly positive outlook on the situation and choose to move forward with that until you have solid facts to base your beliefs and feelings on.

You can probably see why I've never written or talked about this publicly—even as I'm reading this I realize how crazy it sounds. However, this has really worked for me. Besides helping me out in moments of frustration, it's slowly changing me for the better. I'm starting to naturally assume positive things and I'm less likely to assign undeserved meaning to people, words, and situations. This has been a powerful part of my transformation and has impacted my professional as well as my personal life.

I have since learned that this technique is closely aligned with a process psychologists call "reframing." You could Google that term to find out more about why this might work so well.

Happiness Independence

I have three big goals that constantly drive me to succeed. I strive to achieve:

1. Financial independence
2. Location independence
3. Happiness independence

Tony Robbins said one thing that above all else has really stuck with me. He said, "How you feel determines the quality of your life." This was mind-blowing for me. This is why you see people who seem to have everything looking so miserable and other people who seemingly have nothing so full of joy and happiness. I already had financial and location independence as two of my big life goals, but in that moment, I decided I needed to add happiness independence to the list.

Happiness independence means that your happiness is not dependent on any outside factor. If you can only be happy if you have money, then losing your money destroys your happiness. If you can only be happy with a certain person in your life, then that person has full control over your happiness. Don't get me wrong, I can hardly breathe to think about life without my husband and children, but I feel we must all learn to feel happy regardless of our circumstances.

AN INSPIRING STORY

A number of years ago, a leader in my church wrote an article on this very topic. He told a true story about a mother who fled Poland during World War II with her children. She had already lost her husband in the war, and she and her children fled in the winter with other refugees. By the time she reached freedom, she had rags for shoes and had lost most of her children along the way to starvation and the harsh winter elements. The first thing she did upon reaching her destination and safety was proclaim in tears how blessed she was.

She sincerely felt she was blessed, and she was so grateful. She had terrible things happen in her life, but her happiness wasn't dependent on her circumstances. I'm sure her heart hurt every day for the loss of her children, but she had developed an internal ability to tap into happiness regardless of whatever else was happening in her life. I want that. So I have a process I use daily to try to develop this well of internal happiness within myself.

Each day when I feel myself getting angry or frustrated, I stop and turn it into something to be grateful for. Here is a practical example. If I were to feel myself getting frustrated at one of my children, I would stop and acknowledge how grateful I am to be reminded that I need to have patience. If I feel angry at a particularly difficult client, I stop and am thankful for the reminder about how fortunate I am to have clients and a thriving business.

I know this doesn't solve the problem, but it does make it a lot harder to be angry or frustrated when it becomes an automatic part of your thought process to shift it into gratitude or a positive reminder. This is becoming less and less of a conscious effort and more a part of who I naturally am. Calm, happy people make better decisions and tend to be more successful. I started this process for my own personal benefit and out of a desire to have the most happiness possible, but it has had so many other unexpected benefits to my business and personal life.

Intentional Living

Do not allow yourself to be blown along through life like a tumbleweed. Live with intention every day. We all have so much going on in our lives and so many people and priorities vying for our time that if we are not careful, we will just start living reactively. We'll be paying attention to what's happening to us in any given moment and forget where we are headed and why. You always see plaques on walls and quotes in books that say it's not about the destination, it's about the journey. I disagree. While I do think the journey is important, I think losing sight of the destination and why you're headed there can be like a cancer to your dreams.

Yes, experience the journey. Yes, appreciate being in the moment. But don't forget about the destination. In my opinion this is not a one-side-or-the-other philosophy. You really have to strike a balance between experiencing the journey and not losing sight of why you are on it. If you aren't sincerely in tune with your goals, how can you make good decisions that bring you closer to them? This is part of how people get completely derailed from moving their business forward.

I am no exception. That's why every day I take a few minutes to focus on my destination and my "why." I also purchased *Power Thought Cards* and *Wisdom Cards* by Louise Hays. Each day I pick a couple that resonate with how I want to think and what I want to accomplish, and they sit on my desk reminding me to be intentional about my day. Keeping my focus and intent and eye on the prize has REALLY helped me to make good decisions and keep growing into a better version of me.

CHOOSE YOUR OWN ADVENTURE

These are parts of my daily routine. You don't have to do what I do, but I encourage you to find a few things you can do to keep you focused on what you want to accomplish and foster the mindset you need to achieve your goals and dreams. While not part of my daily routine, I do have a few more nuggets to share with you that have really helped me along the way.

Never Waste a Good Failure

I know you have all heard this, but if you're like most people you say you know it, but still struggle with failure when it happens. It's true—failing is hard. There's nothing fun about it. But it IS part of the process of finding success. You can minimize failure by finding good mentors and surrounding yourself with loving, successful people you admire, but I don't know of anyone who has successfully eliminated failures from their personal history. I don't like failing, but because I know it happens my new theory is: If you're going to fail, fail fast. Because the more time you spend leading up to the failure, the harder that fall is.

The most important thing about failure is never let it go to waste. Learn from it. Not all lessons are fun. I am a MUCH more savvy businessperson after losing my house and nearly losing my business when the economy tanked. It's true I couldn't control what happened with the economy, but I certainly could have had myself set up differently so the hit wasn't so hard. I learned from that. I bloomed out of the ashes, and now my businesses are much better because of that. You may create a handful of "unintentional nonprofits" in pursuit of your perfect Profit Path. That's OK—just don't let that failure go to waste!

It Is OK to Want to Be Rich

It is infuriating how much our culture depicts the wealthy as evil, greedy, and selfish. Are there greedy, selfish rich people? Yes. Are there greedy, selfish poor people? Absolutely. There is nothing wrong with wanting to be wealthy. It's a positive desire. We can do more good for the world if we have more money. That's indisputable. You just have more options when you have expendable income. Do not feel bad for wanting to be wealthy.

If you're one of the people who struggle with this internally, it might help if you write down the things you could do for other people if you had extra income. What could you do for your children, family, friends, community, and the world as a whole? More important, if you have negative attitudes about money, you're likely passing that on to your children, whether you realize it or not. Let's raise a generation of children who want to be wealthy AND generous.

Balance

Achieve balance. I dare you. I double-dog dare you. Think it's easy? Think again! It's not. It's hard. But it has to happen. This goes back to intention. The time to think about balance is not when you have a frustrated spouse and parental guilt over lost time with your kids. Go into this assuming that balance will be a struggle, and put a plan in place to help keep the scales evened out. I don't mean to sound negative,

CHECK IT OUT

My friend Jay Kubassek runs a successful podcast called *Wake Up!* and has devoted a portion of his life to inspiring people to get real with themselves and create the life they want. He was generous enough to write up some of his favorite tips about having a Profit Path Mindset for us. Visit the resource section of www.MoonlightingontheInternet.com.

but even those of you reading this and thinking to yourself that you absolutely will have balance will struggle.

I don't know a single business owner or entrepreneur who has not routinely struggled to keep ideal balance in their lives. You're just going to have to trust me on this one. Right now, right from the beginning as you are mapping out your plans for implementing your Profit Path, add to your list ways that you will strive to keep balance and what the red flags will be to alert you that things are off-kilter. It's no fun when the realization finally hits you because you have disharmony in your family or your business feels like it's falling apart. Do yourself a huge favor and plan for it from the onset.

Smile, You Can Do This

You can do this. It's going to be a learning process, but surround yourself with intentional positivity. Be confident and determined. You can do this. Trust me: If I can do this, anyone can. There is nothing extra special about me. I dove in and figured it out on the way down. It's not the ideal path, but you have this book, you have my website, you have LOTS of resources. Don't give up. I promise, you have what it takes, you just have to push through even when it's not very fun.

There are no limits to what you can accomplish. Chase your dream. If you're interested in business coaching that addresses both your business and your mindset, you can check out the coaching business I run with my friend Joshua Lee at www.scaliversity.com.

CHAPTER 17

ANALYSIS PARALYSIS: DON'T FALL INTO THIS TRAP

The purpose of this last chapter is to help you put the book down and take action toward starting your Profit Path.

PLEASE TAKE ACTION

Here's the deal. It is so common for people to find a good book or attend a good conference and get really excited about the possibilities, but never actually move toward applying the knowledge they learned to their own lives. Many times it's because while the information they received got them excited, it didn't actually give them a path that enabled them to work toward their goals. Other times it's because while people have good intentions, they don't have drive.

If you're serious about creating a Profit Path and changing your life, taking action is non-negotiable. The journey is uncertain and there are a lot of variables, but if you do nothing, you get nothing. In everyone's life there are moments that pivot their journey in one direction or another. Often we can look back and identify where those pivots were. However, when we miss an opportunity, often we never even know. This could be one of those times. You have this book in your hand, encouraging you to pivot.

In a minute, I'm going to outline a path with some suggestions to help you move forward, but if you don't like the suggestions I'm making, that's OK—pick a different route. The important thing is that you get moving right away. Take action while you are motivated and have a bunch of information in your head.

I realize this book doesn't have everything you need to know in it. It would be the size of a set of encyclopedias if it did. But it does have a good foundation to get you started. You're also starting this at the perfect time because with modern technology we can offer you so much support through the process. The amount of information that is at your fingertips to assist you is ridiculous. I know firsthand the difference having a Profit Path can make in your life. Please, don't hold yourself back. Take the leap. I hope this is one of the best pivots of your life!

NEXT STEPS

If you read the entire book, your head might be swimming a bit. So I wanted to outline a few easy next steps to get you headed in the right direction.

You Are Not Alone

You do not need to embark on this journey alone. We have a Facebook group you can join that is a supportive community of people just like you who are working on creating their own Profit Paths. It's a great place to ask questions and share information as you go. I don't know about you, but I think this will be a much more enjoyable process if you have a group of driven, like-minded individuals to do it with.

Did You Pick a Path?

Do you already know which Profit Path you want to start? If not, did you take our Profit Path Assessment that is designed to help you choose the best path for you and your situation? To take the test, visit the assessment section of www.MoonlightingontheInternet.com.

If you are not sure which path to take, take some time to evaluate your Profit Path Profile and think about which one resonates with you the most. Ultimately, sometimes you have to go with your gut and pick one so you can get moving. You definitely don't want to get stuck in Analysis Paralysis. Once you have identified which Profit Path you would like to begin, you have taken the first step!

Profit Path Get Started Sheets

You can visit the resources section on www.MoonlightingontheInternet. com to download the Profit Path Get Started sheet for the Profit Path you have chosen. This will provide you with a quick cheat sheet checklist for the items you need to make decisions about or do. This will help keep you moving in the right direction without worrying about whether you are doing things in the right order.

Need Help?

If you really don't want to do this on your own, we offer training programs and coaches to help you get up and running. For more information, visit the resource section of www.MoonlightingontheInternet.com.

THANK YOU

Finally, I want to thank you for spending some time participating in my Profit Path. I'm so grateful for the opportunity to write this perfectly imperfect book and help you create Profit Paths that will change your life forever, the way it has mine.

What are you waiting for? Get started!

I don't only want to blow the roof off the possibilities you see in your life. I want to prevent you from even thinking possibility has a roof in the first place.

INDEX

freelance graphic design;
freelance technical
paths; freelance writing;
freelancing; reselling;
virtual assistants
Shopify, 221
single parents, 14
SmartMarketer.com, 210,
225, 232
social media marketing,
130–132, 148–151, 188–
189, 241, 273–274
social proof, 71–72, 231,
232, 235, 240. *See also*
credibility; reviews;
testimonials; trust
social proof jacking, 143
specialization, 78, 110,
114–117, 119
sponsored posts, 272
stay-at-home parents, 13
subheads, 58–59
support systems, 33

T
Tech Guys Who Get
Marketing, 96
technical profit paths. *See*
freelance technical paths
testimonials, 71–72, 81–82,
104, 106, 134, 164. *See
also* social proof
time as a resource, 31–32
titles, 58–59
traffic generation, 151–152,
232, 240–241, 270–274
training resources, 289
trust, 80, 231. *See also*
credibility; social proof
trust jacking, 234–235
Tumblr, 157, 188. *See also*
social media marketing
Twitter, 130, 149, 187, 207,
241, 271. *See also* social
media marketing
Twitter Ads, 188

U
unattached affiliates, 189

underpaid employees, 13–14
unemployable people, 15

V
video marketing, 156–157,
188
Villalobos, Michelle, 116
virtual assistant companies,
120–122
virtual assistants (VA),
109–126
about, 109–110
certification programs,
119–120
characteristics needed,
123–125
examples of tasks of,
111–114
finding clients, 122
managing clients,
125–126
professional organiza-
tions for, 119
setting rates, 118–119
skills needed, 110–111
specialization and, 110,
114–117, 119
virtual assistant compa-
nies, 120–122
Volusion, 221

W
warehousing, 217–218
WatchCount, 224
wealth, 285
web developers, 97, 99–101.
See also freelance
technical paths
website audit services, 153
websites, 80–81, 153, 219,
224, 230–231, 262,
273. *See also* online
presence; search engine
optimization
white labeling, 218–219
white papers, 47–48
wholesale directories, 224
wholesaling, 217–218
WooCommerce, 222

Write Jobs, 63
WritersDepartment, 63
writing, freelance. *See*
freelance writing

Y
Yahoo! Bing Network
advertising, 271
youths, 14–15
YouTube, 156–157, 164,
188, 206, 279. *See also*
social media marketing
YouTube partner program,
188